Science of Mind Archives & Library Foundation

Extension Study Course In the Science Of Mind

Volume 1: Lessons 1-12

by Ernest Holmes

Copyright © 1953 Ernest Holmes and Reginald Armor.
Questions and Answers by Reginald C. Armor

ISBN # 978-0-9897300-1-3

SCIENCE OF MIND®
ARCHIVES & LIBRARY FOUNDATION

Where the Past Illuminates the Future

Published by Science of Mind Archives & Library Foundation
573 Park Point Drive
Golden, CO 80401
http://scienceofmindarchives.org

For further information on Science of Mind®, visit Science of Mind
Archives & Library Foundation at http://scienceofmindarchives.org.
573 Park Point Drive, Golden, Colorado, 80401, phone: (720) 496-1361,
or via email at info@somarchives.org.

Contents

> ➢ Please note that page numbers with in the following lessons are in reference to the revised 1938 edition of *The Science of Mind*, by Ernest Holmes. The 1938 edition became a classic and is now used worldwide as the standard teaching text and reference for the Science of Mind philosophy.

Creation
Office of the Dean

My Dear Friend,

You are about to start on the most interesting quest the human mind has ever made, the discovery of the Life Principle, the way It works, and your relationship to It. You are about to make the greatest discovery of your life, which is how to use the Creative Power of your thought for definite purposes; purposes which will benefit you, your family, and your friends.

The lessons which follow are not a revelation to some particular individual nor to anyone group of persons. Rather they are an outcome or a putting together of the best that the ages have discovered. We all believe that there is a Power greater than we are. We all hope that we may be able to use this Power.

Throughout the ages certain individuals have discovered some secret relationship between themselves and the Universe which other people have not known about, and because of this they have either consciously or unconsciously used a power that to the ordinary individual seems miraculous because of its effects. Others have stood in awe before them, feeling that God has delivered some message to them which is withheld from others.

This age of superstition, of fear, and of ignorance is passing out of existence and intelligent people are beginning to say, "My relationship to God, to the Universe, and to the Power which is greater than I am must be as immediate to me as to any other person who ever lived. There is a secret, the great secret of Life Itself, and I expect to discover it. And when I do, I know that it will be immediate and personal to me; something that I can live by and use; something that I can benefit by and demonstrate; something that will take the uncertainties out of life.

You are about to engage in a study of the Science of Mind which deals with a Principle and a Power in the Universe as immediate as your own breath. Of necessity such a study is something to which you must give your complete attention, something that you must enthusiastically enter into. All the while it will be something that brings a daily satisfaction, a sense of well being, and the gratification of knowing that you are in league with the Power that creates and sustains everything.

These lessons start with the simple proposition that God, which means the Life Principle or the Creative Cause, is an immediate Presence not only around but within you. Therefore do not be afraid that perhaps you are being coerced into accepting a new religion, for such is not the case. You, like all normal people, already believe in some Power greater than you are. You already understand that everything in the universe is governed by some invisible law, force, and intelligence which sanity compels you to accept, and you are going to discover your immediate relationship to this Power, to establish yourself in such conscious unity with It that you too will become a partner in Its activities.

You should approach your study with a calm determination and a buoyant hope. We believe that as you study these lessons and the various explanations that go with them, you will find yourself agreeing with their content and meaning. You may be certain that this meaning has been accepted by the deep thinkers of every age.

In presenting such a vast subject as this, it is necessary that there be considerable repetition. The ideas must be presented in many forms for clarity. We hope that you will begin at once to apply these lessons. If you do, long before your studies are finished you will have demonstrated that there is a Power greater than you are and you can use It.

Your first lesson starts on page 63 of The Science of Mind Textbook and runs to the top of page 68. You will get the best results if you faithfully follow the Textbook with each lesson, explaining to yourself the meaning of each paragraph and each word.

Starting with this lesson and running through Lesson 12 is an explanation of the inner meaning of the Bible. This explanation is based on what we consider the finest authority. With each lesson you will find supplementary material on specific subjects which are of great importance in coming to comprehend the whole meaning of this course.

While our first lesson starts with page 63, it will be well for you to study the whole Introductory Section of The Science of Mind Textbook from pages 25 to 60 inclusive. The sum and substance of this section of our Textbook resolves itself into this: The Universe is made up of a Divine Intelligence Presence, an Intelligence and supreme Spirit which responds to everyone because It is incarnated in everyone. This response is immediate and personal. The Universe is also a system of Law and Order, and you are surrounded by a Creative Principle which responds to the impress of your thought and acts upon it exactly as you think. These are the great realities with which we deal. And now you are ready to start on your adventure. We believe it will be a happy one.

Sincerely,
Ernest Holmes

Lesson 1
p.63 to top of 68

Let us make plain exactly what we mean by *In the Beginning God*. Of course we do not mean that there ever was a time when God began to be or when the Creative Cause first started to function. What we really mean is the beginning of any created thing.

For instance, in the springtime of the year when the farmer sows his grain means in the beginning, before his crop is created by the laws of nature. In the beginning, then, means any springtime of causation, before any particular object is created.

It is impossible to suppose any beginning to Reality Itself. The Ancient of Days referred to in the Bible never began. This Reality to which we have given the name God, is an ever-present fact in every man's experience.

This Infinite and Universal Creative Spirit is Intelligence, Imagination, Knowingness, coupled with an Infinite Law which executes the Self-knowingness of Spirit. The entire Introductory section of our Textbook, *The Science of Mind*, up to page 60 is a simplified exposition of the theory that there is a Creative Intelligence that knows, and a Universal Law that obeys the will of this Creative Intelligence.

It is impossible to explain life without starting with the proposition that Reality or some final Truth already exists; that behind everything which takes form there is an Intelligence that creates all forms. Now within this Intelligence must exist the potentiality or the possibility of everything that is to follow, which is but another way of saying that God is Absolute Intelligence, Limitless Imagination, Perfect Consciousness, and Complete Self-expression.

In the beginning nothing exists other than this Absolute Intelligence. The Bible refers to the Spirit as moving. If we have an Infinite Intelligence that moves, It must move upon Itself since there is nothing outside Itself. All movement, then, is an interior movement. All creation is a result of this interior movement of the Life Principle upon Itself.

We must assume that the pattern for Its movement, the impulse toward self-expression, the idea, or if we choose to call it the thought, exists in the Mind of God before ever it is formed into objective fact. That is what is meant at the top of page 84 in our Textbook where it says: *Spirit makes things out of Itself through some inner act upon Itself*. This inner act must be an act of consciousness, an act of thought or idea. This inner Consciousness moves upon Itself; that is, It thinks or knows within Itself. Within Its own nature there is a Law obeying Its will.

You will learn later that this Law is the Law we use in what we call *demonstration*. By demonstration we mean bringing some good into our personal experience which we have desired but have not yet experienced. You will learn that we all take part in this original creative act; that man, because of his nature, cannot stop creating; it is merely a question of what we wish to create or have created for us.

This inner movement of the Spirit upon Itself we call self-contemplation. Since we shall speak a great deal about self-contemplation it is well to analyze exactly what we mean by it. Self-contemplation is an inner awareness, an inner sense of being, and this inner awareness in God must of course be complete. Therefore God must forever be expressed, and God's expression must always be harmonious and perfect because God is harmonious and perfect.

If someone should ask how we know that God must be harmonious and perfect our answer would be that it is a self-evident proposition that if the original Creative Cause were anything other than perfect It would be self-destructive. No matter which way we look at this or how often we turn it over for re-examination, we shall always be impelled to return to the self-evident starting point that the Truth is that which is; that there is an Eternal Reality which makes things out of Itself by becoming what It makes.

When we read the story of creation we should realize that we are reading the thoughts of someone who, like ourselves, attempted to put into words what creation meant to him. He arrived at the self-evident proposition that there is an original Creative Cause. He also asserted that this original Creative

Cause must work through Self-knowingness. He described the result of God's thought as a perfect and harmonious creation or manifestation of the Infinite Harmony, the Infinite Wholeness. Naturally he had to put his ideas into human language, as we all must, and in so doing made rather a human narrative, which is also necessary. It is impossible for us to talk unless we use words to symbolize our meaning.

All words are symbols, and when we use the words *First Cause, Absolute Intelligence, God, Spirit*, or *Reality* they are but vehicles conveying the meaning back of the words, and in this instance the meaning is that there must be, and is, a Universal Creative Intelligence which was never born, which never came into being, but which always existed.

While you and I with our finite minds do not grasp the significance of Infinite Being, certainly not in Its entirety, we do understand something of Its meaning, and out of the little that we grasp are born such ideas of God as we possess. From the great and inspired literature of the ages and from many findings in scientific research we are led to the legitimate and justifiable conclusion that God is an Omnipresent Reality; that this Creative Cause which produces all form also exists at the center of our own being, carrying on Its creative work in us; that we are co-partners in Its Infinitude, some part of Its Eternal Reality.

Jesus simplified it in these words: *The words that I speak unto you, I speak not of myself: but the Father, that dwelleth in me, he doeth the works*. He meant that the same Creative Intelligence which gives form to all things also worked in him, and through him gave form to substance, therefore he said that the very words which he spoke were Spirit and they were Life.

You will discover that a spiritual interpretation of the Science of Mind leads to the acceptance of the thought that the Creative Spirit works in and through each one of us, that the Power which we seek we already possess, and that the recognition of this Power is certain to demonstrate the reality of Its presence through a betterment in all outward circumstances. These are the tools we use and most amazing results are obtained when they are used definitely and for specific purposes.

Now the *Word of God* means the consciousness of God doing something. It is God in the act of creation. I am sure that we all believe that God is in and through all people and all things. As a matter of fact there is nothing else that we could be made of, is there, except God?

On page 393 you will find these words: *The correct understanding that Mind in Its unformed state can be called forth into individual use is the key to all proper mental and spiritual work from a practical viewpoint*. This means that every time we think we use the energy of God. And on page 414: *Thoughts are more than things, they are the cause of things*.

The Self-contemplation of God referred to on page 64 means the Thought of God; and the story of Creation on pages 64 and 65 needs no further elaboration. For a clear understanding read these pages carefully several times and put a great deal of thought into their true meaning. While the narrative seems rather human, remember that we are putting into human language that which can be only imagined.

The paragraph on page 66 under the heading, *Describing the Infinite*, explains that God or Spirit is the final answer to all inquiries into the nature of the Universe. Every science has a principle governing it. This principle and the way it works is what science studies. The purpose of philosophy is to inquire into the nature of Reality, while religion is an expression of our belief in God.

You will notice we come to the idea of Absolute Intelligence. Let us examine the meaning of the word *Absolute* as defined in our Glossary on page 575: *The Unconditioned—that which nothing can limit.* Again on page 390 we find these words: *The mind of man is some part of the Mind of God, therefore it contains within itself unlimited possibility of expansion and self-expression.*

You see, then, that Absolute Intelligence means the limitless power of self-expression. There is a Principle of Mind at the very center of our own thought which is infinite in Its ability and limitless in Its power and ever available to us. When we call upon this inner self we are at the same time calling upon God, and when we call upon God we are calling upon this inner self. For both God and man emerge in a complete unity of Mind and Spirit. This is the great secret of all the ages, and you will at once recognize that to have a true and comprehensive understanding of this is exactly what you, and all of us, are seeking.

To understand the meaning of this is your object in taking this course, and to be able to use the Power that already is within you is the thing in which you are interested. We all wish more power, greater happiness, more beauty in our lives, and a greater sense of security. There is something within us which is always whispering to our inner ear that all these things are for us.

The great quest of man has been to solve the riddle of the Universe and see where he, himself, fits into the great design. Knowledge alone can guarantee freedom, and self-recognition can produce knowledge. Is it not true that all knowledge comes from the inner perception of our relationship to the Universe?

Next you will notice these words in paragraph 4, page 66: *Creation means the giving of form to the Substance of Mind or Spirit.* In other words, creation is not making something out of nothing, but rather the giving of form to something that already exists. The electric light is a manifestation of an energy which already exists. The energy is not depleted by using it. No matter how much we use there is still just as much left as there was before we made use of it. There is no limit to the amount that can be generated.

There is a creative energy at the very center of your thought waiting to be called into manifestation. To learn how to use this creative principle is the whole purpose of your study. When the artist paints he gives form to his thought through the medium of his brush and oils. He produces different manifestations of pigments. So in our thoughts we use a creative power by drawing out the latent possibilities of the great Mind in which we live and which finds expression through us.

When the Spirit creates form out of Itself, at the same time, It creates space, for as you can plainly see, form is outline while space is the physical distance between any two forms. If there were no forms there would be no space. Both exist in the great Mind of God as means to His Self-expression. They exist in our minds also, because we too are some part of the Universe in which we are living.

If you draw two lines on a blackboard you also create the space existing between these two lines. But if these two particular forms or lines remained uncreated, then the space which might exist between them would have no existence.

Let us avoid confusion by saying that both space and form are created by the action of the thought of God upon Himself. And let us hasten to add that we also are created in the image, mentally and spiritually, of the Great Spirit. You will at once see that it is because of this that your thought is creative. In other words, your thought is creative not because you will it to be so but because it is so. You will learn later that the will is directive only; it is the conviction and the feeling that are the real creative qualities in our minds.

If form creates space in order that form may be outlined and experienced, then does it not follow that the ideas which give rise to form and space must automatically create time? For time is merely the process of duration in which we experience any given form or forms. This is just another way of saying that time, space, and form are primarily mental concepts.

To understand this is to see how it is that new conditions can be created for us by the invisible Principle which we call Mind or Spirit. We know that the Power we all seek to use is not limited by any present form nor in any present form, nor is It limited by any element of time. What a wonderful thing for us to realize! We may use a Power which makes new conditions and new situations and when It does this It also creates all the things necessary to our well-being.

So we come to the conclusion that spirit, or God, is forever making and remaking time, space, and form, as you and I are forever thinking some kind of thought. Just as we are always aware of ourselves and of our environment, so there is a greater Mind which is aware of all things. The past, the present, and the future flow from this Mind as a result of the creative activity of Its thought.

On page 495 under the heading, *The Mind that Jesus Used*, you will find these words: *We are to let the mind be in us which was in Christ Jesus*. This means the Mind of God. And on the following page are the words: *This Mind is God working in and through us. God can work for us only by working through us*. To understand this is to partake of the Divine Nature and to make conscious use of the same Power to which Jesus had access.

When we come to inquire into the many different great systems of religious thought which have been given to the world, we shall find that this is the central theme of most of them. Man's thought is creative because his thought is God-Power flowing through his individual will and imagination. That is why it is true that *as a man thinketh in his heart so is he*.

Summary

Let us sum up our first lesson and see what we have discovered:

First: There is a Creative Power in the Universe that manifests Itself through imagination, will and feeling.

Second: This Creative Power makes things out of Itself by Itself becoming the thing that It makes.

Third: As the Creative Mind of the Universe operates upon Itself through Its will, imagination, and feeling, It creates forms which are subject to It and to Its laws, but which have no reality apart from the Mind which creates them.

Fourth: This Creative Mind is the mind that Jesus used and that we may all use for conscious purposes just as soon as we come to understand how.

This means that everyone is surrounded by the original Creative Intelligence of the Universe. This Intelligence fills all space, flows through everything and is everything. Therefore there is an intelligence in everything that responds to your thinking. You did not make it this way and you cannot change it. This is the nature of your being and of all being. Consequently by impressing your thought upon It you cause It to do something for you, but whether or not you know it you are always impressing your thought upon It because most of your thought is unconscious and flows out into this Creative Intelligence as a stream of thought which we call the Law of Mind in Action. You are, then, surrounded by a Creative Stuff which makes things out of Itself through the simple act of Itself becoming what It makes.

But this same Principle is also in you and is your mind. You are a center of consciousness or self-knowingness in It. Your mind is some part of It. It is not separate from you. Consequently when you think within and upon yourself, you are thinking within and upon It. This puts the use of this Mind Principle in the only place where it could possibly benefit you and that is within yourself. This is why Jesus said that there is a truth which known will automatically demonstrate itself. We can know only within our own minds. But here within ourselves is our share of the Universal Mind, the One Power, the One Presence, which is God.

Questions

Brief answers to these questions should be written out by the student after studying this lesson, and the answers compared with those which will be included in next week's lesson.

1. What do we mean by the phrase, *In the beginning God*?
2. In the Science of Mind how do we define God?
3. What do we mean by a creative series through which anything is brought into being?
4. Can an effect ever be the cause of another creative series?
5. When we speak of God as First Cause what do we mean?
6. Can we contact and use First Cause?
7. What is meant by the Spirit of God?
8. Can we say that man partakes of this Spirit of God? If so, how?

9. Does the Spirit within man grow and develop?

10. How can a person use this Principle of Spirit which is within him to definitely direct the course of his life?

Metaphysical Interpretations of the Bible Based On Thomas Troward's *Bible Mystery and Bible Meaning*

Thomas Troward, late Divisional Judge, Punjab, India, is recognized as one of the greatest authorities on the subject of Mental Science. His sincerity, the lucidity and profundity of his thought, his great ability to make the complex simple, his profound faith and complete devotion to truth, make him a rare messenger of God.

Troward opens his *Bible Mystery and Bible Meaning* by saying, *The Bible is the Book of the Emancipation of Man.*

We all remember that Jesus admonished his followers: *Be ye therefore perfect, even as your Father which is in heaven is perfect.* He had already located the Kingdom of Heaven within. Moses affirmed that there is a creative word in our own mouth which is the arbiter of our fate. Again we are told that we shall decree a thing and it will happen; that our word will not return unto us void but that it shall accomplish and prosper.

Troward tells us that these promises are based on the idea of our acquiring a certain type of information. Jesus declared that it depends on our keeping his sayings; Job, that it depends on a right interpretation of the meaning of some law or presence in nature; and Moses said that the gift which he offered his followers would be either a blessing or a curse, according to whether or not they kept the Commandments.

Just what do these sayings mean, and what are these Commandments? It is evident that they must have something to do with Universal Truth and our relationship to It. The Bible begins with the simple proposition that the creative intelligence of the universe, which it calls God, is pure, evenly-distributed Spirit, Mind, or Intelligence. The only instrument of Mind is the movement of Its intelligence within Itself. This we call *thought* or *contemplation*. The Bible clearly states that creation is the result of the Word of God.

The Bible assumes a Law of Mind through which Creative Intelligence works to produce form, thus giving us a trinity which we call *The Thing, the Way It Works*, and *What It Does*. From beginning to end the Bible teaches that everything which happens in our lives depends on an understanding of the right relationship between the Universe and ourselves. It assumes that just as God, or the Creative Spirit, is a Trinity, so is man a trinity: spirit, soul, and body. In other words man is a microcosm within a macrocosm; a little world within a big world. He partakes of the nature of the Creative Principle. This is neither by preference nor by compulsion. Thought is creative not because we will it so but because it is its nature to be creative.

The Bible teaches what might be called a law of parallels. That is, the physical universe is an out-picturing of a mental universe; laws of mind are just as tangible as are laws of physics. Of course both are invisible. The invisible is always the cause of the visible. Spirit passes from the Universal into an individualized consciousness. Whatever form the consciousness of Spirit takes it is always in accord with One Primary Law: *The Word was made flesh and dwelt among us.*

No matter what individualized states of consciousness may be produced in the process of evolution, each individual consciousness is a center of God Consciousness. Hence the individual consciousness is the Consciousness of God operating at the level of the individual's comprehension of life. This is fundamental to all Bible teaching: God is One, and man is made in the image and likeness of God.

The Bible has another unique and interesting presentation which Troward calls the *Law of Selectivity* and to which Jesus referred when he said, . . . *as thou hast believed, so be it done unto thee.* The understanding of these two propositions is simple enough when we have the key to their meaning. We are immersed in an Infinite Spirit which stimulates our imagination to the act of thought. We are also immersed in a Universal Law which, acting creatively upon our thought, presents to us conditions that correspond to such states of thought.

So far as we are concerned this means that wherever we set up a center for thought action, there we are automatically reflecting mental images into the Law. The Law always tends to give form to our thought. From the effects of this creative power of thought we shall never escape.

When the Bible Speaks of the beginning of creation it is referring to an Eternal Beginning and not to some historic time in the cosmos when the Creative Spirit first began to project form. It refers rather to the beginning of any creation; to any seedtime which precedes its following harvest season. Thus Troward tells us that the beginning is a continuous fact, always present, and not to be conceived of as something which has been left behind and done with. It means that previous to any created form there is a universal, equally distributed Mind, Intelligence, or Spirit. This Mind is the potential of all form. There is a Law of Mind acted upon by idea; hence the movement of consciousness as thought is law.

In the beginning was the Word, and the Word was with God, and the Word was God. Again let us remember that this beginning is now, in the moment in which we give our mental treatment for the betterment of circumstances for ourselves or others. There is nothing but God, nothing for us but immutable Law and our own thought. Our thought operating through Law will create the desired form if we permit it to do so. This is the fundamental proposition which the Bible sets before us.

When the Bible refers to the heaven and the earth, it is referring to the unformed and the formed. Jesus placed the Kingdom of Heaven within us, which means within our spiritual perception. The earth is likened to the outward form, to that which is created, to objective conditions, circumstances, situations, etc.

We must then consider a self-evolving Power as the basic Principle of the teachings of the Bible— Something which makes things out of Itself by the very simple and direct act of Itself becoming the thing It makes.

We are told that the earth was without form and that the Spirit moved upon this formlessness, which the Bible likens to *the face of the waters*. The waters of themselves do not move; they are moved upon by the Spirit. This means the movement of thought upon Substance; the movement of Idea as Law into form. We are surrounded by *the waters*, that is, by a universal pool of unformed Substance ready to be moved upon.

This unformed, creative Substance has been likened to the Feminine Principle in nature, the Soul of the Universe as distinguished from the Divine Spirit of the Universe. The Spirit has been called the Masculine and the Soul the Feminine, because it is the projective act of thought moving upon the receptive Principle of Mind which sets creation in motion.

Water is a most interesting symbol as used in the Bible, and indeed in most of the sacred scriptures. In the Upanishads we find this saying: *In the beginning this (world) was water*. From one of the ancient Papyri we read: *I am the great God Who created Himself, which is to say, I am water*. Plutarch says: *Homer, like Thales, had learned from the Egyptians that water was the beginning and origin of all things*. From ancient Babylon we note that *water and earth was to be formed*. This refers to the liquid and the solid in the universe. In the Kabala we find: *The emanation which produced the creation of the universe is like water gushing out from its source and spreading over everything near*. We are told water is the first element in the mundane system of the Chinese. Paul Deussen in his *Philosophy of the Upanishads*; says, *This earth, the air, the heavens, the mountains, gods and men are nothing but the water under solid conditions*. This refers to the invisible fluidic cause back of what appears to be a solid creation.

The turning of water into wine is symbolic of the transmutation at lower forms into higher ones. Water is used to symbolize the action of a passive principle which gives form to that which, of itself, has no form. Hence all forms or created things are placed in the category of effects or results. The Absolute Cause is the Creative Intelligence of the Spirit which moves upon the face of the waters; the Masculine Principle impregnating the Feminine with the Divine Ideas.

Troward tells us: *Thus creation is described as the self-transforming action of the One unanalyzable Spirit passing by successive transitions into all the varieties of manifestations that fill the universe*. And when we realize that we ourselves are some part of this Creative Principle we shall see that our thought is always passing into the varieties of manifestation that fill our universe.

Since this is true, man's mind becomes a reproduction of the Divine Mind operating on the scale of individual perception, and Troward tells us: *It is precisely here that the difficulty comes in*. Since we cannot escape the creative power of our thought we must temporarily be limited to such thought patterns as we have already created. Freedom and expansion lie not in a changed attitude toward us on the part of the Universe or of God, but in a changed mental attitude in our own consciousness, a new outlook upon life, a new vision of Reality.

What Is the Science of Mind?

The Science of Mind as taught in these lessons is an outgrowth of the spiritual faith which people have had throughout the ages. Before science was conceived the Presence of God was felt. Before ever mental actions or reactions were analyzed, history was filled with instances of men and women who had experienced God.

The Science of Mind is comparatively new, but the mental experience of the invisible universe is as old as the history of man. It is new in that for the first time in history we have put together all findings which contribute to the establishment of man's relationship with the universe, to the end that he may be able to apply his spiritual understanding to the everyday problems of human life.

This science necessarily starts with the proposition that we are living in a spiritual universe whose sole government is one of harmony, and that the use of right ideas is the enforcement of its law.

The Science of Mind is built on the theory that there is One Infinite Mind which of necessity includes all that is, whether it be the intelligence in man, the life in the animal, or the invisible Presence which is God. In it we learn to have a spiritual sense of things. This spiritual sense of things is what is meant by the Consciousness of Christ. To be able to discern the spiritual idea back of its physical symbol is to use the mind that Jesus used.

The Science of Mind is intensely practical because it teaches us how to use the Mind Principle for definite purposes, such as helping those who are sick, impoverished, or unhappy. Each one of us should learn to become a practitioner of this science, a demonstrator of its Principle, a conscious user of its Power. Power already exists, but the existence of Power is of no particular value to us until we use it. We must not only be conscious of Power, but we must be actively conscious of it. This is one of the first lessons we learn in the Science of Mind.

This science is more than mental; it is also spiritual, since we live in a spiritual universe. The Science of Mind declares the Truth about this spiritual universe and it also declares the Truth about false belief, considering everything which is opposed to good as an accumulation of human thought, the collective negative suggestion of the race.

Wrong conditions are resolved into false beliefs, and through the use of **right ideas** a transformation of thought takes place. We learn to build our ideas upon an affirmative rather than a negative factor. To state the Truth and deny or disregard that which in belief is opposed to it, is to prove that the Principle of the Science of Mind is actual.

The ever increasing thousands of persons who are daily proving this Principle add to our conviction that we are dealing with the most intense reality the human mind has ever conceived. As you will learn later, the practice of this science is the application of a definite technique, the law of right thought, of true spiritual understanding.

It is necessary to start these studies with the complete conviction that there is such a Principle and that you understand the scientific use and application of it. Conscious knowledge alone gives you the conscious control of the laws of nature. The advance in any science always corresponds to the conscious use made of the laws of nature. There could be no advance in science without such conscious use of nature's laws.

It would be unwise to approach a study of the Science of Mind with superstition. You must approach it with understanding. Above all, you must approach it with the definite intention in mind of making conscious use of its Principle. You must come to realize at the very start of your inquiry that Mind exists as a Principle in the universe, just as electricity exists as a principle.

Once you understand this it will not be difficult to see that thought is the tool of Mind, that right ideas enforce the Law of Mind; nor will it be difficult to see that physical objects are fundamentally spiritual in their nature, that an objective fact is but a symbol of a subjective or an invisible cause. It certainly follows that if you are to make practical use of the Science of Mind you must be able to convert things into thoughts, and by changing the stream of consciousness produce a corresponding change in an objective situation, whether this be used for helping those who are sick or to meet any other need.

The question naturally arises whether or not man has a right to use his thought for whatever purpose he wills. The more sincere one is the more likely he is to ask this question. Strangely enough, he would not ask this relative to any other science but would feel that all laws exist to be used, and any sane person would naturally desire to benefit himself and others through the use of nature's laws. Why should any exception be made to the greatest of all laws—the Law of Mind in action, and the enforcement of this Law through right ideas?

One of our fundamental propositions is that God is all there is. When you say God is all there is, that includes everything, all possibility and all action, for Spirit is the invisible essence and substance of all form. It is impossible to separate the highest use of this science from the most exalted conception of an immanent Spirit, a transcendent Spirit, an available Spirit.

Perhaps one might at first have an aversion to the idea of using spiritual power for material purposes, but in the Science of Mind we discover that there are no final material purposes; that whether life exists in an objective or a subjective state, whether it is visible or invisible, all is Spirit; that Spirit or Intelligence, plus what It does, constitutes the entire universe, including man.

The Science of Mind reveals that every man is a potential Christ. Every man has inherent God-power within him. And how could this God-power be used other than through his thought? Since it would be impossible for a man to act as an intelligent being unless he could first think, the very idea of man supposes a center of consciousness, a center of thought activity. The Science of Mind reveals that this center of God activity within each one is a complete and a unique manifestation of the Parent Mind; that the Power of God does actually exist in man.

It is a basic proposition in our philosophy that we live in a mental or spiritual universe and that things can be resolved into thoughts. This is the foundation upon which all scientific practice must be established, and when you are able to establish this premise in your own thought, you at once find yourself equipped with an instrument through which you can change your environment.

The Science of Mind does not deny the physical universe. The objective universe is the Body of God. That Body includes our physical being. In reality every idea of our physical being is a Divine idea.

The misconception of the spiritual universe causes our universe to appear separated from good, and in fact we experience this separation. But that which is a fact in experience is not necessarily true in principle. Bondage cannot be conceived by the Divine, and yet we all know that bondage is a part of man's experience.

In trying to seek a solution for this enigma we must either conclude that there is an ultimate good and an ultimate evil in the universe, or we must conclude that there is but one Ultimate, which is good, and that this Ultimate by Its very nature and by our very nature is compelled to appear to each one of us in the form of our belief. If you can accept this proposition it will be easy enough for you to see how it is that false belief binds humanity.

If that which binds is false belief and not the Truth, then you will see why Jesus told us that a knowledge of the Truth would produce freedom. He did not mean that knowledge of the Truth creates freedom, but that knowledge of the Truth makes us free by aligning us with that which was never bound.

Accepting the foregoing conclusions as true it follows that the Divine Creative Principle is already perfect, having neither confusion nor chaos within It. It was, is, and will remain exactly perfect. Our individual universe shall be redeemed from its bondage in such degree as we become actively conscious of the Truth of our being. We must use the Law as a Law of Liberty; else we shall be using It as a law of bondage.

The Science of Mind provides us with a definite technique for the use of this Law and teaches how each one can use It in freeing himself and demonstrating to his complete satisfaction that right ideas, correctly used, can and must produce right conditions.

So far, neither science, revelation, nor philosophy has arrived at any conclusion which could disturb this proposition, and every day the physical sciences are more completely proving that the physical universe in which we live is more like a *gigantic thought* than anything else. Now if the physical universe, or the cosmos as a whole, is more like a gigantic thought than anything else, it follows that our immediate world is a part of this thought.

How amazed we all should be if we awoke some fine morning, not only with the absolute conviction that this is so, but also with the inner insight which would enable us to see exactly what it means. Then we too should be able to say to the paralyzed man, "Stretch forth thine hand!" But before we can do this we must see the principle of freedom instead of the belief in a paralysis of this principle.

The Science of Mind is a reinterpretation of the universe by a process of thought which Jesus used. We learn that there is one body, the body of right ideas. Jesus sensed this Body of God, which includes man's body, as a perfect, harmonious unit, and he realized that the evil which binds man is not a principle within itself nor a thing of itself, and most certainly not a person, but merely a false system of thought. He understood that his knowledge of good annihilated that which denied good. This fundamental fact he clearly brought out in his teaching; the Truth known is followed by the Truth demonstrated.

The Science of Mind does not necessarily create a new religion or sect, for it may be added to any spiritual system of thought since it is a complement to all. The person who already has the greatest spiritual faith will make the most active demonstrator of Truth. The person who naturally has a spiritual insight or who has already trained himself to have spiritual insight, will more quickly sense the truths which the Science of Mind portrays. He will more quickly lay hold of its technique and more perfectly demonstrate for himself and others that the invisible is the cause of the visible.

For every science there must be a technique or a way of proving its truth. Science of itself is a knowledge of laws and principles and systematic arrangement. And the technique of any science is the way in which we use this knowledge of laws and principles.

Applying this rule (which is common to all sciences) to the science of Mind, it naturally follows that if there is such a principle as Universal Mind, and if It does work according to the Law of Cause and effect, and if thought, self-contemplation, or self-knowingness is that which stimulates Its action, then correct thinking can and must produce objective or visible results.

We must lay even more stress on the *use* of the Science of Mind than we do on seeking to establish its Principle. As a matter of fact its Principle is self-evident; its use is exactly what we make it. And the first thing that any student of this science should do is determine to make daily use of it. In this, as in all other things, we should be practical. Too much study of any principle without making conscious use of it will lead to mere theorizing, and I am sure we all wish practical results.

You are ready to use the Principle governing the Science of Mind the very moment you accept the fact that there is such a principle and that it does operate through your thought. But this seems to be the place where many fall down. They talk so much about the Principle and use It so little. They permit themselves to become confused by the introduction of contradictory ideas. They spend too much time in merely philosophizing, theorizing, speculating, until finally they live in a world of wistful wishing, of day dreams.

You must come to see that the Science of Mind is an actual Principle to be definitely used; that no matter how much good may exist in the universe, only as much good can come to you as you can conceive. Above all things, determine now to use this science. Do not say, "Well, this is but the first lesson and I expect to have understanding enough within a year to use it." Seize upon whatever facts present themselves to your mind today, begin to use such truth as you grasp out of your first lesson, and before the year is over you will have become an effective practitioner.

How to Give a Spiritual Treatment

You may as well begin right now to use the Science of Mind for practical purposes to help yourself and your friends or to change any condition which needs to be improved.

So why not choose one or two persons or conditions, and using the following instructions, take a definite time each day for a period of treatment. If you do this I am certain that before you finish this course you will have discovered the secret of secrets and you will have demonstrated the greatest truth ever discovered.

For Physical Healing

Take a definite time at least twice each day to be alone, sit down, compose your mind, and think about God. Try to arrive at a deep sense of peace and calm. Then assume an attitude of faith in a Power greater than you are.

Say: *The words I speak are the Law of Good and they will produce the desired result because they are operated on by a Power greater than I am. Good alone goes from me and good alone returns to me.*

You are now ready to give a specific treatment for yourself. Begin by saying: *This word is for myself. Everything I say is for me and about me. It is the truth about my real self.* (You are thinking about your spiritual nature, the Divine Reality of yourself, the God in you.) Say: *There is One Life, that Life is God, that Life is perfect, that Life is my life now.* Say this slowly and with deep meaning.

Next say: *My body is a manifestation of the Living Spirit. It is created and sustained by the One Presence and the One Power. That Power is flowing in and through me now, animating every organ, every action and every function of my physical being. There is perfect circulation, perfect assimilation, and perfect elimination. There is no congestion, no confusion, and no inaction. I am one with the Infinite Rhythm of life, which flows through me in love, in harmony, and in peace. There is no fear, no doubt, and no uncertainty in my mind. I am letting that Life which is perfect flow through me and become my life. It is my life now. There is One Life, that Life is God, that Life is perfect, that Life is my life now.*

Next, deny everything that contradicts this. Follow each denial with a direct affirmation of its opposite. In a certain sense you are presenting a logical argument to your own mind, based on the belief that there is but One Life, which is perfect and which is your life now. The evidence that you bring out in your argument should reach a conclusion which causes your own mind to accept the verdict of perfection. Remember you are not talking about your physical body as though it were separate from the spirit, but about God in you; therefore you will have no difficulty in convincing yourself that this God in you is perfect.

You have now reached a place of realization in which you enter into a feeling of assurance that comes from a consciousness of the Divine Presence in, around, and through you. This period of realization should last for several moments, during which you sit quietly accepting the meaning of what you have said. Then say: *It is now done. It is now complete. It is now perfect. There is One Life, that Life is God, that Life is perfect, that Life is my life now.*

Between these periods of meditation try to keep your mind poised in such a way that you do not contradict what you have said in your treatment. Keep your mind open at all times to a Divine influx of new inspiration, new power, and new life. Accept what you have said with joy and gratitude.

For Betterment of Conditions

In treating for the betterment of conditions you are using the same Principle but for a different purpose, therefore you would say something like this:

Everything that I do, say or think is governed by Divine Intelligence and inspired by Divine Wisdom. I am guided into right action. I am surrounded with friendship, love, and beauty. Enthusiastic joy, vitality, and inspiration are in everything I do. I am aware of my partnership with the Infinite.

Every thought of not being wanted, or being afraid, of uncertainty and doubt is cast out of my mind. My memory goes back to God alone, in whom I live, move, and have my being. A complete sense of happiness, peace, and certainty floods me with light. I have confidence in myself because I have confidence in God. I am sure of myself because I am sure of God.

The Spirit within me knows the answer to any problem which confronts me. I know that the answer is here and now. It is within my own mind because God is right where I am. I now turn from the problem to the Spirit, accepting the answer. In calm confidence, in perfect trust, in abiding faith and with complete peace I let go of the problem and receive the answer.

I know exactly what to do in every situation. Every idea necessary to successful living is brought to my attention. The doorway to ever increasing opportunities for self-expression is open before me. I am continuously meeting new and larger experiences. Every day brings some greater good. Every day brings more blessing and greater self-expression. I am prospered in everything I do. There is no deferment, no delay, no obstruction or obstacle, nothing to impede the progress of right action.

I identify myself with abundance. I surrender all fear and doubt. I let go of all uncertainty. I know there is no confusion, no lack of confidence. I know that what is mine will claim me, know me, rush to me. The Presence of God is with me. The Mind of God is my mind. The Freedom of God is my freedom.

Today I bestow the essence of love upon everything. Everyone I meet shall be lovely to me. My soul meets the Soul of the Universe in everyone. This love is a healing power touching everything into wholeness. I am one with the rhythm of Life. There is nothing to be afraid of. There is nothing to be uncertain about. God is over all, in all, and through all. God is right where I am. I am at peace with the world in which I live. I am at home with the Divine Spirit in which I am immersed.

NOTE: When treating another, say: "This word is for him (or her)," then continue exactly as though you were treating yourself.

Bibles of the World
Fragments from the spiritual history of the race revealing fundamental UNITY of religious thought and experience

JUDAISM and CHRISTIANITY -- In God have I put my trust. I will not be afraid what man can do unto me. Fear thou not; for I am with thee; be not dismayed; for I am thy God. He giveth power to the faint; and to them that have no might he increaseth strength. Even the youths shall faint and be weary, and the young men shall utterly fall. But they that wait upon the Lord shall renew their strength; they shall mount up with wings as eagles; they shall run, and not be weary, and they shall walk, and not faint.

ZOROASTRIANISM -- For the three excellent things be never slack, namely: good thoughts, good words, and good deeds; for the three abominable things be ever slack, namely: bad thoughts, bad words, and bad deeds. I will pray unto thee for help, with many consecrations, with good consecrations of libations: that we, abiding in thee, may long inhabit a good abode, full of all the riches that can be wished for.

HELLENISTIC THEOSOPHY -- Now thinking-manifest deals with things made alone, for thinking manifest is nothing else than making. . . And as He thinketh all things manifest, He manifests through all things and in all, and most of all in whatsoever things He wills to manifest. With Reason (Logos), not with hands, did the World-maker make the universal world; so that thou thus shouldst think of Him as everywhere and ever-being, the Author of all things, and One and Only, who by His Will all things hath created.

RAJA-YOGA PHILOSOPHY -- Therefore it is clear that Ignorance can be removed only by Wisdom.

ISLAM -- If God help you, none shall overcome you; but if He abandon you, who is he that shall help you when He is gone? In God, then, let the faithful trust. We created man: and we know what his soul whispereth to him, and we are closer to him than his neck-vein.

Self-Contemplation of Spirit
Office of the Dean

My Dear Friend,
We hope you enjoyed your first lesson and that you have read it over carefully several times.

In this lesson please give special attention to the commentary titled *A Science of Religion and a Religion of Science*, for in it you will learn that law governs everything in the spiritual and mental world just as it does in the physical, and that a combination of deep spiritual feeling added to a definite conscious knowledge of the Law of Mind in Action will always produce the best results.

We are sure that you have started using the spiritual treatment sent you in the last lesson. We shall not repeat this, but shall rest assured that you do turn each week to the simple instructions and follow them carefully. It is only as you apply the practice outlined in these lessons that you will really come to understand its deep meaning and its practical application, and it is this application that we are all interested in, for theories are of no use unless they are used.

We trust that you are interested in the Bible interpretations based on Troward's *Bible Mystery and Bible Meaning* and that you will realize that this is more than a Bible story. It is the story of every man's life. The *Great Mistake* referred to in this lesson is the mistake we all make and one that each must correct within himself. We must all come to see that there is but one Final Power in the Universe, which is God.

Sincerely,
Ernest Holmes

Lesson 2
p.68 through p.70

That there is One Ultimate Reality back of all things is a conclusion we cannot avoid. It is self-evident that two ultimate powers in the universe would be impossible. For if these two powers were just alike they would be one and not two, and if they were different from each other, and each were infinite, they would cancel each other and nothing would be left.

It is perhaps hard for us to comprehend the real meaning of unity. But we do inwardly sense that unity is absolutely necessary to Infinite Being. That the Infinite, or the Life Principle is One, all the deep spiritual thinkers of the ages have declared.

As a matter of fact it really is not difficult to see that Spirit must be One Perfect Unit. We know that all physical forms are made of one universal energy. This energy is undivided. It takes form but it is never divided against itself. Even while the form changes, the energy remains the same.

It is self-evident that the inner movement of Life upon Itself can be likened to a mental movement. Just as we must think before we can do anything, so thought must precede all action. This inner movement has been called the Word of God.

The starting point of creation is the Word of Spirit. If you turn to page 392, lower paragraph, you will read: *In Universal Mind is contained the essence of everything that ever was, is or shall be . . . Things exist in the Universal Mind as ideas. Ideas take form and become things in the concrete or the visible world*. This means that for every visible fact in the objective world there must be an invisible idea which is the cause of the fact. To understand how properly to create ideas is to understand how to experience those facts which we wish to experience.

Fear and faith, success and failure, are tied up in our thinking, and all because we are some part of the Whole and partake of Its nature. One thing we must understand is that man is some part of the experience of God, since the Thought of God must be the cause of all that exists.

Our text states that since there are many things there must be many ideas. But these ideas do not interfere with each other. There is plenty of room in creation for all created objects and since the Creative Principle which we use is infinite, no matter how much we use It or how many people use It, It will never be exhausted.

In the principle of mathematics we may all use the figure two as many times as we wish without exhausting it. So the Life Principle back of our thought is not depleted when we draw upon It. And as there is no limit to the possible combination of numbers, so we cannot conceive of any limit to the number of ideas that can exist in the Universe. This is what our text means when it speaks of an infinite variety of ideas.

We should be careful to realize that many different ideas can proceed from the One Mind without in any way confusing the One Mind, or without in any way producing a quality or a division in this One Mind. Just as we can think many thoughts without dividing the mind against itself, so the Mind of God projects many ideas without confusion.

One of the most important things to understand at the very beginning of our lessons is the unity of all life. On page 493, second paragraph, you will find these words: *There is one Body and one Spirit. The entire creation is this body . . . Within this one Body are all bodies; that is, within the one creation— which is the product of the One Spirit—are all bodies.*

If you will study page 493 I am sure it will be clear to you that we all live in One Mind and that this One Mind is manifesting through each of us in an individualized way. This concept of Unity is the mystical secret of the ages. It is the key to the spiritual wisdom and the teachings of Jesus.

It was because Jesus perfectly understood his union with life that he knew man to be one with God. Because of this he had power, for any man's word will have power in such degree as he is conscious of his unity with Spirit.

Turn to page 646 and read our definition of *The Word*. The secret of our use of spiritual mind power lies in our ability to sense the Mind of God and to realize that It is operating through us. This will give us a conviction that nothing else can, and it will give us a power equal to our conviction.

You will soon perceive that the more conscious you are that good is supreme over apparent evil, and the more completely convinced you are that you are immersed in this good and that this good is working through you, the more quickly and easily you can dissipate evil.

On page 413, paragraph 3, you will find this expression: *To practice the Presence of the Divine in others is to practice mental healing for it is a recognition of this Divine Presence which heals. All the words used in the process of healing are for the purpose of building up this realization*. Please note the definition of *Divine Principle* on page 586 in connection with this idea.

Next we come to a paragraph on page 69 which states that *the Word of God is also the Law of God*. This means that the creative word, whether we think of it as the Word of God or as the word of man, acts in accord with an exact and mathematical law.

It also says in this paragraph*: It is evident that First Cause must be Self-Existent*. "Self-Existent" is defined in our Glossary (page 632) as *living by virtue of its own being*, which means that it is necessary for us to suppose a Final Power in the universe, or an Omnipotence. In other words, how could we explain anything unless we accepted the proposition that Life is, and that Life creates through the medium of Its own Being?

This conclusion is more far-reaching than it appears to be. For if we are dealing with a Power which actually makes things out of Itself by Itself becoming or taking the form of the thing that It makes, and if this Power is Spirit, then it follows that the Word of God is also the Law of God. The Word of God is a conscious act, and the Law of God is a mechanical reaction.

It is necessary to understand as a basic principle in our science that there is both an engine and an engineer; that is, the universe is volitional and mechanical. *Volitional* means having the attributes of consciousness and choice and self-determination; and by *mechanical* we mean an arbitrary, mechanical, automatic reaction. Thus we see that man as spirit is a free moral agent, but the Law of Mind which reacts to this free agent is merely another kind of mechanical force.

The more you think about these things the more thoroughly convinced you will be that this must be true. Does not the gardener plant his seed consciously? We cannot believe that the soil has any choice in the matter but it is an intelligent creative medium and does produce a crop. God as Spirit must be Conscious Life. The Universe as Law must be mechanical reaction.

If you will turn to page 488, *How to Demonstrate Liberty*, you will see how this principle works. In the third paragraph are these words: *Do not will or try to compel things to happen. Things happen by an immutable law and you do not need to energize the Essence of Being*. The wisest man who ever lived said. *Ye shall know the truth, and the truth shall make you free*.

What a marvelous concept to realize that there is something which, when known, automatically becomes demonstrated. This is exactly what you must come to realize, that your word is law. It is not law because you will it to be; it is law because that is its nature. There is no coercion in the process. Realization is quite different from coercion, and conviction is more than an act of the will. Feeling was born millions of years before the intellect came into being.

Let us consider the meaning of the word *Volition* as defined at the bottom of page 69): *There is but one volitional factor in the Universe, and this is Spirit, or the Self-Knowing Mind.* Our Glossary defines *Volition* (page 645) as *the power of conscious choice*. Hence our text might read: There is but One Power in the Universe which has self-choice, and that is the Self-Knowing Mind.

No doubt you have already discovered in the study of psychology that the conscious mind alone may choose and have independent action; while the subconscious, which really is the Law obeying the will of the conscious mind, has no volition whatsoever. The Self-Knowing Mind alone can choose. That is why it says, under the General Summary, page 396, third paragraph: *Mind as Law is helpless without direction. It has nowhere to go and nothing to do of Itself. It must be directed or It will do nothing.*

Read also the second paragraph on page 397: *God as Conscious Mind is Spirit. God as Subjective Mind is Law.* The Universe is a dual unity consisting of an active and a passive Principle. The projective power of Spirit is the active Principle, conscious, volitional; the receptive and creative Law is the doer of the Will of Spirit. We are surrounded by both the Spirit and the Law.

As a matter of fact we are some part of both. But is it not a wonderful thing to conceive of ourselves as having access to an Infinite Law as well as to a Divine Wisdom? It would be well for us to listen to the Divine Wisdom, and by the inspiration and guidance we receive from It learn how to give conscious direction to the Law. The Law, being mechanical and having no choice of Its own, must obey the Will of the Spirit.

On page 70 it says that God did not make Law or Substance; they are coexistent and coeternal with God. They always existed; they are without beginning and without end. Law and Substance, like God, always were. I am sure this is easy to understand since we all must realize that there never could have been a time when two and two began to make four. In this way we can say that the principle of mathematics is coexistent and coeternal with the Spirit.

But our text says that God is always creating forms and that nothing is moved unless Intelligence moves it in accord with Law. This means that Mind is the final Actor; Intelligence alone is the Originating Creative Cause. Whether this Intelligence is in what we call man or what we call God, It is the same Intelligence, since all Intelligence must finally be One.

To teach this creative power of thought is the whole purpose of the Bible. The Bible starts with the assumption that God is Spirit or Absolute Intelligence; that God's thought is creative; that man is made out of God and is like God. It follows that man's thought is creative.

On page 448 under the heading, *The Purpose of the Science of Mind*, you will find an explanation of the spiritual world as being the cause of the material. It follows that everything that Spirit thinks must take form. In other words the forms of nature are the thoughts of God outlined. Infinite Mind has brought this physical world into being. Therefore our thought interprets the physical world, and decides what our relationship to it shall be. What innumerable forms there must be which we do not yet look upon "for now we see through a glass, darkly."

This brings us to the end of Chapter 1 of the Textbook, and I suggest that you read it again in the light of this explanation.

Summary

It is impossible that there should be two creative powers in the universe, because if there were, one would destroy the other. Since there is but One Power in the universe, all action takes place within It. All things are made of It by movement of thought, mind, or consciousness within Itself. This is the meaning of *In the beginning was the Word*.

The fundamental cause of everything is an idea. There are infinite varieties of ideas in the Divine Mind. We are in the Divine Mind, and these ideas operate through us at the level of our own belief. Many ideas and many personalities, however, do not contradict the fundamental idea of the One Unity. It is the Mind of God in everything that makes everything what it is. There is One Body, One Mind, and One Spirit. We individualize this One, each in a unique manner. It was the knowledge of this that was the secret of the power of Jesus.

Good is at the base of everything. The more we recognize this good the more it will respond to us and the more power our words will have. The Word of God is the Law of God, or the Law of Mind in Action.

We are free agents in this Principle, and the conscious mind alone chooses. All subconscious reaction is automatic, mathematical, and mechanical. The thinker chooses. The Law of Mind in Action has no volition of Its own; It must respond.

Questions

Brief answers to these questions should be written out by the student after studying the lesson and the answers compared with those which will be included in next week's lesson.

1. Give two principal reasons why we believe in One Infinite Reality or Power behind all creation.
2. How can we have the many manifestations or creations from the One Ultimate Reality? Is this not duality?
3. What are the chief characteristics of the Ultimate Reality and of the world of manifestation?
4. What is the law by which these manifestations or creations are brought into being? How can man use this law?
5. Is Ultimate Reality ever depleted by becoming form?
6. Is all thought creative?
7. If thought is creative, why is it that some of our treatments are more effective than others?

8. What is meant by the saying that *God is the engine and the engineer*?
9. What do we mean by: (1) Conscious mind? (2) Subjective mind?
10. Are the conscious and subjective minds two separate minds?

Answers to Questions on Lesson 1

1. God never had a beginning. God has always existed and always will. *In the beginning God* means the beginning of any creative series. Any creative series begins in and emerges from God.

2. We think of God as Infinite Mind or Intelligence in and through all creation. We may think of God as Nature, and embodying all the laws of Nature. In our system of thought God is All in All. He is immanent in all and is everywhere present. Our conclusion is that we are unified with and at one with God, for if God is the All in All, then He must be in us.

3. A creative series means from cause to effect. All things which we see, touch, taste, and handle are effects; that is, they have a preceding cause. For every visible effect there must be an invisible cause. A creative series, then, means cause, medium, and effect. For instance, in an invention the series would be the cause (the idea in the inventor's mind); the medium (the intelligent activity on the part of the inventor); and the effect (the result or the completed invention).

4. Yes. Any effect may be the beginning of a new creative series. For instance, the invention, or effect of the inventor, may be an electric light globe, which in turn becomes the cause of a brilliantly lighted room. Such relative causes are termed *secondary causes*.

5. We mean the final Cause which is back of everything. It is first because nothing precedes It and It is therefore Its own reason for being. Hence when we say, "In the beginning God," we mean God as First Cause. If we reason from effect back to cause we shall arrive at the necessary conclusion that pure Intelligence is the Final Cause. For example, back of all figures as we use them there is a principle or law of mathematics, which is its own reason for being. All we can say about it is that it is because it is.

6. Being unified with God we are at one with First Cause; hence First Cause is always ready to respond to us by bringing new experiences into our lives.

7. Spirit is that which knows. Therefore It is Consciousness. Spirit is the originator of all ideas. The Spirit of God creates ideas, and these ideas become things. Spirit, then, as Conscious Intelligence is the first step in any creative series. It is that Mind which knows Itself to be. The Spirit of God in operation is the movement of Intelligence (Mind) upon Itself, producing creation.

8. Since Spirit is the original Intelligence or the Mind in everything, Spirit must be present in man. The conscious knowingness of man is the Spirit of God in him. This Spirit in man is the thinker. Hence man is a creative agent. Man is a center of God's thought. There is nothing else he could be. His thought is creative because God in him is the Creator.

9. Strictly speaking, the Spirit within man is God, the Infinite Potential of all wisdom, the Source of all intelligence and ideas, and we cannot say It grows or develops. That which develops in man is a growing capacity to comprehend more life, power, and action. In this sense man's use of Spirit does develop, his power increases, and his mind expands through

meditation which is mental attention, through prayer which is communion, and through intuition which is God talking to him. As these mind faculties develop, man evolves, or the God idea in him expands. And right action follows right knowing.

10. If Spirit is Consciousness, and if the movement of Spirit is thought or idea, then it follows that thought is creative. We are constantly thinking, and thought is creative power and it does create the conditions in our lives and affairs. All thought is creative, and when we realize that by our thinking we are shaping the course of our lives, then we shall consciously direct this thought power in such a way that it will result in an orderly and happy manifestation. *As a man thinketh in his heart, so is he.*

The Great Mistake

In his comments on *The Fall*, Troward says that the story of Eden is an allegory which represents the Garden of the Soul. In this symbolic garden grew two trees, the Tree of the Knowledge of Good and Evil, and the Tree of Life.

The Tree of Life symbolizes the Divine Nature, referred to in the Upanishads. . . *This is the ancient tree whose roots grow upward and whose branches grow downward, that is called Brahma. . . . All worlds are contained in it and no one goes beyond.* It symbolizes the current of Divine Life flowing through man's nature which the allegory calls the Garden of the Soul.

Philo said, *The Tree of Life is that most general virtue . . . from which the particular virtues are derived.* His reference to the Tree of Life has the same meaning which Troward gives it when he says that the Tree of Life is that innermost perception of spirit.

If in speaking of the Garden of the Soul, which the Bible calls the Garden of the Lord, one has reference to the Creative Principle of Mind both in nature and in man, then naturally we should recognize the fruit which grows in the Garden of the Soul as being the fruit of thoughts and ideas which man must plant, cultivate, and from which he must reap a harvest. The Garden then is a thing of consciousness.

The Tree of the Knowledge of Good and Evil represents the possibility of a dual experience which arises out of man's freedom of choice. For even though our nature is rooted in the Divine, the immutable Law of Cause and Effect brings into our experience those conditions which correspond to the use we make of life; otherwise we could not be free.

Troward draws our attention to the thought that the story of Adam and Eve in the Garden is not the tradition of some bygone age, but the symbolical representation of what we all are in our innermost being. Thus Adam and Eve do not represent two persons, but rather two principles in human nature.

It is interesting that Eve was tempted, and that Adam was cast out of the Garden of Eden because he shared with her in the sin of partaking of the forbidden fruit. It becomes necessary, then, to investigate the meaning of fruit. Here we find a rich symbolism. Fruit represents the results of action, whether they be good or bad. It represents the operation of the Karmic Law, which is the Law of Cause and Effect.

Thus Jeremiah says, *I the Lord search the heart, I try the reins, even to give every man according to his ways, and according to the fruit of his doings*. The fruit of the Spirit is symbolic of the higher nature; . . . *the fruit of the Spirit is love, joy, peace, longsuffering, gentleness, goodness, faith, meekness, temperance: against such there is no law* (Galatians 5:22, 23).

In ancient symbology the fruit of the ground represented the physical nature, which must be transmuted into the fruit of the Spirit. The fruit of the Tree of the Knowledge of Good and Evil symbolizes the mixed experiences of the individual on the pathway of his evolution from lower to higher planes.

Let us inquire into the meaning of the word Adam. Adam is symbolic of the lower aspect of mind, which Philo called the intellect. The word Adam also had a higher meaning and was symbolic of the higher nature, the Archetypal Man. The Kabala says, *In reading the first and second chapters of Genesis, a distinction was made by the learned of the Israelites between the higher Adam, i.e., the Adam Quadmon or . . . ideal man, and the inferior Adam*. The higher Adam also symbolizes the Christ. Thus in Corinthians we are told: *The first man Adam was made a living soul; the last Adam was made a quickening Spirit . . . The first man is of the earth, earthy: the second man is the Lord from heaven*. It also tells us that we must put off the old man, which is the first Adam, and put on the New Man, the last Adam, which is Christ. The last Adam, the prototype of the celestial, is the Universal Christ incarnated in every soul, waiting the redemption from the Fall, that through transition man may become redeemed and sit at the right hand of the Lord. Here *Lord* refers to the Law of Mind or the government of the Karmic Law through the just decisions of Divine Wisdom.

The Chaldeans, Hebrews, and several other religious groups of antiquity spoke of the first man as Adam, and also spoke of the other Adam, which in some of the ancient sayings is referred to as *the First Adam who extended from the earth to the firmament*, for it is said that he was created upon or above the earth. In this illustration the Divine Image, or the Heavenly Adam, precedes and transcends the Adam of the dust. This means that Christ rules the Adam nature.

It is the Adam of the dust who makes the Great Mistake. This is the first man who is of the earth, earthy. But the Christ Adam, the Divine Image, lifts the lower Adam into salvation. Thus it is written: *For as in Adam all die, even so in Christ shall all be made alive.*

Let us now turn to the meaning of Eve. Eve refers to the emotional nature of the mind functioning in the lower aspects, referred to in Genesis as the Mother of Creation*: And Adam called his wife's name Eve; because she was the mother of all living.*

Troward tells us that Adam and Eve represent two principles existent within us, one which can be deceived, can make mistakes, and the other which is incapable of being deceived but yet is involved in the fall of the former. This represents the active and passive principles in all people, or what today we call the conscious and subjective faculties of the mind. Eve, or the receptive side of our nature, receives the argument of error, represented by the temptation of the serpent, and in her turn extends the fruit of duality to the intellect, or the self-conscious faculties, represented by Adam. If we were to modernize this story it would be quite correct to say that the subconscious, being a medium for the activity of thought but having no choice or will of its own, is liable to receive any suggestion, and once having received such suggestion, to act as though it were true. Hence the intellect itself becomes coerced. It is temporarily held captive.

Most of our reactions are subconscious; by far the largest portion of the mind is submerged. In our allegory there is a vast field of subjective reaction, represented by Eve; creative but not selective, not discriminating. Hence it is Eve who listens to the serpent, who eats of the fruit of the Tree of the Knowledge of Duality, and who, having eaten, seduces the husband. The intellect stands for the husband.

From a psychological viewpoint the subconscious controls the conscious. That which today we call the subconscious, in antiquity was sometimes referred to as the *great feminine illusion*, that part of our nature which can be fooled. This does not refer to some external force operating upon us but to some part of our own nature. Plotinus said, *The universal law under which the individual falls is not outside but within each.* Also from the Talmud: *Not God but ye yourselves are the creators and supporters of evils.* But because we are ignorant of our Divine nature and of the consequent power that accompanies it, we use this nature destructively rather than constructively. As the narrative states, we listen to the argument of the serpent.

Inquiring into the meaning and nature of the serpent we must again look into ancient symbolism. In ancient mythology the serpent was sometimes an emblem of good, while at other times it designated the subtlety of evil. From one of the ancient Papyri we have this saying: *Heaven was on earth . . . the good and evil serpents did not exist,* which means that prior to any manifestation there is no duality. Everything emanates from one fundamental Unity which must be the essence of Goodness, Truth, and Beauty. When this One Pure Essence passes through incarnation into individualized spirit, It carries with It the limitless creative power of Its own consciousness. Thus, automatically, man becomes endowed with creative thought.

Troward tells us that this creative power of thought is perfectly unlimited in itself, but its action is limited by the particular conception which it is sent forth to embody. Ignorance of the Law excuses no one from its results. If in ignorance we use the Life Principle destructively, our own creative thought-power externalizes conditions representative of our conceptions, and we become involved in a network of circumstances from which we can find no way of escape. The key to the whole situation lies in the realization that these circumstances are self-imposed rather than imposed on us through some external force, power, or intelligence.

We judge according to appearances. This is what Troward calls the Great Deception, and this is what ancient symbolism depicts as the serpent. The serpent argues that evil is equal to good; that there is a power separated from the living creative Spirit and opposed to It. Ancient literature also speaks of serpents which not only appear on the earth but in the air and sky. In John 3:14 we find: *And as Moses lifted up the serpent in the wilderness, even so must the Son of man be lifted up.*

We see, then, that the serpent is symbolized both as good and evil. Barlow, in his *Essays on Symbolism*, says, *The serpent has had a good meaning given to it and a very bad one. It has been the emblem of wisdom, and par excellence, the symbol of sin. With a pair of wings it became the Seraph. Curled up in a circle it has stood for time without end.*

The three-headed serpent symbolized the threefold nature of Reality, just as does the Christian Trinity. It was the Triad. It is evident, then that the serpent symbolized the Life Principle Itself and the different viewpoints which one may take of It, together with the inevitable corresponding results. This is why Troward tells us that by thinking of evil as a thing in itself we give it the very power which we pray it may be robbed of. By the act of our creative thought, the evil which we experience is brought into existence.

Listening to the serpent may be construed as listening to what Troward calls secondary causes; judging according to appearances rather than righteously; judging from the viewpoint that there is more than One Causation, thus making evil equal to good.

The story of Adam and Eve then, becomes the story of every individual's life. That part of his psychological nature which can be fooled, symbolized by Eve, receives the suggestion of separation, and through continuous repetition gradually coerces the intellect or the self-conscious faculties, represented by Adam, until the whole psychological man is brought under the influence of subjective thought patterns. It is generally considered that much, if not most, of our conscious actions are definitely influenced by this unconscious field of thought, which rising from the habit nature tends to control our actions.

This does not mean that evil is a thing in itself. And yet it is more than a belief. It is a solid conviction. In our science we learn to separate the evil from the one experiencing it, since evil itself is neither person, place, nor thing, and belongs to no one. The Talmud states*: Pray not that sinners may perish, but that the sin itself may disappear.*

The knowledge that good is supreme will automatically destroy evil. *By knowledge of God all bonds are destroyed. . . .* The Koran says, *I say: Truth is come and falsehood vanished. Verily falsehood is a thing that vanisheth.* From the Zend-Avesta: *The word of falsehood smites, but the Word of Truth shall smite it.* From the Gita: *I destroy the ignorance-born darkness by the shining lamp of wisdom.* And in II Corinthians: . . . *for what fellowship hath righteousness with unrighteousness? and what communion hath light with darkness?* Again the Koran states: *Whatever good betideth thee is from God, and whatever betideth thee, if evil, is from thyself.*

Such passages might be endlessly quoted. It is sufficient to know that the deep spiritual thinkers of all time have realized that the problem of evil is not a problem concerning something that has power within itself. It deals with the creative power of our own thought. The argument of the serpent is any argument in our consciousness which denies the supremacy of good. For as Troward tells us, if God, or the Originating Creative Principle, is One, then any suppositional opposite to this One is zero.

It would be impossible for . . . *two principles to neutralize each other, one of which is, and the other of which is not.* We can never suppose that the great nothing is equal to the Great Something. And yet this is exactly what we often do when we judge according to appearances. For instance, we say that since poverty has always existed, it always must exist.

Now this is just where we make our mistake. We eat from the fruit of the Tree of the Knowledge of Good and Evil and it is really the Law of Liberty that permits us to do this. The fruit of the Tree of Life Itself is not evil, but merely a result of action. The Tree of Life which grows in the garden of our own soul is a tree which bears many types of fruit. All manifestations come from One Final Power. Our own divine individuality differentiates this Power into innumerable experiences. If our thoughts are always received from the Great Reality and from the knowledge that the One is ever expressing Itself in many forms, then we shall come to see that It can as easily express beauty for us as ugliness. But if we have not yet learned how to see beauty instead of ugliness, then because thought is creative, ugliness appears in our experience. Hence the One Power appears to us as evil.

The evil, however, is merely a result of our own confused thought and is never a thing in itself. Hence we discover this paradox, that the very fear of evil creates its experience, while faith in good is enduring. The Truth always neutralizes fear and dissolves evil experience.

One of the most difficult things for us to learn is that each one individualizes the Spirit, and as such each is a law in his own life under the One Great Law of all life. Life becomes a mirror reflecting those conditions into our experience which mathematically correspond to our subjective attitudes of thought. In such degree as we come to see that God or Good is the only positive and absolute Power and Presence, and in such measure as we perceive this Divine Presence in our experience as Goodness, Truth, Beauty, Harmony, etc., in this measure we shall experience Reality, not as duality but as unity.

The idea in Genesis that if one eats from the fruit of the Tree of the Knowledge of Good and Evil he shall be as God and live forever, has a hidden but an interesting meaning, and one of utmost simplicity. It resolves itself into this: Man, a center of God Consciousness, gradually becoming aware of himself and of his relationship to the universe, is on the pathway of experience, evolution, or unfoldment (whichever expression one chooses to use). His thought is creative, and because he has freedom of choice, that which he chooses, either through fear or faith, tends to become part of his experience.

Since evil and good are not two ultimate powers arrayed against each other, for evil is merely an inverted use of good, it follows that by experience we all shall learn to live constructively. Meanwhile we suffer the experience of a destructive use of the Law of Life—this is *The Fall. Redemption*, of course, means just the opposite. It means a complete salvation from everything designated by the Fall.

Troward concludes: *If then it were possible for him (man) to attain the knowledge which could enable him to live forever before gaining this experience, the result would be an immortality of misery.* This would be true because it would make evil equal in power with good. Hence there is a judgment pronounced against the serpent, which stands for the lower use of the Life Principle, until the day of salvation, that is, the elevation of the serpent, which then becomes the Savior. Serpent and Savior designate two possible uses of One Life Principle.

Troward summarizes his findings: *Thus the story of The Fall contains also the statement of the principle of the Rising-again*. So we come back to the old saying: *For as in Adam all die, even so in Christ shall all be made alive*. No more definite statement could be made than that man himself is both heaven and hell. While duality exists only in our imagination, our belief in it becomes an experience which is real enough while it lasts, but by lifting up *the serpent in the wilderness*, that is, by elevating the Life Principle in the midst of fear, pain, and impoverishment, we may look upon It and be made whole.

A Science of Religion and a Religion of Science

There are three channels through which knowledge comes to us, namely, science, philosophy, and religion. By *science* we mean an organized knowledge of natural law and its application to life. By *philosophy* we mean the opinions one holds about the world, life, and reality. Although we generally speak of philosophy in relation to those statements which have been put down in writing by men whose opinions we respect, as a matter of fact, philosophy is anybody's opinion about anything. By *religion* we mean any man's belief about his relation to the invisible universe. Or we might say religion is a man's idea of God or gods.

It follows, then, that there are many philosophies and many religions, since in both instances they constitute opinions. But not so with science, for science is a knowledge of the laws of nature. We also speak of *pure science* and *applied science*. Pure science means the application of these natural principles to human needs. Thus pure science is a knowledge of principles, while applied science is a technique for using universal principles.

A scientist, in whatever field of investigation he may be engaged, is one who uses universal principles. Once a principle is discovered and the laws governing it are ascertained, he maintains absolute faith in that principle.

Science is not an investigation into the *why*, but into the *how*. The why of anything, that is, the reason for its being, the reason for Being Itself, science makes no attempt to answer. Should it shift its field from the knowledge of principles and facts to the field of inquiry into why these principles exist, then science would become philosophy.

Today scientific minds are beginning to speculate on their own principles. And as they do this their speculations fall into two generalized classifications, philosophically speaking. These speculations lead them either to a philosophic basis of *materialism* or to a philosophic basis of *idealism*. For all philosophy finally falls into these two branches of thought—idealism and materialism.

Both the idealist and the materialist believe that the universe is a thing of intelligence. The only difference is that the materialist refuses to admit that the intelligence operating through the laws of nature is backed by or permeated with any form of consciousness; that is, the intelligence is merely a blind but intelligent force, a conglomeration of immutable laws of cause and effect with no element of consciousness, no sentiment, no feeling. He sees only blind force but he sees blind force intelligently organized.

The idealist feels that back of and operating in and through the laws of nature there is volition and consciousness, for he argues that the manifestation of physical life upon this planet always is in accord with organized intelligence. He argues that organized intelligence can be accounted for only on the basis that there is an engineer as well as an engine.

There are, then, these two branches of philosophy—the idealistic and the materialistic. The idealist believes in consciousness, hence an Oversoul or a Spiritual Universe, while the materialist does not. Naturally the scientist who is philosophically a materialist believes in no God, no spiritual universe, and no consciousness in the universe which responds to man. He does not believe in the immortality of the individual soul, nor can he give any real meaning to life. He may be a humanitarian and a very good man, but his ultimate philosophy is: "Six feet under and all is over."

The scientist who feels that there is consciousness in the universe finds no difficulty in believing in God or in the universe as a spiritual system, permeated with a consciousness which responds to man. Therefore he believes in prayer, faith, immortality, and a definite meaning to life. An increasing number of scientific men are taking this position. The scientist who is a materialist has no religion unless it be one of humanitarianism, while the idealist can scarcely get along without some religion.

But if the idealist is a scientific man, believing as he must that everything is governed by law, his religion cannot be superstitious. Being a scientific person he cannot believe in a God who specializes on one person more than on another, or who esteems one person above another, nor can he believe that the laws of nature can be broken or modified through anyone's prayer or faith. Therefore the scientific mind which happens at the same time to be idealistic, that is, believes that the universe is not only intelligent but that it is also consciousness, will be satisfied with no religion which contradicts reason, common sense, and a cosmos of law and order.

When the first discoveries of science refuted ancient superstitions and proved that this world was not the center of the universe, that it was round and not flat, the faith which many people held began to wane. The ancient shibboleths, dogmas, and superstitions could no longer be held valid for intelligent men. So they were discarded, and religion began to lose its hold on the scientific mind.

This marked but a certain stage in the evolution of science, for today we find increasing numbers of scientific men emerging from this age of materialism, particularly since science has now theoretically resolved the material universe into organized energy and has discovered that the smallest particles which it supposes to exist exercise a sort of volition, which of course leaves room for freedom. Once you establish freedom and volition operating upon, in, or through the energy which creates form, then you have established a universe of consciousness. And once you establish a universe of consciousness you establish the possibility of communion, and arrive at a logical basis for faith, prayer, the religious and the mystical life.

During this mental and spiritual controversy which has taken place in the world in the last few hundred years, a vast majority of people have given but little thought to the subtle intricacies and the deep abstractions which we have been considering. To most people religion was either superstitiously entertained—and no doubt with great benefit to those who believed in it—or else it was rejected.

Today, however, there is a certain and rather swift return to religious convictions. The reason for this appears to be twofold. It has been discovered that when all religious atmosphere disappears, when every mystical element is eliminated, and when man views the universe merely as blind force, he loses hope. He views life as an unfortunate experience and looks forward to death as a happy oblivion. No mental attitude could be designed which would create a more forlorn outlook than this.

Moreover, when the mass consciousness becomes irreligious, unmystical, unbelieving, and without faith in God, without any conviction as to the meaning of life, it becomes chaotic, anarchistic, irresponsible, and in effect says, "Eat, drink and be merry, for tomorrow we die." Therefore it again becomes necessary that some form of religion shall be given to the world which scientific men need not reject and which the unscientific man may accept without superstition.

This is exactly what we mean when we speak of a *scientific religion*. We do not mean that we reduce religion to coldness, without sentiment or feeling, but that we add law and order to the sentiment and the feeling. We have a perfect right to speak of a scientific religion or a religion of science. But upon what natural principle should a scientific religion be based? It must be based upon the principle of Mind, Intelligence, and Consciousness.

A scientific religion may still affirm consciousness in the universe, that is, a spiritual Presence and an Intelligence which responds to the individual approach. Therefore a scientific religion does not exclude what we call prayer or communion even though it lays greater stress on communion than on petition. For instance, a scientific religion does not believe that man's petitions to God can change the natural order of the universe or reverse the laws of nature.

It does believe, however, that prayer is the communion of the soul with the Oversoul or with God, which makes it possible for man, not to reverse natural law but to reverse his position in it in such a way that bondage becomes freedom.

We might speak of *pure Religious Science* as we would speak of a *pure natural science*, which means the study of natural causes. We might speak of pure Religious Science as that branch of science which studies the nature of the Divine Principle, the nature of Mind and Consciousness. Then we would think of *applied Religious Science* as the application of this Divine Principle to human needs for practical purposes, and this is where the Religious Scientist, in applying his Principle, would study the nature of prayer, of faith, and of mental actions and reactions.

He would discover that in using faith, prayer, communion, or what we call mental treatment, he would be applying the Principle of Mind, Spirit, Intelligence, Consciousness, Law and Order to the persistent problems of everyday life. He would, then, be more than a theoretical religionist; he would have an applied and a practical religion.

This is exactly what we mean when we speak of a science of religion and a religion of science, for we are using this term in its broadest sense. We are using the term *religion* from the standpoint of universal religion, including all religious beliefs—Christian, Buddhist, Mohammedan, or any other faith—and we are thinking of prayer, communion, and the laws of consciousness as applied to any and all people. In short, we are universalizing the Principle. Thus each religion approaches the same God, all religions ultimately believe in the same God, but a scientific religion cannot believe in any concept of God which denies a universe of Law and Order, or which attempts to exclude anyone from its benefits.

It would be unscientific as well as irrational to believe that God, or the Supreme Intelligence, holds one man in higher esteem than another. For as the Bible so truthfully and boldly declares: *And let him that is athirst come. And whosoever will, let him take the water of life freely.*

A Religious Scientist believes with Robert Browning that *all's love, yet all's law.* He believes in an impersonal Law as well as in a personal relationship to the Spirit. And he must believe that this Law exists for all, like the law of mathematics or any other natural law, but that this personal relationship is personified through each at the level of his consciousness, at the level of his comprehension of what God means to him. In a scientific religion, superstition and dogma find no place. They must be discarded.

Intelligence and reason must be the rule of thought, and God must be accessible to all on equal terms. The scientific man cannot believe in special revelations nor in special dispensations of Providence. He does not believe that Joshua made the sun stand still nor that Moses parted the Red Sea. He believes that these are but symbols of spiritual power, probably intended to teach us that the Spirit in man is supreme over all apparent material resistance.

The scientific religionist cannot believe in miracles, but he does not deny the power of spiritual thought. He believes that the so-called miracles performed as a result of spiritual faith have been in accord with natural law and cosmic order. He believes that they should be reproduced at will. That which the illumined have experienced and that which men of great spiritual power have proved, the scientific religionist feels should be deliberately used in everyday life.

He believes there is a Principle governing all things. He feels that he understands the laws, or at least some of the laws, of this Principle; hence he feels that it is intensely sane as well as humanly practical to supply faith, consciousness, and spiritual conviction to the solution of human problems. This is what is meant by *spiritual mind healing.*

Spiritual mind healing is based on the belief or the theory, which we now consider to be proved, that there is a Principle of Intelligence in the universe which is not only creative, giving rise to objective form, but It is immediately sensitive to our desires, and being universal It is omnipresent, and being omnipresent It is not only where we are but It is what we are. The difference is in degree and not in essence. Hence the scientific religionist feels that he understands what Jesus meant when he said, *The words that I speak unto you I speak not of myself, but the Father, that dwelleth in me, he doeth the works.*

Just as all pure science, before it can be of any use to humanity must pass into applied science, so pure religion, before it can have a practical application, must pass into applied religion. And it is the application of religion to the solution of our problems which we speak of as *demonstrating* the Principle.

What, then, is the Principle of pure and applied Religious Science? The Principle of pure Religious Science is that there is an Absolute Intelligence in the universe—one, undivided, birthless, deathless, changeless Reality. Since no one made God and since God did not make Himself, that which was, is, and is to be, will remain.

That which is, according to our first axiom of truth which says that the Truth is all there is, means that there is nothing else beside It. Hence the entire manifestation of Life is an evolution or an unfoldment of form from that which is formless, primordial, and eternal. This intelligent Cause, this undifferentiated and undistributed God-Principle, one and complete within Itself but yet from which all action proceeds and in which all creation takes place, this original and originating One is the absolute Principle of Religious Science.

In the philosophy of Religious Science we rightly deduce that since man lives, and moves, and has his being in states of consciousness, that is, since man can think, he exists. Since he can proclaim he must be, and since he is, he must be made out of that which is, by reason of the fact that you can get out of a bag only what is in it. It was this perception, we believe, which was back of what Jesus meant when he said, *He that hath seen me hath seen the Father*.

The philosophy of Religious Science, then, consists in the belief, the opinion, or the certainty that God as man, in man, is man, and that when man makes a proclamation it is still God proclaiming, but now at the level of man's consciousness. Therefore the cosmos is reflected in or manifested by or through the individual. You cannot say, "Why is man?" any more than you can say, "Why is God?" Intelligence exists and man interprets It. Therefore man is Its mouthpiece; man is a personification of the Infinite, governed by the same laws. But man is more than law; he is consciousness.

The application of this science of religion and this philosophy of its thought to our everyday problems is the practical end of Religious Science, just as there is a practical end to every other science. It is not enough merely to speculate or philosophize. It is certainly not enough to abstract our thought and announce an Infinite, for the Infinite can never mean more to us at any time than the use which we make of It, just as electricity can never mean more to us than the use we make of it. This is true of any and all principles of nature.

Religious Science rightly argues that if there is an Infinite Creative Intelligence which makes things out of Itself by Itself becoming the thing that It makes, and if man exists and is conscious, then the creative Genius of this Universal Mind is also the creative genius of Its individualization, which we call man.

From the above stated propositions intelligence cannot escape, correct induction and deduction cannot escape. Thus most of the great intellectual geniuses who have ever lived on this planet have proclaimed these truths, each in his own tongue, in his own language, in his own day, for his own age, and we believe that Jesus proclaimed them for all ages since he was so universal in his concept.

Religious Science does not belong to any sect, to any group, to any class, and most certainly not to any person. It lays no claim to special revelation, but does announce that in its particular system of thought there have been gathered together facts from all ages, from all people, from all philosophies and religions, and using the practical methods which any other scientific research would use it is able to, and does, deliver a message of freedom.

Meditation

Since God is Love, and God is All in All, Love must be the underlying Principle of life, and therefore in all. This Life is my life. This Love I am. It is the very essence of my being.

I know that Love is harmony and peace and joy. In it is all good, all that is true, all that is beautiful. It is perfect balance, perfect poise.

Love heals everything, every imperfection of mind or body or environment. Love overcomes hatred, anger, envy, criticism. Where Love is there is no room for any negative emotion. Love is the Great Adjuster.

I empty my mind and heart of all but Love. I let Love express in me, through me, and flow out into my world of thought and action. *I AM Love.*

I AM Love—that is harmony,

I AM Love—that is peace,

I AM Love—that is joy,

I AM Love—that is freedom,

I AM Love—that is wisdom,

I AM that Love that is in all.

I AM LOVE

Creative Thought—the Greatest Discovery
Office of the Dean

My Dear Friend,

We take great pleasure in sending you Lesson No. 3 in the Principle and Practice of the Science of Mind. This lesson deals with mental laws and how they operate, and we should like to be certain that you are beginning to differentiate between the Law of Mind in Action as a mathematical principle, and the Living Spirit as a Divine Presence. We are surrounded by an intelligent, creative Principle which acts upon our thinking, and also by a Divine Presence which inspires this thinking. We commune with God but we use the Law.

These are the two foundations upon which this whole course is built. They are both simple and profound and have been taught by all of the deep thinkers of the ages.

As you will notice in our Supplement on the Bible, there is no danger in using laws of nature or Laws of Mind when they are used constructively. We should be careful to use our thought for life-giving purposes only, and with the desire that we bless everything we touch. If we do this, nothing but good can come to us.

Please note carefully the article, *The Use and Meaning of Words in Mental Treatment*, for this is of vital importance.

Also examine the several pages from *Bibles of the World*, and you will find that there is almost complete agreement among them, which goes to show that all great spiritual thinkers of the ages have agreed on fundamental truths. They have all communed with the same God, and received the same answer. We too must do this.

Sincerely,
Ernest Holmes

Lesson 3
(page 71 to *Mental Laws,* page 77)

Our lesson begins with the thought that nature waits on man's self-recognition. The laws of nature have always existed. Moses might have had electric lights instead of torches, but Moses did not know anything about electricity although electric energy filled the universe then as now. We might say that electricity waited man's recognition of it and his conscious cooperation with the law governing it. Man did not have it to use until he first recognized its existence and understood how it worked.

This of course is true of every law of nature; any law that ever has been discovered by the scientific world must first have existed and in a sense waited to be used. All advance in science is a result of gaining more knowledge and a deeper understanding of the laws of nature and how they work. What untold possibilities lie before the scientific world only the imagination can depict. Everything happens as though the evolution of man were the result of a gradual awakening of his relationship to the universe and to the laws governing all life.

We do not believe that the Principle of Life has evolved; we cannot believe that God is more complete than He was a million years ago. What we do believe is that the manifestation of God is forever unfolding before us. As man's vision gradually increases, new laws and new conditions are revealed to him which in his former ignorance he neither believed in nor understood.

The laws of nature have always existed and the possibility of using them has always existed, for principles never change—what changes is the practice of principles. It is marvelous to consider the possibility of such an infinite and endless unfoldment. There must be beings as far in advance of us as we in our present state have evolved beyond the tadpole or the crocodile. Jesus said, *In my Father's house are many mansions*. There are many states of consciousness, many planes of self-expression. Man's being is founded on a limitless Principle; hence the evolution or unfoldment of his becoming— that is, of his manifestation—must also be without limit.

There will always be new worlds to conquer, the horizon of previous experiences will ever be rising over a new day. *Life waits on man's discovery of natural laws, his discovery of himself, and his discovery of his relationship to the great Whole* (top of page 72).

Next we have this thought: *The* principle *of any science is invisible*. On page 631 in the Glossary you will find *Science* defined as *knowledge of laws and principles; organized knowledge*. The principle of science is invisible. We do not see Life; we experience it. And because we experience It, we know that we live. Life must forever remain invisible, and yet what intelligent person would deny Its reality? (Read very carefully the definition of *Life*, page 606 and the whole paragraph on page 490, *The Ascending Scale of Life*.)

There is no end to our evolution, but the invisible Principle of Life we experience without seeing It. We can analyze how It works, but not what It is. You will readily see that in the last analysis we must accept Life rather than explain It. For instance, the united intelligence of the human race does not know how it is that we can eat lamb stew and apple pie and have it converted into whiskers and fingernails. We may watch the process, but the principle of that process we cannot see.

It is written: *No man hath seen God at any time; the only begotten Son, which is in the bosom of the Father, he hath declared him* (John 1:18). We do not see Causation; but the Son, which is the creation, does reflect or manifest or prove the existence of Causation. In this way God is revealed to us. Who is there who has ever seen love? Yet no one doubts its reality. (This is the meaning of the second paragraph on page 406, General Summary, in which we discuss the idea that Pure Spirit exists at the center of all form. We see the form but not the Spirit.)

Now turn to page 74 under the heading *Science*. One thing we must keep in mind is that God as Pure Spirit is an Infinite Presence, while the Universe as Law is mechanical. Science is the study of the mechanics of the Universe, just as religion is the study of real values and the relationship between God and man. Science, of necessity, must deal only with cold facts. There may be a sentiment in the mind of the scientist, but there cannot be any sentiment in his approach to Universal Principles. He discovers they are always exact, always mathematical, and always responsive to him, but they will never work for him until he has first discovered their nature and the mode of their response .

Is this not true in dealing with all the laws of life? We must first obey the laws of nature, then they will serve us. In the unfoldment of any science the laws governing that science must first be discovered, and then through careful, painstaking, and patient investigation, ways, methods, and means of using those laws are finally worked out.

The knowledge of law as principle is the foundation of any science; the knowledge of how this law works is the technique of that science. The science itself does not belong to anyone. It is always impersonal; it does not care who uses it. (Read the definition of *Impersonal* on page 601). It is always neutral, it does not care for what purpose it is used; but it is always effective when we approach it in its own nature. The laws of science being universal belong to everyone. We might truly say that each of us possesses all the laws of nature. They are, in a sense, a personal belonging since each may use all of them, but since they are universal they are impersonal in that no person can ever exhaust them.

We rob no man when we seek our own good. Life exists for the purpose of self-expression—the more we express, the more completely God is expressed. It does no one any good for us to remain poor, weak, sick, or unhappy. Rather we glorify God in such degree as we become emancipated from our bondage. I am sure we all believe this final emancipation can be attained only through the closest cooperation with the purpose of nature; only by a more complete sense of our unity with the Divine Spirit, which is the Infinite Presence of Life, Truth, Love, and Wisdom.

When it comes to the scientific use of any law, whether it is the science of electricity or the Science of Mind, let us forswear superstitions and approach it with intelligent understanding, for this is the only way we shall ever derive any benefit from our studies. As our text says in the second paragraph, page 75, *The Science of Mind, then, is the study of Life and the nature of the laws of thought*.

When we make the claim that there is a Universal Mind and a Universal Spirit we are announcing that there is a Principle back of all thought. We are announcing that the Spirit operating upon the mental Principle produces all forms. We are announcing the presence of a Divine Knower and the certainty of a mechanical response—the Law and the Word. (Turn to page 641 and carefully study the definition of *Universal Spirit*.)

We must be careful in this connection not to confuse the idea of the Spirit of God and the Law of God with any concept of duality. They are really two attributes of the same thing, just as seedtime and harvest are but two ends of one process of evolution. In the interpretation of Romans 12:2, referred to on page 486 under the heading *The Renewing of Your Mind*, you will find a discussion of the thought that mental healing is subject to the exact laws of Mind and Spirit and is accomplished by correct knowing. This knowing is a mental attitude toward the Truth. It is the Truth which makes free and it is the mind which knows the Truth.

On page 407, second paragraph, is the statement, *We cannot account for the seen without having faith in the unseen*. Therefore in dealing with the Science of Mind as a study of life and the nature of the laws of thought, we must never forget that we are dealing with a definite Principle. We must learn how to deal with it consciously, knowing that as a result of our conscious thought there will be a subjective reaction in the Law which will exactly balance and equal that conscious thought.

The reaction of the Law is in the nature of a reflection of the image held in thought. Both the reflection in the mirror and the image in front of it are effects. Someone has placed the image in front of the mirror and the mirror must automatically reflect its exact likeness. The invisible cause of both the image and the reflection is the image maker. Here we have a perfect analogy of our use of mental law and of the mechanical reaction to our thought.

But again we must be careful not to confuse this with any system of duality. The mechanical reaction of the Law is a part of Being Itself and is in no way separated from It. Always we must be careful to avoid any confusion which arises from a belief in duality. (Read very carefully the definition of *Duality* on page 587 and the definition of *Unity* on page 640.)

When you say that there is a Universal Mind and someone asks you if you have ever seen It, be quite frank and say no and then ask him if he has ever seen Reason, Love, Integrity, or Beauty. Of course you have never seen the Universal Mind! Our text says (page 75), *The Eternal Principle is forever hidden* and *The only proof we have of Mind is that we think*. We are undoubtedly living in the Universal Mind. Everything happens exactly as though we were living in a universe of Pure Spirit from which we may receive intuitive perceptions and inspiration and Divine guidance.

At the same time, we are surrounded by a Universal Law of Mind which reacts creatively to our images of thought. From this standpoint you will better understand the statement on page 76 to the effect that what appears to be outside is really inside. That is, nothing is external to mind. Mind is both individual and Universal. (Read the explanation of *Mind* on page 612 and of *I Am* on page 598. Also study page 391 of the General Summary and the first three paragraphs of page 392.)

One of the most difficult things for us to understand, and yet one which is absolutely essential, is the saying at the end of the second paragraph, page 76: *The Mind which is personified is the same Mind which is Universal*. Also read the thought at the bottom of the page, that the Intelligence which perceives nature is the same Intelligence that created it. Is not this really what Jesus meant when he said, *I and my Father are one*? In the first paragraph on page 77 you will notice these words: *God exists in me, and because God exists in me, I am able to recognize other beings in whom God exists*. We must never fail to realize that the Divine Creative Medium which is the Principle back of the movement of thought, is governed by the Divine Creative Presence which is the Spirit of God. And as we more and more completely sense the Divine Spirit as being our spirit, we shall have an increasing power in our use of the Law.

Summary

The Principle of Mind has not evolved. We are merely coming to understand how It works. All scientific research is in the realm of laws that pre-existed the human inquiry.

The laws of nature wait our recognition but respond to us the moment we use them. This is true of the Law of Mind with which we are dealing. This will always be true because evolution is eternal.

There are limitless possibilities within the human being because he is not merely human, he is Divine. These possibilities wait for our recognition. This recognition is a spiritual act of the mind.

It is not strange that we do not see God, Spiritual Mind, or First Cause. Neither do we see mathematics, harmony, love, or beauty. All we see is the effect of these things. We have just as much reason to believe in the Universal Mind Principle that responds to us as we do in the law of gravitational force.

There is no sentiment in our approach to the Law of Mind, since it is mathematical, mechanical, and exact. The sentiment is in the way we use this Law. We must get it firmly established in our thought that there is a Principle of Mind and a science or a way to use It.

 This science does not belong to any individual but it belongs to whoever uses it.

We have no superstition about this any more than a mechanic is superstitious about his engine. We are the mechanic using the engine, or the force and energy of a Creative Intelligence. We have access to this whole Creative Intelligence, even as each one of us has access to the whole of God.

Questions

Brief answers to these questions should be written out by the student after studying the lesson and the answers compared with those which will be included in next week's lesson.

1. What is the basic truth about any law of nature?
2. When can we use the laws of nature?
3. Does the Principle of Life or God evolve?
4. Does the Creative Spirit make something out of nothing?
5. Will man ever reach the apex of his evolution?
6. How does man progress?
7. Do we see natural causes, principles, or spiritual realities?
8. (a) Can we explain life? (b) How then is God revealed to us?
9. What main idea should we keep in mind in studying this science?
10. How do we utilize the laws of nature?
11. To whom do the laws of nature belong?
12. What is the purpose of life?
13. How do we glorify God?
14. How can final emancipation from bondage be accomplished?
15. What is the Science of Mind?
16. What do we mean by the Law and the Word?
17. How is mental healing accomplished?
18. Does the idea of Spirit as Knower and Law as Doer imply duality?
19. What is the result of conscious thought?
20. Has anyone ever seen the Universal Mind?

21. Is man's mind separate from the Universal Mind?
22. How should we increase our use of creative Mind?

Answers to Questions on Lesson 2

1. (1) If there were two ultimate powers neither would be infinite, for if each were infinite they would neutralize each other and the result would be zero. (2) Scientific findings now indicate that all form comes from a common source, Universal Energy, which is undivided, has always existed, and always will exist. So we say all that is or ever shall be has as its source one Ultimate Reality, which is Unity.

2. The created forms may be many and varied, but coming from the One Source they cannot be different in essence, hence there cannot be duality. To use an example, let us take water which is one form of substance, and subject it to heat. The form changes as the water becomes steam. If we lower the temperature of the water it becomes solid ice, which is another form. Here we have three different forms of the one substance. The form of each is different but the essence remains the same.

3. We cannot see Ultimate Reality. We can only sense It through inner feeling. We constantly see and experience the forms of Reality. For instance, we cannot see love, beauty, harmony, etc., but we are constantly experiencing what these qualities do. The resulting forms are the outer symbols of the inner Reality. The realm of Reality is the unseen world of thought and idea that is behind the world of form which we experience.

4. The Law is a law of cause and effect. Thought or idea is the invisible cause. Manifestation or the created form is the effect. The form is an outer symbol expressing the idea. Thoughts are acted upon by a Subjective Law which responds with mathematical exactness to the ideas of Spirit. Man may use this Law because It is an aspect of Infinite Mind and everywhere present. Hence It is present within man. Man's thought or Spirit in operation is acted upon by this Law of Cause and Effect to manifest definite conditions in his body and his affairs.

5. The Infinite, being all, cannot be depleted in any way. There is always more and still more substance, wisdom, and creative ability. The possibility of creation is limitless.

6. If any thought is creative it must follow that all thought is creative. The Law is exact, not capricious. However, since man's belief is his use of the Law, it must follow that the greater the conviction the more power his word will have. Therefore conscious prayer, treatment, or meditation is more powerful than mere idle words.

7. The answer is that our conviction is not always completely sustained. We may reach a point of acceptance during a treatment, and immediately neutralize it. In this case we have not arrived at complete conviction. We must always remember the Law is exact and cannot show favoritism.

8. In observing the universal nature of God we view both volitional and mechanical activity. The Word of God is the engineer directing the Law of God, which in Its turn is the mechanical activity or the engine. The Word and the Law are coexistent. Before an engine can be effective there must be an engineer. Both are necessary.

9.   (1) The conscious mind of man is the volitional, self-conscious faculty. It is self-conscious mind. Man thinks, forms ideas, and consciously directs the law of his life with his conscious mind. It is the engineer. (2) The subjective mind of man is not volitional, but mechanical. It is the law of his being. It accepts ideas and thought, and is subject to the conscious mind. It knows only to do. It is the engine which responds to the engineer.

10. No. There is only One Universal Mind with two aspects—Spirit and Law. In man's mind, which is his point of identity in Universal Mind, we call Spirit the conscious mind and Law the subjective mind.

God Power and the New Name

In his chapter on Israel, Troward explains the necessity of bringing all psychic forces under control. He says, *The psychic world is an integral part of the universe.*

This psychic world is frequently referred to in the Bible as water. As already stated, the story of the flood or deluge is symbolic of what might happen when the psychic life controls an individual or the race. Troward says . . . *a deluge would indicate a total submergence in a psychic environment which had become too powerful to be held under control.* Psychologically, in the case of an individual, this would mean when subjective thought patterns actually take possession of him and obsess him—a psychic confusion so complete that there is no longer a true integration of personality. Some form of insanity would follow such a condition.

If we can conceive of a world psyche, or what some psychologists might call a collective unconscious which largely dominates the race thought and action, we shall see that limitless confusion in this field would produce something akin to race insanity.

But the deluge referred to in the Bible, according to Troward, is attributed to the wickedness of mankind. Nearly all scriptures of antiquity refer to some form of deluge; that is, to some universal confusion which follows the misuse of the law of cause and effect, the law of causation and interaction between the higher and lower plane. It is the law which says that we shall reap as we have sown. Hafiz says, *Do not complain, Oh soul! of the injustice of the Beloved, for such is thy law.*

All books of spiritual wisdom, particularly those of antiquity, warn us against a misuse of the Creative Principle. Most of them had some fictitious personage who, like Noah, outrode the turbulent waters of confusion. The ark symbolizes the preservation of Divine individuality even while the lower manifestations of life are swept away. In the *Ark of the Covenant* were kept the books of the law, symbolizing that in the Secret Place of the Most High, in the Christ within us, there is always a spiritual equilibrium.

It does not seem at all strange that universal belief should sway the opinions and acts of the human race, since we know that individual opinions do control to a large degree the actions of an individual.

Consider the reaction in what we call mob psychology. Its fear, hysteria, or heroism, something greater than any individual member, seizes all members. Or we may consider the act of collective faith beneficently healing, bringing peace, etc. This would be Christ walking over the waters—the Ark riding on the waters. The Spiritual Principle walks over, transcends, is above all psychic confusion, ever speaking from the depths of Its mystical Self: *It is I, be not afraid.*

This has been referred to as the movement of the Spirit upon the waters. It is from this movement that the psychic forces are brought under control and made to serve a good purpose. Troward is careful to point out that while there are certain dangers which might arise out of the psychic life, we must not fall under the illusion either of doubting its reality or of refusing to have anything to do with it, for by our nature we are always immersed in it.

Common sense tells us that since this psychic realm is the realm of thought actions and reactions, the Law of Cause and Effect, it is impossible to escape it. We should use it as a servant rather than obey it as though it were a lord. And in order to do this both intelligently and constructively we must first recognize the Divine Principle of our being as one, undivided, harmonious Goodness in which there is no violence whatsoever.

Just as there is no danger in using laws of nature unless they are used either in ignorance or with vicious intention, so no possible harm can come from the use of psychic powers, which are laws of mind, unless they are used either in ignorance or with vicious intention. Fortunately, ignorance soon destroys itself and vicious intention defeats its own purpose. The universe must be foolproof in order to endure. Troward states that we are always safe when we recognize the Divine Spirit as the only source of power. This he implies is brought about by learning to see God in all things. For it is certain that we must accept life either as good or evil.

Perhaps the greatest single mystery in life is the simple fact that life must become to each one of us what we are to it. The Law of Cause and Effect is no respecter of persons. We are at all times surrounded by a Creative Principle which accepts the images of our thoughts and acts creatively upon them. Consequently everything depends on the source from which we derive our thought patterns.

Are we controlled by the suggestion of our external environment? Do we judge according to appearances? If so we cannot hope to escape the limitations which now appear to hold us in their grasp. Suppose we are not controlled entirely by things as they appear objectively but that we are controlled by traditional beliefs which tend to limit us. If we are controlled from this subjective field our reflection in the Law of Cause and Effect is still limited to previous experiences. Whether we are bound by our psychic insight or our physical outsight makes no difference, for each furnishes us with images of limitation.

The Law of Mind like other laws in nature has to be used. But since it happens to be the greatest creative force we shall ever contact and since it is absolutely receptive to our thought, everything depends upon what our thought patterns are like and where they come from. Do they come from a belief that the highest Truth can be reached on only the lower physical or even the lower mental plane? If so we are building our Tower of Babel.

As Troward points out, this tower was built of brick, symbolic of the supposition that the external world is a thing in itself. This naturally leads to confusion, and as our text suggests, is the very opposite of the heavenly Jerusalem which is built of gold and precious stones. Gold is a symbol of spiritual qualities, Divine Wisdom, heavenly treasures— . . . *and the city was pure gold, like unto clear glass* (Revelation 21:18). Swedenborg tells us that frankincense represents spiritual goodness, and myrrh natural goodness. It is when this gold is joined with frankincense and myrrh that we have the true offering to life.

Here again we arrive at the trinity in unity. It is this recognition of the threefold unity of life with all of its implications that the wise men, the Magi, bring from the East to lay before the Babe in the manger at Bethlehem. The Magi came from the mystical East which symbolizes the source of heavenly light. They were guided by the Star. This star is the intuition which Wordsworth called our life's star. It guides us across the pathway of human experience to where the little child lies in the manger of our innermost self. Manger is a symbol of spiritual simplicity and unity with all forms of life.

We also have the story of Moses who was found floating in a little ark. Coupling the mystical meaning of Moses, which Swedenborg tells us represents the Law, we find the symbol is that of the Law of Righteousness riding upon the waters of Mind. This stands for Divine Government. In the case of Jesus we find The Waters not only governed by Law but also by Love. St. John tells us that the Law was given by Moses, but that grace and truth came through Jesus Christ.

Returning to our story of the deluge and the Tower of Babel we find that the whole symbolism represents the operation of natural law directed by a state of confusion which is the result of a sense of disunity with the Creative Principle. The story implies that the more we know of natural law, the worse off we are unless our knowledge is controlled by Divine Wisdom. Nothing could more perfectly describe conditions as they exist in the world today. Knowledge may be power but power without wisdom is confusion; hence the deluge.

Troward points out that the story of the Bible up to this point is an allegory. It is a symbolic word presentation describing the nature of man and the creative power of thought, and telling us what happens as a result of our thought. Troward tells us, *The purpose of the Bible is to convey instruction in the nature and use of . . . principles to those in whose hands this knowledge would be safe and useful.* These principles are few in number but they run through everything. The Bible repeats these few simple principles in innumerable ways, and is ever seeking to instruct the individual to awake to his own sonship.

Next we come to an explanation of the meaning of Jacob wrestling with the angel. Jacob is a symbol of the natural man trying to discover his relationship with the nameless One. Jacob's ladder represents the soul's path from the lower to the higher planes—from earth to heaven. Earth and heaven represent two states of consciousness. We are told that Christ has united heaven with earth.

The nameless One that Jacob wrestled was the great problem of his own relation to the Universal Spirit. He wrestled until the day broke, meaning until the light of Truth dawned upon his consciousness. This light is represented in Egyptian mythology by Ra, the ever-living Principle, symbol of the Higher Self of man and of the Supreme Self, which is God or Spirit. The Supreme Self manifests Itself as the Indwelling Self, which is called Khepera or the Indwelling Christ.

The new name which Jacob received, Troward tells us, signifies man's relationship to the universe of Spirit, soul, and body—the Spiritual, psychical, and physical. The new name is received in such degree as we become consciously aware of the Spiritual, the mental, and the physical. Our text states that it is only in the combination of all three elements that the true Reality is to be found.

Jesus said that we do not live by bread alone, but by every word that proceedeth out of Reality. He did not deny the physical universe, but told us not to judge everything by it. That is, to judge not according to appearances but to judge righteously. It is this righteous judgment which is designated by the word *Israel*, which means a knowledge of the truth of our being.

Troward said that Abraham, Isaac, and Jacob represent the three great Principles of Life—that which we in the Science of Mind often refer to as *The Thing, The Way It Works*, and *What It Does*. The Universe is made up of Spirit, Soul and Body. Spirit is the active Principle of self-assertion. Soul is the neutral, plastic, creative Principle which receives the ideas of the active Principle and gives birth to form. Body is the physical universe or the universe of manifestation. It is the logical, inevitable, and mathematical result of the interaction of Spirit upon Soul.

Man also is spirit, soul, and body, thus partaking of the Divine Nature in each part of Its threefold aspects of cause, medium, and effect. In his evolution man awakes first to only the physical, and believes that he is entirely controlled by his objective surroundings. This is the period which has been referred to as tooth and claw, the survival of the fittest.

If at this point he fails to become aware of spiritual and unifying principles such as love, truth, beauty, and harmony, his awakening to the mental plane as a medium of power produces a confusion even greater than that which existed before he recognized the mental plane. Hence beside awakening from the material to the mental, there must be another awakening—an awakening of the mental to the spiritual.

When the spiritual animates the mental, the mental gives birth to that which is true. Consider this interesting quotation from Hermes: *All things accordingly that are on earth . . . are not the truth; they are copies of the Truth. Whenever the appearance doth receive the influx from above it turns into a copy of the Truth; without its energizing from above, it is false.* The Talmud says, *Unhappy is he who mistakes the branch for the tree, the shadow for the substance.* From the Gita: *The unreal hath no being* (i.e. no being in itself), *the Real never ceaseth to be.*

One could find innumerable sayings from the scriptures of many races descriptive of the transitory nature of the world at experience and the abiding nature of the Truth which governs it. It is not that we should deny the objective world, but rather that spiritual wisdom should inspire us to control it in accord with the laws of harmony.

From the creative power of our thought we can never escape. It is certain that we can neither change nor alter the laws of the universe. Within these laws there is perfect freedom, complete liberty, everlasting happiness, and eternal life. More we could not ask, greater could not be given. The universe, however, is always true to its own nature. We may trust in its integrity; we may rely upon its immutable laws whether we call them physical or metaphysical; and we may be certain that there is one underlying unity governing everything.

If there is any limitation imposed upon man it is only the limitation that the very nature of Reality automatically must impose, which is that we cannot use causation destructively without suffering. This is the whole meaning of sin, mistake, hell, and punishment. Spiritual power is delivered on its own terms and these terms are unity, goodness, love, justice, truth, beauty, etc.

It is not as though there were some deific power waiting for us to bow before its omnipotence, but that real omnipotence cannot be delivered while we use the power derived from it to destroy such omnipotence. We must never mistake liberty for license. God Power is delivered only when It is used in a Godlike way; but this is no restriction. There is nothing in the universe which denies us the right to use the highest Law to promote health, happiness, and success for ourselves and for others, provided our use of the Principle of Truth is constructive. It would be impossible to ask for more; it would be impossible for more to be given.

But how should we receive this great good which has been given? As Troward has suggested, there is only one way that Power can be loosed through us, and that is through the creative act of our own consciousness. We must accept the universe as good or as evil; it will be to us a thing of limitation or of freedom. If our images of thought are generated by personal ambition, disregarding the greater good for all, then we shall be caught in a confusion of thinking.

The God Power which all potentially have can be used to the fullest extent only in a constructive way. Real Power, God Power, is Spiritual. Does this mean that the Spiritual contradicts either the mental or the physical? Not at all. The very word *Spiritual* implies a constructive use of physical and mental powers, and not some separate state of existence.

It is written that to be spiritually minded is life and peace, which means that we are both strong and peaceful when our thought processes are based upon a perception of the Unity of Good. But we are not consciously unified with Good while we desire to use Good for evil purposes. Hence it is written: *Thou shalt have no other gods before me*. That is, our faith should transcend all fear.

Are we daily watching our thought processes, being certain that all negative reactions are transmuted into positive acceptances? Do we really believe that Good is the final and only Power; that Love not only overcomes hate but completely annihilates it even as light converts darkness? These are the questions which daily we should ask ourselves.

We should be certain that our consciousness is continuously being enlarged. The whole purpose of life is to express the Self without fear or hurt to the Self or to anyone else. The gift of Life is made. We now know how to use it. No one else can decide for us but ourselves.

The Use and Meaning of Words in Mental Treatment

The entire basis for spiritual mind healing lies in the assumption that we are now living in a spiritual and mental universe; that law is mind in action; that thinking and action are the same. And if thinking and action equal the same thing, certain kinds of thinking must constitute certain kinds of action. It logically follows that if one kind of thought produces a certain effect, then an opposite thought must produce an opposite effect.

Mental treatment is mind in action. A person should use those words which convey a meaning to his own thought. For instance, if he says, "This word is the law of elimination," he must feel that any condition which does not belong is actually being eliminated.

Since it would be impossible for him to believe that mind could operate upon some matter or substance which is unlike mind, he must first have resolved things into thoughts. For the practitioner does not treat a body separate from consciousness; he treats consciousness alone. Hence the state of inaction which he seeks to remove, so far as mental treatment is concerned, is neither a state of material nor physical inaction; for he has reduced the whole process to a state of mental inaction. It is evident that unless he could do this he could not give an effective mental treatment.

Thought alone can reverse thought, thought alone can handle thought, and only thought can demonstrate over that which is a result of thought. Therefore the mental practitioner theoretically resolves everything into mind and proceeds upon the basis that mind is form, or takes form, and that the form which it takes is still mind. Our work is done in the realm of mind alone. The words that we use should be simple, direct, and to the point, and should signify a meaning to our own consciousness.

The process of reasoning in treatment must be one which establishes man upon a spiritual basis, enthrones him in a kingdom of good, and gives him dominion over all apparent evil.

If you say four and four make eight and eight has a meaning because you have already experienced handling eight marbles or eight oranges or eight chairs, then when you say four and four make eight you understand what those words mean. But do you understand what four million and four million means, even while your intellect announces eight million to be the answer?

Words must have value to the inner comprehension. I am sure Jesus understood this when he spoke of his word as being Spirit and Life. He spoke of his words as though they were entities. The thought and the thing cannot be separated. *The words that I speak unto you, they are spirit and they are life*, implies that the words possess not only power but almost a degree of personalness.

In mathematics a person can correctly use his principle only as far as his understanding goes. This is also true in mental treatment. What is this understanding which he must have and which he must pour into the words which he speaks? He must understand his relationship to Being Itself, to God, to the Universe, and to Reality. There must be an interior awareness, a realization that good is all the power there is.

 A practitioner uses words which imply to his own imagination the idea of movement, of explanation, of action or reaction, or whatever the desire is. That is, when he uses the word *elimination* he must know that something is being eliminated. He must have unqualified faith that there is a movement toward the desired elimination simultaneous with the word he uses. The practitioner must come to realize that thoughts and things are not separated; they are identical.

If he says, "Substance is supply and supply is money," and if he desires to demonstrate money, when he uses the word *substance* he should feel the presence of substance. Otherwise he is merely using a lot of words which have no meaning.

Surely we cannot separate thoughts from things in our treatment and hope to demonstrate things through thinking. For unless thoughts were things, then thoughts could not change what we call *things*. Indeed they would have no power over them whatsoever. It is upon this proposition that our whole science is based. Since thoughts are things, different kinds of thoughts are different kinds of things. When the practitioner uses the idea of substance and supply in his imagination, the idea should not be divorced from the actual presence of whatever he thinks supply is, or whatever supply means to him.

Suppose he were conceiving the idea of *home*. It would not be enough for him to say, "I'm but a stranger here, heaven is my home." In this world *home* means house, tent, a place of residence, a place to live. Therefore if he wishes to demonstrate a home, when he uses the idea *home* there should be some corresponding reaction to the word which means the actual presence of a right place in which to live.

What we can really use with spiritual meaning, significance, and reality, constitutes the stage of consciousness we are entertaining at any particular time. As a matter of fact, our state of consciousness is what we are, and if we happen to be in business and wish to treat for right action we must realize that right action means being busy in the thing that we are doing. Business is the activity of consciousness and the business of mind is never inactive. Neither is the business of mind limited to two, four, six, eight, ten, twelve, etc. It is as limitless as is our concept of it. Spirit is good, therefore business is good, and we should know that our business represents our oneness with supply, with the Creative Cause, with the Creative Givingness, with the limitless activity of the Creator.

Our business enterprise is the demand which we make upon supply, and since the demand is answered, and can be answered only in terms of the demand made, and since there is no gap between, because both supply and demand are mental or spiritual, then it follows that supply follows demand, while demand does not limit supply but measures it out at the level of the demand made.

One man working for success might have the idea of enough money with which to pay the rent; another might have the idea that after the rent was paid he would have a few dollars left over; while still another might have the idea that paying the rent was merely attending to a detail and that out of the limitless abundance he should have money left which he could share with others.

There must be some reason why some succeed and others fail if the universe in which we live is intelligent. It is impossible to conceive of Mind as ever being unexpressed, and wealth and poverty are expressions of Mind, fulfilling an idea. The thought of success will create success. Mind thinks and it is done. Man's business is God's business and God's business is man's business, and there is only one business, which is the business of Life. Life is never inactive, never inadequate; it is always perfect, and your consciousness of right action is perfect. Your word is perfect and the thing to which the word gives form is perfect, and abundance is the only law there is—but your words must have meaning and their meaning is their power.

If you are treating to heal a physical disease, you should realize that material appearance is a mental formation rather than a law unto itself. Your realization that this formation is not necessary, and the significance of the statements which you make in declaring that your word is the law of elimination of the condition, should have the same reaction in your own thought as that which would be produced if, while you were looking at something, it should disappear. You would immediately recognize the omnipresence and the omnipotence of God, and to such degree as your recognition of the omnipresence of Good signifies to your own thought the annihilation of the negative physical condition, the condition will cease to be.

When the practitioner says, "This word is for so and so" or "for such and such a purpose," his definite intention specifies the place or the purpose, and this is all he needs to do. From then on his work is within himself, and his work is a combination of thinking, which through argument or realization brings about a complete acceptance of the desired fact. It would be impossible to do this unless facts could be reduced to states of consciousness.

That which needs to be externally changed is not a thing in itself but a physical state of consciousness. This is the crux of the whole matter; it is the finest of all points in metaphysical practice; it is the essence of the subject, but unfortunately it is too often overlooked. The external condition is not a thing but thought externalized, and thought externalized is still thought. A mental conclusion objectified is still a mental conclusion.

This is the meaning of argument in giving mental treatments. The argument is for the purpose of convincing the mind of the practitioner that the condition, which needs to be changed, is not a thing in itself; that back of it is a perfect universe, God, the All-Being. But unless the words used by a practitioner in such argument have a definite meaning to him, implying life and action, they will have no power.

If we can understand that objective nature is a thing of thought, a Divine language, still plastic in the imagination of its conceiver, we shall know how to liken the laws of nature to the laws of thought, for this a metaphysician must do.

His work is specific in that it meets and repudiates a claim where the claim is—it denies it where it is and affirms the opposite—for he must meet the false argument either with an argument that is directly opposite to it, or by a realization which denies the argument without controversy. This is called *spiritual realization*. Therefore the condition must be met as though it were the surface form of a mental argument or state of consciousness, a suggestion rather than a thing itself.

Getting and Giving

One of the laws of radiation says that the absorbing power of a substance is equal to its emitting power, which means that the ones that absorb the most must be the ones who emit the most. Or to state the proposition in another way, we can take in only what we give out. Jesus said, *Give, and it shall be given unto you.*

Now here is a law in nature verified by science, and we believe that every law in physical nature is reproduced in the laws of mind. This would have to be so if the universe is one system rather than two, and if unity is to be maintained throughout the whole.

There is a reason for these things, and the reason is that everything moves in a circle. Everything bends back upon itself. As a man sows so shall he reap, and so must he reap until he sows differently. Whitman said that the gift is most to the giver and comes back most to him, and we all know that since the universe is in balance nothing can leave any point without an equal something returning to it.

Each one of us is a point in the Infinite Mind, a center in the Consciousness of God or the Living spirit. We do not live because we understand Life or even put Life into our own living; we live because Life lives in us. We could make no greater mistake than to think that we created either Life or Law, but it would be an equal error to suppose that we escape Life or Law. We are subject to it but not in any predetermined sense, for no matter what happened yesterday we can change its sequence today.

If we have given out but little and received only an equal amount, we can begin to give out more, and just as surely as we do this, more will return to us. The giving and receiving are at the center of our own being; going out from us is but one end of the coming back to us, and the coming back to us is merely the other end of the going out from us.

The whole thing is so simple that its very simplicity eludes us, and we look for a more profound reason for the universe being in balance, and why being in balance it automatically proclaims the law of justice.

If the going out and the coming back are equal, then in a certain sense, like the energy and mass of Einstein, they are equal, identical, and interchangeable. To refuse to give is to refuse to live to the fullest extent. To refuse to give love is to refuse to receive love. That which we refuse to give out not only closes the door on the giving but on the receiving as well.

All this sounds like quite a tough proposition until we come to realize that if it were any other way we would not be free, but would be bound by external circumstances. Freedom can exist only on the proposition that it is first of all individual.

If we know that we ourselves are centers of distribution and centers of accumulation and that the two are equally identical and interchangeable, and if we know that nothing interferes with this but ourselves, we are free to act as we would be acted upon. This is why Jesus said, . . . *all things whatsoever ye would that men should do to you, do ye even so to them: for this is the law and the prophets.*

Bibles of the World

Fragments from the spiritual history of the race revealing fundamental UNITY of religious thought and experience

RAJA YOGA PHILOSOPHY—This manifested spiritual consciousness begins to manifest like the dawn in the pure heart, and shining like the midday sun in the *cave of wisdom*. . . illumines the whole universe.

The origin of pain can thus be traced to ignorance and it will not cease until ignorance is entirely dispelled, which will be only when the identity of the Self with the Universal Spirit is fully realized.

JUDAISM and CHRISTIANITY—He brought them out of darkness and the shadow of death, and brake their bands in sunder.

Unto the upright there ariseth light in the darkness.

For what fellowship hath righteousness with unrighteousness? And what communion hath light with darkness? And the light shineth in darkness; and the darkness comprehended it not.

The Lord is nigh unto them who are of a broken heart, and saveth such as be of a contrite spirit. Many are the afflictions of the righteous, but the Lord delivereth him out of them all.

In returning and rest shall be ye saved. In quietness and in confidence shall be your strength.

HELLENISTIC THEOSOPHY—Matter, my son, is separate from God, in order that thou mayst attribute unto it the quality of space. But what thing, else than mass thinkest thou it is, if it is not energized? Whereas, if it be energized, by whom is it made so? For energies, we said, are parts of God.

Then in this way know God; as having all things in Himself as thoughts, the whole Cosmos itself.

TAOISM—He has attained who knows what God is and who knows what man is. Knowing what God is, he knows that he himself proceeded therefrom. Knowing what man is, he rests in the knowledge of the known, waiting for the knowledge of the unknown.

BUDDHISM—Better one day of insight into the deathless state than a hundred years of blindness to this immortality.

Creatures follow the destiny of their deeds.

By the complete destruction of lust, hatred and delusion, devout men are no longer liable to suffering, and are assured of final salvation.

If a religionist desires to be assured of final salvation, let him be devoted to quietness of heart which springs from within; let him not drive back the ecstasy of contemplation; let him look through things.

JAINISM—Freedom from bonds is in your innermost heart. Knowledge, faith and right conduct are the true causes of final liberation.

CONFUCIANISM—The noble man is calm and serene. The inferior man is continually worried and anxious.

The noble man seeks what he wants in himself. The inferior man seeks it from others.

A wise and good man is occupied in the search for truth, not in seeking for a mere living.

A wise man should be solicitous about truth, not anxious about poverty.

HINDUISM—The wise should work desiring to promote the general good.

A wise man should always share with others.

Good words, good deeds and beautiful expressions a wise man ever culls from every quarter, even as a gleaner gathers ears of corn.

SIKHISM—All wealth is obtained by the love of God.

God's design cannot be set aside.

In whose heart the name abideth not—he it is who is poor.

Personal Word and Impersonal Law

My Dear Friend,

May we draw your attention to the Supplement to this lesson, *Desire, Opinion, and Revelation*, because we want you to think this over very carefully and come to realize the vast difference between unconscious desires, conscious opinions, and true spiritual revelation.

Our lesson says that the Spirit is changeless and will never reveal one thing to one person and something else which contradicts this to another. Therefore you must always be careful to discriminate between truth and illusion.

We want you to become a scientific practitioner, which means that we want you to know how to use the Power that is within you to help and bless yourself and others; how to use It definitely for specific purposes. We want to be certain that you know what you are doing, why you do it, and certain that you actually do it.

Again may we remind you to follow the instructions in Lesson 1 on how to give a treatment, and we certainly hope that you are doing this every day. There is nothing to wait for. The Law of Good already is around you, and your word that uses this Law already is in your own mouth. You are going to find that using this word is the most interesting experiment of your life.

May you be blessed in this endeavor.

Sincerely,
Ernest Holmes

Lesson 4
Mental Laws, p.77, to Spirit, the Changeless, p.83

In the study of mental laws we are considering one of the most vital, single points in our whole series of lessons. Your ability to demonstrate the supremacy of spiritual thought force over all apparent material resistance must necessarily depend upon your understanding of mental laws, their nature, and how they operate.

We must come to think of the mental medium, which is the Principle governing spiritual mind healing, in terms of exact law. Our text says at the top of page 78: *While we might think of It as the Mind of God, we could not think of It as the Spirit of God; for the Mental Medium is automatic, while the Spirit must be Self-Knowing.*

Let us then consider this all-important idea of God or Reality in the terms of an Infinite Knower and a Limitless Doer. Even at the expense of repeating one idea a great many times, we reaffirm the thought that the Universe as Pure Spirit is filled with warmth and color. It is illumined with the Divine Presence. It is filled with Divine Ideas. In other words we are surrounded by an atmosphere, a Presence in the universe which is conscious, alive, awake, and aware. In this Divine Presence we live and move and have our being, while It moves through us as inspiration, intuition, and illumination.

This Presence is God, the Living Spirit, Love, the Eternal Reality, the Supreme Being, with whom we communicate in prayer and meditation, and who in the silent places of the soul floods our minds with new and better ideals. (Turn to page 585 and read the definition of *Divine Ideal, Divine Influx,* and *Divine Mind*; and on the following page *Divine Principle*, that you may have still another presentation of the difference between God as Pure Spirit, and Mind as Absolute Law.)

To think of the universe as Pure Spirit, to uplift the thought and open the consciousness to an influx of the Divine, is to achieve communion with God. This has been the office of prayer throughout the ages. It was this Divine Inspiration coming to him as a voice from the Invisible, emanating from the burning bush in the wilderness, to which Moses responded. The wilderness symbolizes the need which Moses felt for inspiration; it typifies the unproductive, uncultivated place of the mind, the extreme need of man met by the consuming fire of Love descending from Heaven.

Moses had gone out into the wilderness to meditate and pray. He sorely needed inspiration. Somehow in his meditation and prayer he must have so completely left the human will behind, that the Divine could speak and make Itself heard. The burning bush signifies that any ordinary object of nature, even a wilderness shrub, is shot through with the warmth and color of Pure Spirit. In this way the most humble event may proclaim the omnipresence of Good. The weakest link of any chain of Cause and Effect may be so tempered by the flame of a new concept that it will have sufficient strength to bind the entire sequence together.

This is also the meaning of Jacob's experience with the angel at the Ford of the Jabbok. He wrestled with the angel of his better self until the day broke, bringing to him a consciousness of the nearness of the Divine. In such spiritual experiences of inner communion with the Most High, even our nearest and dearest cannot be present. But it is then that we receive the conviction that the power within us is the very Power of God.

Jacob's earlier experience on the road to Haran symbolized the same intimate truth. In the experience of aloneness with the Invisible, the soul bares itself to the Divine Influx, heaven and earth are joined together, angels ascend and descend the ladder of intuition. The messenger of Truth, the witness of God, the inspiration of the Almighty descends into our thought and we receive the assurance that the place where we are is the dwelling place of God.

We must be careful not to confuse the Divine Presence with the Universal Law. The Universal Law is a Way, a Principle, an immutable Cause and Effect. Our text points out that the Mental Medium is automatic, but you will notice in the second paragraph on page 78 these words: *As we examine the Subjective, we find It to be both intelligent and conscious, without knowing that It is intelligent, and without being self-conscious.*

(Read carefully page 580 under the definitions of *Consciousness* and *Conscious Mind*; and under the General Summary, page 397, read paragraph 4 beginning, *The Universal Mind in its subjective state is what we mean by the Law of Mind*; and the paragraph beginning at the bottom of page 396 which tells us that while the Law of Mind is subjective, It has Infinite Intelligence.)

One of the most difficult things for us to understand is that while we may consciously deal with the Law, which is creative—may even definitely direct It and set Its creative intelligence in motion for our good—yet the Law is not self-conscious. In other words, even though this Law is intelligent and creative, even though It is conscious of our desire, It has no self-consciousness, no self-choice with regard to such desires. It must execute the directions given It by the self-knowing mind. It must respond to our word.

Jesus was so certain of this that he said, *Heaven and earth shall pass away, but my words shall not pass away*. What a marvelous conception of his unity with Good and his command of the Law! That is why Jesus was different from other men. *He taught them as one having authority, and not as the scribes*. This is why the wind and the waves obeyed his will. He received the inspiration from the Spirit, but he commanded the Law.

That is really what we do every day in all common occurrences in dealing with the laws of nature. We are so accustomed to the reaction of the laws with which we are familiar that we have never stopped to recognize that in using any law of nature we are dealing with a creative agency which knows what to do and how to do it, but which cannot possibly have any self-choice.

Electricity does not know whether it is boiling eggs or furnishing motive power for the streetcar, but we might truly say that in a certain sense it knows how to do these things; as a matter of fact it must do them. We do the deciding; it has power but no decision. It has authority but no volition. It is energy, but of itself remains undirected. It is subject to our desires, and as our text says (page 78), *If this were not true of the laws of nature, we could not depend upon them; we should be confronted with caprice*.

It is because we may depend upon the laws of nature that we can have a science. The Science of Mind is an exact science; it is subject to our conscious use; it is a principle of nature just as chemical affinity is a principle of nature. If we do not understand this we shall never be able to consciously demonstrate. We might, through the prayer of faith, arrive at a conclusion which would be beneficial but to reproduce that conclusion at will, to reduce the occasional experience to a laboratory experiment which may be reproduced whenever and wherever we desire—that is a different thing. One is chance; the other is science. We must be scientific in our approach to the conscious use of the Law of Mind.

The Law of Mind is absolutely impersonal. Anyone who understands it may use it. Once set in motion it tends to produce a logical result. It proceeds in a mathematical manner to create, and unless the tendency set in motion is changed, it will create the logical result of whatever idea is given to it. In our Textbook we read in the last paragraph on page 78, *We cannot destroy the Law but we can redirect Its movement*. In this concept lies the possibility of freedom from bondage, not that we can change the Law but that we can change Its direction.

The spirit of man, being some part of the Spirit of God, has self-consciousness and self-choice. The Law, having neither self-consciousness nor self-choice, automatically reacts to the Spirit. Therefore when you treat someone else you are really treating yourself, and we wish you to know from the very start that this is exactly the way the Law works. You will never have to go outside yourself to treat any person, place, or thing; to think it necessary would be to deny the unity of Good and your access to the Universal Law of Cause and Effect. Within this one Law all events transpire. Emerson rightly said that history is the record of the doings of this Mind on our planet.

While the Law of Mind is a blind force, It is intelligent. We could make no greater mistake than to think that subconscious means unconscious. It does not. Subconscious means below the threshold of the conscious mind. As a matter of fact, the subjective Law of the universe with which we deal in giving treatments has limitless intelligence and limitless power to proceed from cause to effect. It is the creative agency in the universe.

You will notice in the third paragraph on page 79 that reference is made to this Principle as the thing we use in practice, and also that we are cautioned not to be superstitious in our reaction to the Law. Too much emphasis cannot be placed upon this, for if you wish to become a scientific practitioner you must be one who knows what you are doing, why you are doing it, and just how to do it. When you give a treatment to help someone who is sick or in need, no matter what the need may be, you must be conscious that you are making a definite statement in Mind and that Mind is the sole and only actor.

Principle acts upon your thought and projects it into the experience of the one toward whom you direct it. This is the whole theory of mental spiritual practice. This is the meaning of *Be still and know that I am God*. It was back of the illumined thought of Jesus when he said, *Ye shall know the truth, and the truth shall make you free*. The purpose of this course of lessons is to help you understand exactly how to use this Law for yourself and others. You must begin at once to be definite in your use of It, and today consciously set the Law in motion for yourself and for someone else.

At the top of page 80 we point out that God is threefold in His nature: God is Spirit or Self-Knowingness; God is Law or action; God is form or result. You will at once recognize this as the Trinity which has run through all the great religions of the world. I do not know of any great system of spiritual thought which did not include some teaching of the Trinity. We call it *The Thing, The Way It Works*, and *What It Does*.

The Thing Itself is Pure spirit; *The Way It Works* is Absolute Law; and *What It Does* is to give form to substance which is within Itself. This form we call creation. Whenever the Spirit wills or knows, as a result of Its will the Law is set in motion and produces that which the Spirit knows.

God never could do anything which would contradict His own nature. Hence we are certain that God cannot will evil, lack, limitation, or fear, for such thoughts would be self-destructive. If you wish to discover what the will of God is, try to realize what the nature of God must be and then realize that the will of God can never contradict the nature of God.

Turn to page 438 and read what is said under the heading, *God Knows No Evil* and also page 433 under the heading, *Judge Not That Ye Be Not Judged*. These ideas, I think, will help you to see that the nature of God must be Truth, Beauty, and Peace; and if the will of God is always in tune with His nature, which reason, science, and revelation alike tell us must be, then we know that God cannot will evil.

If God cannot will evil, what is evil? On page 590 in the Glossary read the definition of *Evil*. You will learn that of itself it is neither person, place, nor thing and that it will disappear from our experience in exact proportion as we cease using destructive thoughts.

Evil is merely a misconception, a wrong way of using good. God does not will limitation, because the nature of God is Infinite and that which is Infinite cannot will limitation. Nor is God limited merely because we accept what we call a small amount of good. There is just as much life in a flea as there is in an elephant. Size has no meaning to the Infinite. We outline our experience and call it size; we deny the good and call our experience evil; we put the wrong combinations of thoughts together and call the effect pain. But a reorganization of thought removes these discords, showing that the Eternal Reality is ever-present, ever-available. Emerson expressed this beautifully when he said, *The finite alone has wrought and suffered; the Infinite lies stretched in smiling repose.*

Next we turn to page 81, Chapter III, for the definition of Spirit; and to page 633 in the Glossary where *Spirit* is defined as *the Self-Knowing One*. This will help us to understand the conception of the Universe as one limitless sea of Life, animated by a Divine Presence which is the very essence of Life, of Truth, of Beauty, of Joy, of Peace, and of Perfection. While we cannot conceive of Spirit in Its entirety, in our highest moments of exalted thought we do feel this Divine and effulgent Presence. Let us realize that this Supreme Spirit is at the very center of our own being. *Closer is He than breathing, and nearer than hands and feet.*

If you will turn to page 364 under the heading, *The Indivisible Whole* and read through to the top of page 368, you will find a complete description of what this living spiritual Presence has meant to those who have sensed Its divine immanence within themselves. Read also the definition of *Immanent* on page 600; and Jesus' idea of the *New Birth* as presented on page 471. Read also in the General Summary on page 421 the description of the teaching of this great mystic. All of this helps us to feel the reality of this Divine Spirit in which we are immersed and which finds an avenue of self-expression through us.

The last paragraph on page 81 contains the statement: *The Spirit is Self-Propelling*. This means that all initiative proceeds from the Self-Knowing Mind. The Law never initiates anything; It always reacts to the Spirit. As you carefully read the first and second paragraphs on page 82, try to realize the meaning of this marvelous idea that Spirit is both the center and circumference of everything; that there is such a perfect completion within your own soul that you really do have access to the very Soul of the Universe. Daily practice calling upon this inner Intelligence in belief, in faith, in confidence, knowing that It will respond to you, that It will guide you.

We have already considered fully the section of our lesson at the bottom of page 82 and top of page 83, which is a further elaboration of the idea that the Spirit within you, the God within you, commands the Law, which is the Doer of the Word. Now you should immediately put this understanding which you have received into definite and conscious use. Of course you will realize that you may translate these thoughts into your own words, and that you should always use such words as have a definite meaning to your own consciousness, but the treatment should always be definite.

Summary

There is an Infinite Knower and a Limitless Doer in the Universe. The Knower responds to us as feeling. The Doer is a mechanical reaction. These we call the Principle and the Presence. The Principle is the Law of Mind in Action; the Presence is the warmth and color of Infinite Intelligence, personal to each one of us, moving through us as inspiration, intuition, and illumination. Prayer is communion with the Divine Presence.

We never confuse the Presence with the Law or the Principle. The Law is always subjective or subconscious to our conscious thinking. That means it is like our own subconscious mind; it receives the impress of our thought, asking no questions and always tending to create a situation to correspond with our thinking. The subconscious or subjective law of the individual and the Universal is one and the same thing.

Even as there is such a subconscious law within us which we call our individual subconsciousness, we are surrounded by a Universal Law of like nature, and our individual subconsciousness is but a center of attraction and repulsion in It. This is certainly true of every other law in nature. Everyone uses the same gravitational force, the same principle of electricity and mathematics, and all are guided by the same law and order. All that we do is individualize Universalities.

To understand a law of nature is to have a science relative to that law. It is the same with the Science of Mind. It is exact, and we must consciously use it and the Law for definite purposes. We should not leave this to chance but should always make it a question of choice; The Law being impersonal works the same for everyone, but the Spirit is personal to each one of us.

While the Law of Mind is a mechanical force, it is also intelligent and knows how to convert ideas into things. This Law with which we deal is not limited, and knows nothing about big or little, hard or easy, good or bad.

Remember we are talking about the Law. The Presence of the Living Spirit is an entirely different thing. It comes to all of us with warmth, color, and feeling, causing us to initiate new channels of causation in the Law, which automatically responds to our thinking. Daily we should court the Presence of the Spirit and use the Law.

Questions

Brief answers to these questions should be written out by the student after studying the lesson, and the answers compared with those which will be included in next week's lesson.

1. Upon what does our ability to demonstrate the Spiritual Law depend?
2. How should we think of the Principle of Spiritual Mind Healing?
3. How should we think of the Spirit of God?
4. How shall we commune with this Divine Spirit in an intimate way?
5. What does the burning bush which Moses saw represent?
6. What is the meaning of Jacob's experience with the Angel of God's Presence and his experience on the road to Haran?

7. What do the ascending and descending angels represent?

8. How does the Universal Subjective Mind or Law respond to us?

9. Can Subjective Law refuse to act upon our thought?

10. What gave Jesus his authority?

11. (a) What gives us authority over any law of nature? (b) Is this true of mental law?

12. What is mental treatment?

13. Where does mental treatment take place?

14. Do the expressions *subconscious* and *unconscious* have the same meaning?

15. What constitutes scientific mental practice?

16. What do we mean by the Trinity?

17. Can God will evil? If not, why not? What, then, is evil and limitation?

18. What words and thoughts should be used in giving a mental treatment?

Answers to Questions on Lesson 3

1. The basic truth about any law of nature is that all natural laws have always existed.

2. We can use the laws of nature when we recognize them and understand how they work.

3. No, the Principle of Life or God does not evolve. It continuously unfolds.

4. No. The Creative Spirit does not make something out of nothing. Creation means the passing of Spirit into form. It is the play of Life upon Itself.

5. No. Man will eternally unfold. There is no limit to his possible expansion.

6. Man progresses through his discovery of natural laws and his relationship to them.

7. We do not see the spiritual realities or the principles of nature. What we see and experience are their effects.

8. (a) No. We cannot explain life. (b) God is revealed to us through His creation and through our own minds. We see the form but not the Spirit.

9. The main idea to keep in mind in studying this science is that God as Spirit is a Divine Presence, while the principle of this science is a law of cause and effect.

10. We use the laws of nature, first by finding out what a law is; next by cooperating with it, by complying with its mode of operation. In this way we cause it to serve us.

11. Since the laws of nature are universal and impersonal, they belong to whoever uses them.

12. The purpose of life is self-expression.

13. We glorify God by becoming emancipated from bondage.

14. Final emancipation from bondage is accomplished by unifying with the Divine Presence, by understanding Its will and cooperating with Its nature.

15. The Science of Mind is a study of life and the nature of the laws of thought.

16. By the Law and the Word we mean that Spirit, the Divine Knower, operates through a mechanical Law. This Law is Mind in Action; It is the Principle of mental science.

17. Mental healing is accomplished through a correct mental attitude toward the Truth about God and the Truth about man's real being.

18. No. Spirit as Knower is Causation. Law as Doer obeys Spirit as Knower. Hence Law as Doer is subject to Spirit as Knower. They are two attributes of the One Mind.

19. The result of conscious thought is that the mental Law responds and produces a form as the mirror reflects the image held before it.
20. No. No one ever has seen the Universal Mind. We see only what Mind does. Because we can think, we know that Mind is.
21. No. It is some part of It. Man personifies the Universal Mind.
22. We increase our use of Creative Mind through a deeper realization of our unity with the Divine spirit.

The Great Lawgiver

In beginning his discussion on the mission of Moses, Troward again points out that the Bible repeats its few grand principles over and over again, and that its teaching regarding man starts with two great facts, which are *first*, that man is the likeness of God; *second*, that he individualizes the Creative Spirit in his own life. At first he is ignorant of this and consequently brings upon himself both trouble and limitation.

The whole theory of the Bible is based upon these simple propositions. Having shown in the story of The Fall what happens through a negative use of the power of thought, the rest of scripture is devoted to the winning of Redemption, which is the realization of the perfect Self, the archetypal man, or Christ incarnated within every soul.

Troward tells us that the mission of Moses was founded on the conception that God is One self-existent and self-transforming Power of which everything is some mode of manifestation. . . *there is none beside me. . . I am God, and there is none else* (Isaiah 45:21-22). This One, this God beside Whom there is none else, is the Universal Spirit. As Riley points out, *All the sacred books declare that God is One, the First and the Last, from Which nothing can be excluded and to Which nothing can be added.*

In an excerpt from the sacred books on the Fifty-seven Attributes of God, we read: *God is Breath of breath, Spirit, Primeval Fire, Creator and Generator, and being the One great Universal Supreme Soul, all things are threaded on God like pearls on a string. . . . The universe is spread in God's vast form and the Infinite One is the ocean into which all things flow.* From the text of Taoism: *The Tao, considered as unchanging, has no name.* Again from the same text: *That which made things and gave to each its character, was not Itself a thing.* In Hebrews 1:10 we read: *And, Thou, Lord, in the beginning hast laid the foundation of the earth; and the heavens are the works of thine hands.* And in Ephesians 4:6: *One God and Father of all, who is above all, and through all, and in you all.*

It is upon the union of our life with this eternal One that the teaching of Moses was based. The *I AM* Principle which he taught is both universal and individual. *I AM*, as Troward suggests, *is the announcement of Being in the Absolute . . . self-existence without limitation either of space or time.* It was the inspiration of Moses to perceive the meaning of the *I AM* in Its universal sense, the God who is over all and above all.

It was the spiritual genius of Jesus to perceive that the Universal *I AM* is reproduced in the individual *I*. He said, *I and my Father are one* (John 10:30). He knew that we must live in complete union with good before the Power of the One can be delivered in Its fullness. Thus in *Fragments of a Faith Forgotten*, when they asked him when the kingdom of heaven should come he said, *When two shall be One and the without as the within, and the male with the female neither male nor female*. This refers to a consciousness of complete union between God and man.

In studying the lives of both Moses and Jesus we discover that while Moses taught the great Law of Cause and Effect, exemplified by the precept of an eye for an eye and a tooth for a tooth, Jesus, without denying the Mosaic Law, affirmed a Love guided by Wisdom.

Troward tells us that the teaching of the *I AM* had been familiar to Moses since his youth. This teaching was confined to those who had been initiated into the great mysteries of Osiris. Osiris is a symbol of the Higher Self in Egyptian mythology.

It was the mission of Moses, Troward tells us, to make known to the common people the mysteries of the Temple. It was his mission to teach not only that pure Spirit is the ultimate essence of all that is, but that man is included in this all. This Self is the Lord of all, the eternal Ruler, the Source of all things.

In the Upanishads the ancients taught that there is an Absolute Being subsisting under all appearances, but Itself never confined nor conditioned to any experience. They also taught that as the individual attains truth and identifies himself with it, in that degree he passes into the Being of pure Spirit. The Gita says, *Perceiving the same Law present in everything and everywhere . . . and when he realizes perfectly that all things whatsoever in nature are comprehended in One, he attains to the supreme Spirit*.

Undoubtedly the Egyptian priests were well versed in the knowledge of unity. They were also conscious of the psychic life, but just as Osiris represented the symbol of the higher Self or the Wisdom Principle, so the goddess Isis represented the Divine Mother or Bringer Forth. She is representative of what today we call the Subjective Principle. It is evident that even the idols of antiquity must have stood for some symbolic presentation of concealed wisdom.

While the chosen few had knowledge of psychic and spiritual facts, the vast majority were kept in ignorance. Moreover even the priesthood in the temples of Egypt, whose business it should have been to gradually acquaint the whole population with the truth, had themselves degenerated. They had practiced ceremonials without understanding their meaning, until finally the only power they exercised came closer and closer to what has been called *Egyptian Darkness*. Such knowledge as they possessed was exercised largely on the mental plane. And this is exactly what differentiated the teaching of Moses from that of the Egyptian priests who had forgotten the real meaning of *I AM*. Like those who preceded the symbolic Deluge, they had great knowledge of psychic powers but lacked the vision of spiritual realization. Unconscious of the unity of good they used such power as they had for evil purposes.

Symbolically, Moses represents the Higher Principle riding upon the seas of Egyptian darkness. Hence he is discovered in a little ark floating on the water. Since Ark represents the Life Principle in Its transcendent or purely spiritual phase, and since in this instance water is symbolic of the Subjective Principle which is subject to confusion, the symbolic birth of Moses means the appearance of an individual who, while amply conscious of the subjective or psychic life (the realm of Cause and Effect operating as a Law of Mind), is equally conscious of the unifying and coordinating power of spirit.

Whatever viewpoint one may take of ancient symbolism, nothing is more certain than that it taught a few central truths, one of which was the necessity that the Spirit shall dominate the mind. The child Moses is found floating upon the waters, just as the Ark floated on the sea, and we find the man Moses parting the waters of the sea. These are the waters that closed in upon the pursuing Egyptians, immersing and destroying them in its flood. Philo says, *In inward meaning, the flood is symbolically representative of spiritual dissolution*. Swedenborg says, *By the flood is signified an inundation of evil and falsity*. It was this psychic sea of illusion, also referred to as *Maya*, which Moses parted.

The occult knowledge of the Egyptian priests, their knowledge of psychic and mental powers, was tremendous. But being ignorant of or having forgotten the true significance of spiritual power which should be exercised only for beneficent purposes, they became swallowed up in the very power which they had generated, thus proving that the Law of Cause and Effect works with mathematical certainty. Jesus said, . . . *for all they that take the sword shall perish with the sword*.

It was the Staff of Moses, representing the authority of Divine Wisdom, the Word of God in Moses, the Divine Command of the Unity of God, which symbolically parted the sea of confusion, the sum total of all human error. And the Children of Israel, that is, the Children of the *I AM* (which signifies any and all who understand their true relationship to Spirit), walked through the Red Sea on dry land. The pursuing Egyptians, though filled with power, were also covered with confusion. Thus the Deluge—the story of the flood—repeats itself.

We have the same symbol in Zoroastrianism. Mazda is the father of justice. Mazda refers to the Light which overcomes darkness, or the Good which always triumphs over evil. In the same system of thought we have the Light or Truth, the Good completely subduing evil, confusion, and chaos, until finally the Light reigns supreme.

We find Jesus walking upon the water, putting under his feet the sum total of human ignorance, viciousness, and disunion. In Scott's *Lady of the Lake* the symbol is again repeated: *She is calm whatever storms assail the sea, and when the tempest rolls, hath power to walk the waters like our Lord*.

It was the mission of Moses, then, to lead the Children of Israel out of the darkness of the Egyptian night; to lead ignorance into enlightenment. But the Children of Israel murmured, hesitated, drew back. This represents the inertia of our own thought patterns, our habit thought forms which bind us to superstition, fear, ignorance, and bondage.

When a modern metaphysician less than a hundred years ago spoke of the argument of error in the human consciousness, many intellectuals may have smiled. And yet today psychology recognizes what it calls the inertia of thought patterns; that which appears to be an argument emanating from these subjective habitual states of thought. To dislodge these thought patterns is one of the most difficult tasks of the psychologist.

It was the mission of Moses to lead the Children of the *I AM*, those who understood their relationship to God, not only out of the material bondage of objective slavery, but equally out of the psychic bondage of subjective slavery. Maya, or the great illusion, was to be penetrated. And what was this illusion other than the belief in their separation from good? The Great Exodus represents a symbolic rising from the lower to the higher nature, led by an intuitional sense of unity. It was following the Feast of the Passover that this exodus began. The Feast of the Passover is a symbol representing a realization of Truth. It is a symbolic repast of the fruits of Spirit.

The march through the wilderness represents a march through the desolate places of the soul—fear, superstition, want, famine, hunger, and anything that stands for the illusion of separation—to the Promised Land filled with fruit and honey. It is a march from the valley to the mountaintop, which means from the lower to the higher nature.

You will remember that Moses was told that everything his eye looked upon his feet would tread upon. This means that what he beheld with undimmed spiritual vision, he would come into possession of. This, of course, is a statement of cause and effect, as were most of the teachings of Moses.

Troward draws an interesting comparison between the teachings of Moses and those of Jesus. It was, he said, the mission of Moses to lead the Children of the *I AM* (that is, those who recognize their unity with Good) out of the wilderness of their own fear, ignorance, and confusion into the Promised Land of Truth, Beauty, and Light. And it was the mission of Jesus to continue in the footsteps of Moses and in some way repeat the Exodus and reestablish the people of the *I AM*. Hence we find Jesus laying great stress on the Law and the Prophets, on the Law of Cause and Effect, on everything that Moses taught, but tempering the Law of Justice with the realization that Love ever seeks to guide us into pathways of Peace, Joy and Perfection.

Troward tells us that the English version of the Bible which states that Jesus said, *If ye believe not that I am he, ye shall die in your sins*, is misquoted. What Jesus actually said was, *Except ye believe that* I AM, *ye shall die in your sins*. Now this passage means that unless you believe in the Eternal Principle within you as one of complete unity, Divine guidance, etc., you will continue making mistakes. For sin means making a mistake or missing the mark. From the Mahabharata: *In consequence of ignorance, one sinks into hell. Ignorance is the swing of misery. Through ignorance one suffers afflictions and encounters great dangers*. Dying in your sins has no reference to a theological damnation.

Purgatory is symbolic of the purification that is brought about as the fire of Spiritual Truth burns out the dross of human experience. Clement of Alexandria tells us, *The fire of purgatory is the rational spiritual fire that penetrates the soul*. Origen said, *Each sinner himself (which means each person in his own mistakes) lights the flame of his own fire . . . his conscience is agitated and pierced by its own pricks*. Plotinus tells us that purgatory is a way of purification from earthly desires. Hence when Jesus said in effect that except you believe that *I AM* you shall continue to suffer, he was teaching the Law of Cause and Effect. In this he was continuing the teaching of Moses, for it was his mission not only to continue the teaching of the *I AM* but to explain it in terms of its meaning to the individual life. Troward tells us that if *I AM* is the generalized statement of God, it must also be the generalized statement of Man, for man is the image and likeness of God.

The whole teaching of Jesus in following out the instructions of Moses was to show that what is true about God is also true about Man. God is at the center of every man's life. Jesus came, as Troward said, *not to proclaim Himself, but Man; not to tell us of His own Divinity separating Himself from the race and making Him the Great Exception, but to tell us of our Divinity and to show in Himself the Great Example of the* I AM *reaching its full personal expression in Man.*

We find, then, that as it was the mission of Moses to proclaim the Universal Principle of the eternal *I AM*, so it was the purpose of the teaching of Jesus to show the intimate relationship between the Universal and the personal; to show us that our very life is in essence some part of the Being of God and that whatever we believe does for us in very fact exist.

The Egyptians believed in the power of darkness, so out of the creative fertility of their own imagination such an apparent power was conjured up that it confused both themselves and their enemies. Moses perceived that there could be no power of darkness operating against the light; that the people of the *I AM* who believe in the unity of Good were guided by this Unity in which they believed.

The wrong use of the Law of Cause and Effect is called sin or the transgression of the Law. This produces suffering and death, or dissolution, while the knowledge of Truth always produces a resurrection. As Troward points out, *the transgression . . . is the transgression of the Law of the* I AM *in ourselves.* Our punishment does not come from God who is good, nor does the Law, which is merely a law of cause and effect, hold anything against us. Our punishment is an inevitable result of the use we have made of the Law of Cause and Effect.

Hear, O Israel: the Lord our God is one Lord (Deuteronomy 6:4). If God is the Only Being, *I AM* must be the name of this Being, and the conscious knowledge of the meaning of *I AM* is the keynote of liberty. The transgression, Troward tells us, is in supposing there is any power opposed to Good. Once we see through this proposition and realize that there is nothing opposed to Good, but that the Eternal *I AM* is Wisdom, Truth, Love and Beauty forever guiding us, then we are made free. But in such degree as we limit the *I AM* we are limiting ourselves.

When we think of the *I AM* as separate from our own being we feel that we are isolated, each on his own so to speak, disconnected from the central power. It is necessary for us to understand with Moses that the *I AM* is Universal, and to understand with Jesus that the Universal is individualized through, in, and as our own nature. Obeying this nature we are automatically saved or resurrected from our previous mistakes.

In simple, actual, and direct mental practice this would mean that we should daily affirm our union with God, our oneness with the Creative Genius of the Universe, and that we consciously believe in and understand that we are Divinely guided, guarded, protected; that everything we do is made whole, prosperous, and happy.

Desire, Opinion and Revelation

It was John who said, and rightly, *Believe not every spirit, but try the spirits whether they are of God*. Paul said, *God is not the author of confusion, but of peace*. Possibly he knew that our conscious opinions and our subjective desires so frequently confuse the revelations that when an alleged revelation appears, it is so distorted with conflicting opinions that much of its truth is lost.

If we were to put all of the alleged revelations of the ages together we would be amazed to find how contradictory they are. In fact the contradictions would be so complete that practically the whole revelation would be wiped out, and this in face of the fact that each prophet claims to have received his inspiration directly from the Mind of God. The confusion of such alleged revelations is so great that intelligence compels us to put up the sign: *Stop, Look, and Listen*.

We are amazed to discover that some of these revelations which seem to come from God stimulate man to commit the most atrocious crimes, for many crimes that have been committed in the name of Liberty have also been committed in the name of Truth.

It stands to reason that the Author of Peace cannot inspire confusion. And God is the Author of Peace, since a house divided against itself cannot stand. If God stands for that which is rational, the essence of peace and poise; if the Divine means love, beauty, harmony, and reason, it follows that from this Divine Fountain only pure waters can flow. God could not be the author of confusion inspiring men to acts of destruction. God could not be the author of confusion leading men to irrational mental or spiritual conclusions. Therefore a person who would differentiate between subjective hallucination and opinion, between desire and reality, does well to analyze his own feelings, emotions, and mental reactions. And he does well to analyze the reactions of other people, regardless of whether they are numbered among the so-called great, the little known, or even the unknown.

In the pursuit of Truth one seeks to wed oneself to reason, for she is the only mistress who can lead the soul to the altar of Reality. We do not dispute the idea of revelation, since all truth is some revelation of Reality to the mind of man. We do not deny that there is a Spirit which inspires and a Guidance which directs. What we say is that when it seems as though this Guidance directs us chaotically or counsels men to destructive acts, it is not Divine Guidance at all. It is some form of opinion or desire masquerading as reason, seeking to justify itself by claiming to be the Voice of God.

When someone tells you that he has received a revelation direct from the Almighty you will be wise if you analyze his revelation and see whether it really is inspired by the Divine or whether it is merely a rationalization of his own desire. History records many so called revelations by which men have claimed to be directed by God to commit such atrocious crimes that sensitiveness shrinks from the fact and intelligence refuses to accept the verdict.

Life cannot will death. Death is the direct opposite of life. Therefore Jesus said *God is not the God of the dead, but of the living*. Jesus with his clear comprehension of Reality knew that life cannot will death, but many lesser prophets have proclaimed that the Divine Being inspired them to kill. Most nations at war, worshiping tribal gods, react from their collective unconscious with this same motivation. But whether it be an individual or a collective unconscious, the principle operating is the same.

We may be certain that when Cyrus mounted his chariot and rode in front of his legions crying, "Kill! Kill! Kill! and to God be the glory!" after having attended the divinations of the oracle, what he really was proclaiming, but of course unconsciously was, "Kill! Kill! Kill! and to Cyrus be the glory!" Even this barbarian shrank in horror before the terrific carnage about to take place. His desire had first to be rationalized in order that his opinion might be justified; therefore he had to receive, through his imagination, evidence for the belief that his killing of men was done for the glory of God and not for the glory of Cyrus.

We take this instance, so far removed from us personally and from our present history, that we may be impersonal about it. But every day this same performance takes place in our own consciousness. We certainly should realize that all is not revelation which masquerades under its name. In the present day when we are privileged to understand more about psychic reactions, history is better explained on the basis of human will to power.

Today more than ever, psychic revelations are imposed upon our consciousness through the sincerity of those receiving such messages in automatic writings, in séances, and by various other media through which such revelations come, and again we must put up the sign: *Stop, Look, and Listen*. To one who has, over a period of many years, carefully studied such apparent revelations, it is evident that too frequently these revelations are largely governed by the mental background of the one through whom they come. Generally we find in them elements of the philosophies, religions, social, political, and economic systems which the author has believed in, theorized over, toward which he has aspired, or in which he was born. This in no way contradicts the sincerity of those through whom these messages come. Therefore it is not a question of condemning or criticizing the individual; it is merely a question of right judgment and a sane perspective.

We certainly should believe in no revelation which contradicts the final unity, goodness, and perfection of the Supreme Being. In analyzing such revelations we should carry them right back to the point of reason and unity, and whenever they contradict reason we may know that they are not revelations but hallucinations or the rationalizations of desire. They may emanate directly from the consciousness of an individual or from the conscious reactions of an entire race.

We are told that Martin Luther saw the devil. One day he presented himself in Luther's study. Now what was it that this reverend gentleman saw? Not an actual devil, since intelligence compels us to admit that the devil is a mythological figure with no reality outside man's consciousness.

What Luther saw was a personification of the then universal belief about the devil. If we could ask the average man of that period what the devil looked like, his description would be similar to what Luther saw. Strange as it may seem, what he saw was an idea, but this idea had its roots deeper than his own personal consciousness. It arose from the sum total of the opinion of his day. Everybody believed the devil looked like that; therefore the devil did look like that in belief, and what Luther saw was the belief personified; a picture in imagination, but a picture of an imagination more real than his personal one, more dynamic than his individual thought. This picture was impressed upon his psyche, and in some moment when he was subjective to it, it appeared.

With all sincerity Luther may have believed that he saw an actual devil, but with equal sincerity the man who is suffering from an hallucination believes that he sees some grotesque form. It is real enough as far as the experience is concerned, but it is nevertheless an illusion as far as reality is concerned. Luther and all his contemporaries believed in an actual devil, and what they believed in he saw. Hence seeing, he doubly believed.

This is one of the reasons why many people believe that God ordains suffering, impoverishment, and unhappiness, and that He even demands murder. When we subject such a concept to the rule of reason and common sense we soon discover that the All-Creative Principle could not will martyrdom, suffering, or impoverishment, for this would not be to the glory, but to the degradation of the Creative Principle. God would not be honored, but dishonored; not made whole, but limited.

Yet what countless thousands of sincere and well-meaning persons suffer the illusion of such a belief and actually condemn the desire for happiness in this world. The very thought of the crucifixion of Jesus has, in innumerable instances, stimulated such morbid introspection that the resurrected form of Christ is but dimly seen through the clouds of darkness and despair. Too often the cross and the tomb overshadow the resurrection.

We must not forget that when we are dealing with this psychic life of ours we are dealing with a very tricky thing. It will just as quickly provide us with an illusion as with a reality. But deeper than this psychic life there is a Spiritual Intelligence which transcends even our objective processes of reasoning, and it can distinguish between illusion and reality.

Our subconscious reactions will coerce us unless we control them, will cause us to believe all kinds of fantastic things unless reason sits in judgment. Therefore we should be careful at all times to study any alleged revelation in the light of this truth, knowing as we do that one's personal opinion may masquerade as any revelation which one's unconscious desire may order, for the entire race thought is more or less active in all of us.

One of the most prolific fields for race hallucination, strange as it may seem, is in the field of so-called revealed religion. Accumulated acceptances of pronounced beliefs have finally created such a subjective reaction to them that people believe all sorts of things, reasonable and unreasonable. Usually it takes a strong new belief to shatter the old. Fortunately, back of most revelations, especially the great spiritual ones, there has always been enough reality, that is, enough of the nature of Truth has been revealed, not only to give vitality to the belief but to equip it with power and give it a performance which has been good.

Thus in analyzing the great revelations we do not need to recheck them in their entirety, but merely to recheck those parts which arise from human opinion, human desire, or psychological rationalization.

We shall find that reality is at least partly revealed through most of these great systems of thought, but we shall also find a great deal of illusion. Nowhere was this more apparent than in the ancient caste system, which did not rise out of reality since there can be no God who holds one person superior to another. It was an economic thing, and what is more natural than that the dominant minded should have rationalized their desire and even had it seemingly revealed to them that some were of lower origin than others, and therefore were outcasts. In Psalm 82:6 we read, *I have said, Ye are gods; and all of you children of the most High*. In the days of slavery in America many of our Southern brethren rationalized their belief in slavery as God's will. It could not be the will of God that some men should be free while others were bound, since God is the Author of freedom and not of bondage.

It is interesting to note with what dynamic authority many of our so-called great seers have spoken. With sincere conviction they have proclaimed, "Thus saith the Lord." It was not until the advent of science that reason began to deny these theological assumptions. Science deals with facts and not with opinions, and must reduce these facts into principles which never vary and which are always impersonal.

With the advent of science we have the beginning of the destruction of superstition. This does not mean that science will destroy religion. Nothing can do that, for true religion is man's immediate experience of Reality. Science will merely destroy distorted beliefs, and in so doing it will render true religion a great service since it will reveal the nature of Reality to be entirely impersonal, responsive alike to each and to all.

As science proclaims the rule of reason and a government of law, new revelations come. These new revelations, even as the old, the student of Truth must carefully scrutinize. He must remain master in his own household. Unless he does so, he will be a mental puppet dancing to other people's thoughts, coerced by the ideas which have already hypnotized them, and if the blind lead the blind, shall they not both fall into the ditch?

Bibles of the World

Fragments from the spiritual history of the race revealing fundamental UNITY of religious thought and experience

TAOISM—The right way leads forward; the wrong way backward. Do not proceed on an evil path. Do not sin in secret. Accumulate virtue. Increase merit. Turn toward all creatures with a compassionate heart.

Assist those in need and rescue those in danger.

Regard your neighbor's gain as your own gain, and regard your neighbor's loss as your own loss.

CONFUCIANISM—Put away evil without hesitation. Do not carry out plans, the wisdom of which you have doubts.

The way of the superior man is threefold: virtuous, he is free from anxieties; wise, he is free from perplexities; bold, he is free from fear.

BUDDHISM—The giving hand, the kindly speech, the life of service, impartiality to one as to another: these be the things that make the world go round.

Growth in faith, growth in virtue, growth in insight: these are the three attainments.

JUDAISM and CHRISTIANITY—Execute true justice, and show mercy and compassion every man to his brother.

And oppress not the widow, nor the fatherless, the stranger, nor the poor; and let none of you imagine evil against his brother in your heart.

Be perfect, be of good comfort, be of one mind, live in peace; and the God of love and peace shall be with you.

HINDUISM—The peaceful mind soon becomes well-established in wisdom.

Like the body that is made up of different limbs and organs, all mortal creatures exist depending upon one another.

Spirit—Its Meaning, Action and Use
Office of the Dean

My Dear Friend,

One of the principal things you will learn in this lesson is that you are not concentrating any power when you use the Science of Mind, but rather through belief and faith and communion with the Spirit in you and around you, you are using a Power that is already centered everywhere. You do not have to take It from one place to another. What you are learning is that you use this Power at the very center of your own being, for this is the only place that you meet the Divine Presence or use the Universal Principle, and it is always a combination of these two fundamental realities with which you are dealing.

We have discovered that some people wait for years before they realize the simplicity of this thing. We trust that you are not such a person and that you have already proved to some degree that you neither wish, will, supplicate, coerce, nor concentrate anything; that you do not send out thoughts, or hold thoughts, or influence people. Your prayers, your thoughts, your beliefs, your affirmations, your treatments are all at the center of your own being. They could be nowhere else.

But what does this mean other than the act of convincing yourself? The only reason that this sometimes seems difficult is that there are so many unconscious denials in every man's life. As you penetrate these and rise to an attitude of simple acceptance you will get remarkable results.

We wish you all the success in the world in doing this.

Sincerely,
Ernest Holmes

Lesson 5
Spirit, the Changeless, p.83, to Only One Kind, p.87

As already explained in our previous lessons, creation does not mean making something out of nothing. Creation means the giving of form to the formless. It is the act whereby the invisible becomes visible. Turn to the Glossary and read the definition of *Creation* and *The Creative Medium*. You will notice that the first definition contains the thought that creation is God making something out of Himself by becoming the thing He creates. It is necessary for us to conceive of a single Power which, by the act of mental projection within Itself, gives birth to form.

The paragraph dealing with *The Endless Creation* (page 492) makes clear the fact that while particular objects may have a beginning and an end, yet creation itself is endless. This gives a new meaning to the old phrase, *World without end*. This endless creation is a continuous mental projection of the Universe within Itself.

This mental projection within the One is what is meant by the Word of God, the Contemplation of Spirit, the Self-recognition of Reality. This we must keep in mind when we seek to demonstrate or prove our principle in actual practice. We must be sure that the thought will give rise to the form. In order to do this, in our imagination we must resolve things into thoughts and thoughts into things. This is what might be called making a mental diagnosis of wrong conditions in order that we may treat them scientifically and effectively to make them right. We must realize that the Spirit is the Active Principle and that, as our lesson explains, all else is subject to Its will.

In order that you may understand this more fully, turn to the section dealing with *The Law of Correspondents* (page 483). You will note that back of every visible form there is a mental concept or thought form which is an exact counterpart of the object. The subjective word is the Word of Causation and it contains a picture of the objective. In fact the objective world is really a manifestation of the subjective world. The thought and the thing are but the two ends of the same sequence.

This subjective world is the medium of Law. Into it we drop the images of thought which tend to objectify in our experience. It is desirable that we know how to use this Power and how to control It in order that we may actually get the most out of life. (See page 29, *Limitless Power at Man's Disposal*.) We are really using this Divine Creative Power every time we think. The only way to stop using It is to stop thinking, and that is impossible. What we all wish to do is to use this limitless Power consciously and constructively for definite purposes.

We spoke in a previous paragraph of a changing universe. This idea of change is dealt with under the heading, *Spirit, the Changeless* (page 83). The Creative Principle is conscious of that which It manifests, but It is not conscious of any effort or process in Its manifestation. For instance, when we plant a seed in the ground we are invoking the creative agency of the soil, which in conjunction with sun, rain, and atmosphere will produce a plant for us. The process whereby the seed unfolds into a plant is a mechanical and not a self-conscious one. It is its nature to do this according to a certain mathematical law, the law of evolution.

Involution is conscious. Evolution is automatic. We must never forget this when we come to the point of treating either ourselves or others. We plant the seed; the Law of Mind produces the desired result. We do not have to be conscious of the process, but we should be conscious of the idea we desire to see projected into our experience.

The Law of the Lord being perfect, it is our business to believe that It is working for us and not against us. On page 414, the first paragraph, are these words: *Effective treatment must be independent of any existing circumstance.* This means that when you give a treatment you must know what you wish to have done or what you desire the effect to be, but the treatment itself must be given in complete independence of anything that now exists in your experience. This of course calls for faith, but in this instance you will find it is a faith based on understanding rather than superstition. It is faith reduced to science.

Let us examine another thought in this same paragraph: *From this viewpoint there is no hard and no easy.* How wonderful it will be when we no longer think that one thing in our spiritual work is hard and another is easy. Since with God all things are possible, since the Law of the Lord is perfect, and since there is a Perfect Presence and a Perfect Principle, what more could we desire? We are not to think of some things being hard while others are easy, but we are to know that the Truth responds immediately and perfectly to any demand made upon It.

Because this is true, and because the Law works impersonally and automatically, we can see that negative impulses will produce results as surely as positive ones. Therefore we need to watch the character and quality of our thought. Attention is drawn to this idea in the second paragraph on page 412 in these words: *The Objective form to which we give our attention is created from the very attention which we give to it*. In other words, to look at a wrong condition and to fear it is to perpetuate it. To contemplate limitation is to create it.

Jesus told us that when we pray we must enter the closet and shut the door. We should approach life inwardly and not outwardly, for to look only at the outward is to perpetuate the form we desire to dissolve. Here is the crux of the whole matter. On what is our faith and confidence based? Surely not on outward appearance, but on the inward Reality. This is why we are told never to count our enemies, but as Isaiah said, *Look unto me (the God within) and be ye saved*. How well this spiritual genius knew what he was talking about, and how wise for us to follow his example. His contemplation of the Perfection of God, and the fact of man's unity with God led to demonstrations of healing and deeds of power.

Read the section on page 456 headed, *As Little Children*. We should cultivate the acceptance of the little child. We must learn to believe, for as Jesus said, *Go thy way; and as thou hast believed, so be it done unto thee* (Matthew 8:13). Today you should not only believe but begin to practice what you have already learned. No matter what else you do, be sure to take ten or fifteen minutes twice a day to center your thought serenely and peacefully on the invisible, and to believe that the form of experience which you wish in your life is being created for you. Mentally see its objective manifestation. Accept it completely and try never to deny it, for this is correct practice.

It may assist you to obtain inner conviction if you contemplate the words, *God, the Self-Existent First Cause, speaks and it is done* (page 84). Intelligence decrees and the Immutable Law executes. We must use this Law definitely and consciously. For as individualizations of the Self-Existent Spirit, we decree, and the Law executes our commands. But read page 51 and you will realize that we know only as much as we can prove by actual demonstration.

Throughout the period of study based on these lessons and in your daily experience from now on, believe that you can demonstrate. (Read the definition of *Demonstration* on page 583.) We need to prove the Principle. It is easy to believe in an underlying Power or Principle in the universe which governs all things and is all-powerful, but for ourselves *it is not enough to confess that God is the only Power there is* (page 563). In our personal experience, at least, we must prove the supremacy of good over apparent evil. We must prove that the God Principle is in us and so is available to us. We must recognize our unity with the Divine Principle of Being.

If we look at love long enough we shall become lovely (page 491). It is not enough merely to declare that God is Love. This was true before we made the declaration. Whatever statements we may make about the Divine Being in a treatment, we must unify with It inwardly in thought and imagination or the treatment will not be complete and effective. If you say that there is only One Life and that Life is the

Life of God, you have made an abstract statement about a Universal Principle. When you add, "That Life is my life now," you have connected this Principle with your own experience; you have unified with It. Be sure to do this every day.

God speaks, and it is done. God, the Universal Mind, is manifest in man, the individual mind. Man is an individualized center of God Consciousness; he repeats the Divine Creative Order in his own experience, but he must learn to identify his experience with his desire. That is why we say, *In practice we state clearly in words what these ideas mean to us and then we relate these statements to some needed experience or to some desired good which we have not been experiencing* (page 410). Unless we learn to do this definitely our statements will be up in the air instead of being clear and concrete. Just an abstract statement such as "God is all the Power there is," even though it is true will not demonstrate the good we desire.

The abstract statement of a fundamental truth and the realization of its meaning generate spiritual power, but do not distribute it. As with electricity we must not only generate power but we must direct it. Our conscious statements and acceptances give conscious direction to the power generated. *There is One Life, that Life is God.* This is true. But we must complete the statement by distributing it, by saying, *That Life is my life now.*

An additional statement in regard to the matter of demonstration is found on page 84: *We have, then, an Infinite Spirit and an Infinite Law . . . Intelligence and the Way It works. God working through Law, which is unfailing and certain.* We must realize that it is this God Principle within us which is the power back of our thought. We must never try to hold thoughts or will things to happen. Do not even try practicing any form of mental concentration, for without any desire to criticize these methods we wish you to understand that they are not what we are trying to teach.

We are trying to teach you how to become a practitioner, how to demonstrate in your everyday experience the fact that you can produce results by calling upon a higher Creative Power, without any act of coercion or concentration. The Power is already concentrated and needs but to be definitely used. What does a gardener concentrate when he plants his crop? He does not concentrate anything. He plants the seed, that is all. You must use the Power that is within you. Be sure to make conscious use of this Power; otherwise you will reap no advantage for yourself from this study, nor will you be able to help anyone else. Of course you will endeavor to use it both for yourself and those who come to you for help. The Power is within you, and *Today is the day of salvation.*

The whole action of Spirit must be within Itself (page 84). I suppose that one of the most difficult things to thoroughly understand is the simplicity of the operation of the Law which we are using. It is just the interaction between thought and the Law. We might state the Principle in this way: God moves upon God, Spirit moves upon Itself, Life sets Its own law in motion and out of Itself produces form. This is the art, the act, and the science of all creation.

Spirit moved upon the face of the deep. How marvelous and exalting is this idea of reality, for we also move upon the face of the deep and out of the seeming void form emerges. Both cause and effect are spiritual. Read the last two paragraphs on page 413 and carefully consider the meaning of the words you will find there, because they are fraught with the utmost Significance in your everyday practice.

An excellent method of procedure for your mental work will be found on page 49 under the heading, *Hope a Subtle Illusion*. The Spirit creates by Self-Contemplation, that is by Self-Knowingness and because we are Spirit, our self-knowingness also creates. *And the Word was with God and the Word was God.* This Word is your good, or rather the use you make of the God-Self within you. *I and my Father are one.* A knowledge of this was the secret of the power of Jesus.

Jesus exercised an authority in the invisible world which the Centurion recognized and at which he marveled. Read the account of this most interesting incident on page 437 and you will see that Jesus exercised actual authority on the invisible plane, but he did it with the utmost simplicity. He knew the secret of power (page 431). The Secret Place of the Most High was to him a place where he daily walked and communed with the Invisible Presence. Thus do the meek inherit the earth (page 427).

In the second and third paragraphs on page 85, carefully consider the idea of the original Energy and Intelligence moving as a mathematical law. As you consider the meaning of the last two lines in the third paragraph, *the Infinite or abstract Essence of concrete personality, and the Cause of all objective and subjective manifestation*, realize that this means that the Invisible Principle acts through the Immutable Law. This is also invisible but creates form because the Word always tends to produce form. This is the meaning of the statement in John: *And the Word was made flesh, and dwelt among us.*

In paragraph 2, page 395 you will find the thought that the Universal Mind can do for us only that which we know It is doing. The very fact that we are made out of Spirit presupposes the thought that we are free to express liberty or bondage. As a matter of fact, both liberty and bondage come from the same source, being different degrees of the same thing. Since Reality Itself knows no big and no little and since we give form to It in our own experience, we give to the form of our experience the size which we conceive mentally from day to day.

For instance, you will find that on some days you will do better work than on others. Thought is always creative, but some days your thought will conceive of a greater good than at other times. The more positive and certain it is, the more effective it will be, but the movement of your thought will always be mathematical. That movement takes place in a mechanical field of cause and effect—intelligent, responsive, but unvolitional.

You must decide what you wish to have happen. Be sure it is in accord with the nature of harmony and then convince yourself that this desired good is already an experience in your life. This is the secret of spiritual mind healing and demonstration. To believe more in the Invisible than in the visible and to judge not according to appearances, but to judge aright, is to use the Principle which gave Jesus his power. You doubtless understand this, but how effective is understanding unless you use it? Our motto should always be: *To do is to know.*

No limit can be placed upon the spirit of man (page 87). We should place no limit on the possibility of our use of this Divine Power. *If God be for us, who can be against us?* Therefore let us turn to the source of all personal power, the Infinite Spirit which has Its Being at the center of our own life, and daily in meditation commune with It.

Summary

Creation is the manifestation of Spirit in form and is eternally going on. We are always creating something. Creation itself is an automatic, mechanical, and mathematical response to our thinking. We may choose what we want to think but the Law cannot refuse to accept what we think. Thoughts and things are but two ends of the same proposition. Since it is impossible to stop thinking, we cannot stop creating. Our choice is whether we shall create constructively or destructively.

There should be no more effort in this process than there is in planting a seed. The Law of Creativity responds to us in the way we approach It. We can reduce faith and prayer to an exact science when we know how the Law of Mind works.

The more attention we give to negative conditions the more they will become associated with our thinking. It may be difficult to turn from appearance but it is necessary. Each deals with the Divine Presence and the Creative Law in the silence of his own mind as he shuts the door to outward appearances and accepts his unity with the Whole.

You will never know that this is true until you try it. It must pass from theory into practice. You must prove this Principle in your personal experience and in helping others, for this is the purpose of your study.

It is not enough merely to state an abstract principle or to say that God is all there is, for while this is true it is not making a definite use of the Law of Mind in Action. But because the Principle exists, or because God is all there is, you can both know God and use the Principle.

Questions

Brief answers to these questions should be written out by the student after studying the lesson and the answers compared with those which will be included in next week's lesson.

1. What is meant by creation?
2. What is meant by the endless creation?
3. What do we mean by resolving things into thoughts?
4. How does the practice of resolving things into thoughts apply to mental science?
5. What is meant by mental diagnosis?
6. What do we mean by mental correspondents?
7. When do we use the Divine Creative Power?
8. What do we mean by involution?
9. What do we mean by evolution?
10. What do we mean by faith reduced to science?
11. What do we mean by *entering the closet and closing the door* when we pray?
12. What is meant by *Intelligence decrees and Law executes*?
13. What is meant by a unity of thought and imagination in treatment?

14. What does *man as a creative center of God Consciousness* mean?

15. Why is it that abstract statements, without specific realization and direction, will not demonstrate?

16. Why must we make conscious use of the Creative Power of Mind?

17. Why are both cause and effect spiritual?

18. What was the secret of the power of Jesus?

19. What is meant by *energy and intelligence moving as mathematical law*?

20. Why do we get better results through mental treatment on some days than on others?

Answers to Questions on Lesson 4

1. Our ability to demonstrate Spiritual Law depends upon our belief in the use of, compliance with, and dependence on the mental Law of Cause and Effect.

2. We should think of the principle of Spiritual Mind Healing in terms of exact Law automatically responding to Spirit.

3. We should think of the Spirit of God as a Divine Presence within and around us, personal to us and personified through us.

4. We commune with Spirit through prayer and meditation; through opening our consciousness to Its influx.

5. The burning bush symbolizes the Divine Presence in all nature.

6. Jacob's experience symbolizes that God is personal to all people, and that each comes to Him individually without the aid of mediators.

7. The angels represent the ladder of intuition or the influx of Divine Ideas into the mind of man.

8. The Subjective Law responds to us by intelligently acting upon our thought.

9. No. This Law must respond to our word and execute directions given It. The Law of Itself has no volition.

10. The power of Jesus was the result of his faith in God, and his understanding of spiritual and mental law.

11. (a) We derive authority over any law through the knowledge that all laws of nature are exact. They never are a thing of caprice, and may be depended upon with mathematical certainty. (b) Yes, mental law being a natural law is like any other law of nature.

12. Mental treatment is using the Law of Mind for definite purposes.

13. Mental treatment takes place in the mind of the one treating.

14. No. Unconscious means without consciousness, or nonexistent. Subconscious means below the threshold of, and the servant of conscious mind.

15. Scientific mental practice is a conscious and definite use of mental law.

16. By the Trinity we mean cause, medium, and effect—Spirit, Law, and Form.

17. (a) No. God cannot will evil or limitation because His nature is wholeness, and because the Will of God cannot contradict the Nature of God. (b) Evil is a misinterpretation of God. Limitation is a restricted concept of God.

18. In giving a mental treatment one should use the words and thoughts which convey the desired meaning to one's own mind.

The Great Wayshower

The point that Troward stresses in Chapter V, *The Mission of Jesus*, is *Universal Mind, as the all-pervading, undistributed Creative Power must be subjective mind . . . its relation to the individual mind must always be in exact correspondence to what the individual mind conceives of it.*

It was the mission of Moses to teach the Universal Law of Cause and Effect. It was the mission of Jesus not only to continue this teaching of the Law of Cause and Effect, but to show how it can be more intimately applied to individual and human relationships. He added beauty to power and put feeling into that which of itself is merely a mechanical law. The Law of Mind, being a doer and not a knower, automatically responds to us by corresponding with our mental attitudes.

One of the chief difficulties in presenting the Science of Mind is the tendency which people have to confuse the laws of nature with the Spirit. When we speak of the Law of Mind as being a blind force, people are liable to think we are speaking of God, the Spirit, as merely a blind force. We should be careful to differentiate between the Law as a way, and the Spirit as a presence. It is from this Divine Presence that we receive inspiration, illumination, intuition, and guidance. As this inspiration images itself in our thought, its reflection is automatically cast into the Law which responds by corresponding.

Troward points out that we may view the Universal *I AM* as merely an unconscious Force which blindly follows our dictation without any sense of responsibility, or we may view It as being the only Principle which has decision and will, thus reducing the individual to a mechanical automaton. Or again we may view the Spirit as forever flowing into our spirit, merging with it. This enables us to set in motion sequences of causation, which we have decided we wish to experience. When our thought has been built on a conscious recognition of the unity of good, this sequence of Cause and Effect will never be destructive.

Troward tells us that the Bible teaches that *from the center of his own smaller circle of perception the individual is free to make any selection that he will and if he acts from a clear recognition of the true relations of things, the first use he will make of this power will be to guard himself against any misuse of it . . .* We must all come to see with Emerson that there is One Mind common to all individual men. Moreover, as Troward points out, we must come to realize *a higher and more far-seeing Wisdom* than that which we consciously possess. We must believe in Divine Guidance and have complete trust in the Universal Creative Spirit as an active Presence of Consciousness and Intelligence, and the Universal Law as a servant of both God and man. We must come to see that God and man are One.

Troward makes plain that the institution of sacrifice is the most effective way of impressing the proper mental attitude on people's thoughts because it implies the desire of the worshiper to submit himself to Divine Guidance. It is not that the All Supreme Wisdom demands this recognition, but because such recognition is necessary if we are consciously to unify ourselves with the All Power as well as the All Wisdom.

Sacrifice symbolizes the offering of the lower self to the Higher. It symbolizes the surrender of the human to the Divine. It means the transmutation of lower qualities, animal desires, into a new birth. It signifies a condition of spiritual improvement as a result of having made the sacrifice. The burnt offering signified purification by fire, by which lower qualities were transmuted into higher ones. As the intellect advances in its evolution, it begins to realize that the sacrifice of animals, *the blood of bulls and goats and the ashes of an heifer can have no power in themselves*. We awake to the realization that this cruder form of sacrifice is no longer necessary, and we say with the Psalmist, *Burnt offering and sin offering hast thou not required*. But instead of these, *I delight to do thy will, O my God; yea, thy law is within my heart.*

Troward states that the act of sacrifice carries with it the idea of making a covenant with God. Covenant means recognizing the true relationship between the Divine and the human as something which is eternally taking place. *And I will establish my covenant with thee*. This is a discloser of the unity of all life. Jeremiah says, *Come, and let us join ourselves to the Lord in a perpetual covenant that shall not be forgotten*. The sacrifice and covenant announce a surrender of the lower nature, which feels itself to be separated from Spirit, to the higher nature which is forever being One with God. Troward points out that as this Divine At-one-ment is consciously recognized, we come into the knowledge that the Divine Mind is Life in Itself, the very Essence of Being.

It is the recognition of our life as being forever one with God which results in what Jesus meant when he said, *I am come that they might have life, and that they might have it more abundantly*. This would have to be the case if the Law is something which reacts mechanically to our thought. If our patterns of thought arise from a consciousness of our unity with good, then in whatever direction they turn we shall be reflecting this unity of good. If our thought is rooted in Beauty our acts will be beautiful; if we have a consciousness that Love is at the base of everything, we shall not only love but we shall be loved. Thus we have not destroyed the Law, but have sacrificed the lower to the higher, and in doing so we have made a perpetual covenant with the Eternal. Job says; *Acquaint now thyself with him and be at peace: thereby good shall come unto thee . . . For then shalt thou have thy delight in the Almighty and shalt lift up thy face unto God*. The Koran states the same truth when it says, *But God will increase the guidance of the already guided*. And the Text of Taoism, *In the way of Heaven there is no partiality of Love; it is always on the side of the good man.*

Troward explains that from this conception of Unity arises the idea of guidance and protection, which he reminds us recurs throughout the Bible under the emblem of the Shepherd and the Sheep. *The Lord is my shepherd; I shall not want . . . I am the good shepherd . . . Give ear, O shepherd of Israel . . .* Often we fail to be guided by the Good Shepherd, which is the indwelling Christ referred to in Psalm 119:176: *I have gone astray like a lost sheep*. And in Isaiah, *All we like sheep have gone astray; we have turned every one to his own way*. It is only when the higher qualities are guided by the Divine Instinct, which is the Christ Mind within us, that we have discovered true guidance.

Troward tells us that just as Israel represented the attitude of the Shepherd and the Sheep, so Egypt represented a principle of disunion with good. Genesis 46:34*: . . . every shepherd is an abomination unto* *the Egyptians*. What is this but a veiled statement referring to man's lack of the knowledge of Divine Guidance, or desire for it?

This Divine Guidance must be found in Universal Mind, and Troward is careful to point out that such Guidance is impossible unless the individual mind first recognizes the Universal Mind as an Intelligence capable of giving the highest instruction. Why, we might ask, does not Universal Mind impose this knowledge upon us willy-nilly? And the answer again takes us back to the starting point of all philosophic discussion relative to the freedom of man. Ecclesiastes says, *Lo, this only have I found, that God hath made man upright, but they have sought out many inventions*. Here is a clear statement that even the Divine Creative Wisdom cannot impose full-fledged individuality but that such individuality must be left alone to discover itself.

From the teachings of Hermes we read, *But the All Father Mind being Life and Light did bring forth Man coequal to Himself*. And in the Koran: *You created man and You know what his soul whispereth to him, and You are closer to him than his neck vein*. And from *Fragments of a Faith Forgotten*: *Thou hast begotten Man in Thy self-born Mind, and in Thy reflection . . . he is the man begotten of Mind . . . Thou hast given all things to the Man*. In Chaldean Oracles we find these words: *The Father of man and gods placed Mind in Soul and Soul in inert Body*. Again in St. John 1:5: *And the light shineth in darkness and the darkness comprehended it not*. The Text of Taoism asks why the darkness comprehended it not when it says, *But how can the Tao be so obscure that there should be a true and a false in It . . . Tao becomes obscured through the small comprehension*. Surely this means that perfection already exists but we do not realize it.

We find Christ described as the Good Shepherd who giveth his life for his sheep. This could not mean the actual giving of life, since Life is that which cannot be either taken or given. To give life would be to suppose death. The Bible clearly states that man is the author of the idea of death and of resurrection: *For as in Adam all die, even so in Christ shall all be made alive*. It is evident that death refers not to an actual cessation of existence or to the destruction of Being, but rather to the transmutation of the lower into the higher. Troward tells us that Jesus stands before us as the Grand Master of Mental Science.

The Great Sacrifice which Jesus made was what Troward calls The Great Suggestion. That is, the entire mission of Jesus points to the necessity of Divine Guidance through our conscious cooperation with the Supreme Spirit. It was his mission to become the Wayshower. He said, *I am the way, the truth, and the life; no man cometh unto the Father but by me*. He was referring to the Universal *I AM* individualized in each one of us as the individualized *I*. The two are One.

It was the purpose of Jesus to reveal the Self to the Self or as an ancient scripture says, *to raise the self by the Self*. He told his disciples: *God is not the God of the dead but of the living*. God, being the very Life Principle, does not perceive death. There is no death. It is evident that Jesus as the Wayshower was not trying to show the way from death into life but rather from one state of existence into another; from a lower to a higher plane.

We read in the Zend-Avesta, *If death come at eve, may healing come at daybreak. Let showers shower down new waters, new earth, new trees, new health and new healing powers*. What does this mean other than that the higher shall govern the lower; evil shall give way to good; the beneficence of the outpouring of the Spirit shall fill the upturned bowl of acceptance from Its universal horn of plenty. *The eternal God is thy refuge, and underneath are the everlasting arms* (Deuteronomy 33:27). Job said, *Yea, surely God will not do wickedly, neither will the Almighty pervert judgment.* And in Psalm 19:7,8: *The law of the Lord is perfect, converting the soul . . . The statutes of the Lord are right, rejoicing the heart: the commandment of the Lord is sure, enlightening the eyes.* From the Chaldean Oracles: *For the Self begotten One, the Father Mind, perceiving His own Works sowed into all . . . so that all might continue living on for endless time. And that . . . the Father's Light might never fail.*

The great mission of Jesus was not to convert death into life nor to transmute a material universe into a spiritual one, for either of these propositions would be impossible. He plainly told his disciples that God is not the author of death; that God, being the spiritual Principle of Life, cannot conceive death. Therefore there are no dead men. He also told them to look about them and rightly estimate the universe in which they lived, which they thought to be separated from pure Spirit. *Behold, the kingdom of God is within you.*

Varying degrees of intellectual and spiritual comprehension automatically divide people into different levels of consciousness, from which level each must interpret Life as he sees It. Kipling says, *And each, in his separate star, shall draw the Thing as he sees It, for the God of Things as They are.* We must interpret the mission of Jesus from the viewpoint of a Supreme Being who consciously sacrificed the Beloved Son in atonement for the sins of the world, or else we must believe that the Beloved Son himself offered the sacrifice, not as a propitiation to the Universal Creative Spirit but as an example to man. This latter viewpoint seems the more intelligent one. But if an individual has not yet reached a spiritual perspective where he recognizes the true significance of sacrificing the lower nature to the higher, there is still a great lesson in the act of Jesus delivering his human life to the needs of those whose philosophy is one of materialism.

Thus the sacrifice of Jesus is designed to meet the need of all classes. The human body sacrificed on the cross symbolizes the union of God with man, of heaven with earth. It is surrendering the lower to the higher nature, the lesser to the greater. The *not being* is sacrificed to *Being*.

It is never enough, however, to leave principles strung on symbolic meanings. Unless our Bible, like other bibles of the world, delivers a message which is practical as well as idealistic, then it is of little value to us while we live in this world. But Troward tells us that the Bible is the Book of the Emancipation of Man. It teaches a Principle which we can demonstrate in our individual experience. Assuming the creative power of thought, it tells us in many ways how to use this creative power constructively and how to avoid using it destructively.

Moses the Lawgiver taught an immutable Law of Cause and Effect; Jesus the Wayshower, without denying the Mosaic Law, told us that we must add Love to the Law. In these two great central figures of the Bible we find a clear, comprehensive teaching of the nature of the universe and the relationship between the Creative Spirit and ourselves. Moses proclaimed this relationship to be one of absolute, mathematical, cold, unfailing Cause and Effect. There is something that grinds out every act to its logical conclusion. This same law Buddha cleverly taught. Moses, looking down the corridors of time and peering into the future, declared that God would raise up another prophet like unto him. He perceived either by logical deduction or through intuition that his teachings would not be complete until some personal element had been added to his concept of the Law of Cause and Effect.

Science has proved the universe in action to be a mechanical force, but does not disprove a spontaneous Presence in addition to the mechanical force. A modern scientist has inferred that we think of the universe in terms of an Infinite Thinker thinking mathematically, meaning that we may think of the universe as a dual unity of spontaneous self-knowingness and reactive self-manifesting law. Here we have the Infinite Thinker and the mathematical thought. We have both an engine and an engineer. We have a universe not only of law and order, but also of feeling, love, consciousness, truth, and beauty.

Science observes a mechanical universe because it studies the universe in action. Whether we study physical or mechanical laws or the movement of thought, we shall always find a mechanical movement. However, it does not seem intelligent to leave out the Thinker. The artist is superior to his art; the engineer controls his engine. One of our great scientists tells us that science has not discovered anything which denies a Universal Consciousness in which the relationship of the Supreme Creative Spirit is to us as a parent to its offspring.

So we find that the mission of Jesus was to complete the Law of Moses. He explained that he came not to destroy but to fulfill. He breathed beauty, warmth, and color into life, and thus the very law which had produced bondage, by the divine alchemy of his creative touch was transmuted into freedom.

Belief, Faith and Prayer

And the prayer of faith shall save the sick and the Lord shall raise him up (James 5: 15). What, then, is the prayer of faith?

Jesus clearly taught that spiritual power works through man at the level of his belief, implying that it would work as he believed and while he believed. He ascribed a mighty power to belief and to faith, and we find that throughout the ages faith has been honored. Most certainly some people's prayers have been answered but not all persons' prayers have been answered in the way in which they wished them to be answered.

How are we going to account for the fact that one person's prayers are answered and another's are not? Must we admit that there are degrees in which prayers are answered? And if so, why? Is one man's faith better than another's? Is God more pleased with one man's petition than another's?

It seems a pretty tough problem, until we understand what Jesus meant when he said, *Go thy way, and as thou hast believed, so be it done unto thee.*

What did he imply? He implied that it is done unto us by some impersonal Principle, a Principle which knows neither Jew nor Gentile, but knows only Its own ability to do. It will do as quickly for one as for another. The Law is no respecter of persons but works alike for each and all.

Jesus not only said, *So be it done unto thee*. He said, *As thou hast believed*. The impersonal Law, which is the actor, does it unto us, but only as we believe. Immediately we recognize our old friend the Law of Cause and Effect. It is done unto us as we believe and if we can believe only a little, then only what we call a little is done. But if we believe in what the consensus of human opinion has called a lot, then a lot is done. Not that there is a big or little in the Truth but that we measure it. Well did the Great Teacher say, *With what measure ye mete, it shall be measured to you again*. It is done unto us, but only as we believe.

What is belief? Most surely belief is a certain way of thinking; it is an activity of consciousness. Belief is a thing of thought, and being a thing of thought we can change belief. And if what a man believes decides what is going to happen to him, the most important thing for him to do is regulate his belief so that what happens will be good for him, and he will be glad to have it happen and joyously welcome it.

What is most likely to change our belief from a negative to a positive viewpoint? What thought, what hope, what expression, what stimulus is most likely to change our belief? This Jesus established in the Sermon on the Mount when he said that the meek shall inherit the earth; that the peacemakers shall be called the children of God. In other statements he showed us how to reform our belief so that it could partake of the nature of Reality and would contain within itself everything necessary for our well-being. This is also what the Apostle meant when he said that we should think on whatsoever things are good, true, and beautiful.

Faith is an affirmative mode of thought. Faith says, "I can," rather than "I cannot" or "I shall not." We can learn to have faith in abundance rather than in poverty. We can change our thought in regard to lack. This is what treatment is for. Instead of saying, "There is not enough good to go around" we say, "All the power there is, is devoted to my good. I am not afraid of poverty because all the power there is, is devoted to giving me abundance. God provides me with every good thing today, every day, always." Such statements as these will change our belief from denial to one of positive faith. Whatever we can have faith in, and having faith in can understand, we may experience according to the Law of Cause and Effect. This Law is immutable, invariable, unassailable, and absolute.

"But," someone might ask, "is faith in lack equal to faith in abundance?" The answer to this question is that there is neither lack nor abundance, as such; there is merely what is and the way it works. We are so constituted that faith in love overcomes the belief in hate. Our nature is such that faith in life destroys our fear of death. Our nature is such that faith routs fear all along the line. The great affirmations of life must, of necessity, destroy their apparent opposites. Nevertheless we cannot overlook the fact that all statements are positive, all statements are affirmations, since each is a statement of one's belief in something.

Right here is where prayer comes in, and of course we are thinking of prayer in its broadest connotation and its most realistic meaning. We are thinking of prayer as the communion of the soul with the Oversoul, with the Divine Creative Presence which is not only in the soul but which *is* the soul. It is more than an individualization; it is also a Universality.

Prayer in its truest sense is not a petition, not a supplication, not a wail of despair; it is rather an alignment, a unifying process which takes place in the mind as it reaches to its Divine Self and to that Power which is greater than human understanding. In the act of such prayerful and reverent communion with God one senses the unity of good, the completeness of life, and at times the veil of doubt is lifted and the face of Reality appears. This consciousness, which has been referred to as the Secret Place of the Most High, is an experience rising out of the conviction that God is all there is, beside whom there is none else.

Prayer, then, is communion, and this communion pronounces life to be good. Prayerful communion ascends to that place where unity has not yet become variety, where the unformed One is ready to take any specific shape. In this act of communion the individual becomes copartner with the Eternal and gives birth to time, space, and conditions.

But what could Jesus have meant when he referred to fasting in connection with prayer? It seems evident that he was not necessarily referring to a physical fact, for one of the accusations laid against him was that he drank wine with sinners. He was also accused of breaking the Sabbath by permitting his disciples to pluck corn on the Sabbath day. In fact he seemed to disregard many of the outward forms which were common in his day. He referred to some deeper Principle which physical fasting was intended to symbolize.

This is what he meant when he said that it was not sufficient to make the outside of the platter clean and again when he said, *Not every one that saith unto me, Lord, Lord, shall enter into the kingdom of heaven.* Perhaps by fasting and prayer Jesus meant such a complete consecration to the ideal that the creative Genius of the universe passed immediately into self-expression through man's imagination.

Such a high altitude of thought could not be described other than by using the symbol of fasting and prayer, and possibly that is why Jesus used it. Suppose we call fasting a determination to refuse further contemplation of the negative. This would be passing from death into life, from negation into affirmation, from denial into acceptance. In this transformation of thought through faith and belief the communion of the soul with its Source would become a pronouncement rather than a petition. This is the position which the enlightened of all ages have taken.

If a person feels that the act of physical fasting is necessary to the consummation of such a devout communion, let him fast, and no person should be so rash as to deny him this privilege. If, on the other hand, he feels that he is not fighting his way but singing a song, let no one deny him the joyous pathway to freedom. For sooner or later all must discover that it is neither fasting nor feasting, but belief, faith, and acceptance which cause one to transcend the lesser good and ascend into that holy mount within where the eye views the world *as one vast plain and one boundless reach of sky.*

We must never forget to make a practical application of this science. In our philosophy it is not enough merely to state a principle. We must apply such a principle to our everyday living, and wherever a need appears we must meet it, not by accepting the inevitability of such a need but by affirming its exact opposite. The need is met when we no longer recognize it as a need but seeing through it, envision that Principle which could just as easily remold the need into an acceptance of good. Therefore we are told to think on whatsoever things are true, lovely, and of good report; we should dwell on these things rather than on their apparent opposites.

To put this into practice should be the desire of every sincere seeker after spiritual truth. He must come to believe that there is such a Divine Power waiting his use. He must fully understand that he is the one who knows how to use It and then he must proceed definitely to make use of this Power which is within all men. In actual practice one's life should become a continuous communion with good.

One's mind should be continuously acknowledging the presence of good and the power of good in one's experience. A practitioner should acknowledge the power and presence of this good in the experience of the one he seeks to help. For the acknowledgment of good is a creative act making possible its manifestation in human experience. We should *fast* to the idea of lack and *feast* with the idea of plenty. We should *fast* from the idea of poverty and *feast* upon the belief in wealth, and most surely we should abstain from contemplating uncertainties and enter into a long and eternal period of feasting upon certainty. And when the world cries, "Whither goest thou?" something within us should answer, "We know in whom we have believed."

At first this fasting and feasting, this prayer and communion may seem a little difficult. We all are more or less surrounded by negation and this is where the office of prayer enters. It establishes a serenity within the soul enabling it to have confidence in that spirit of acceptance without which the Divine gift is never complete. For how can the Divine gift become complete until one accepts it? There is no song without a singer. And so we must learn joyfully to enter into our Divine inheritance.

What does all this mean other than that we should learn to have confidence in life, to believe in the eternal goodness, and to accept the Divine Bounty? This transformation of thought from negation to affirmation is seldom instantaneous, so one must maintain a flexibility of thought, being willing to bend somewhat before the storms of life but refusing to break. His thought should have an elasticity which permits it to spring back into place, but it cannot do so unless it is first fully convinced that it does know in whom it has believed, unless it is completely convinced that the universe is a spiritual system governed by a Beneficent Consciousness.

This greater vision seldom transpires in one flash of consciousness, although it may do so. More often than not, the ascent from our valley of negation to the mountaintop of realization is slow. But each step on the road entices us with the enchantment of a new vista and judging from past experiences and former transformations, the pathway upon which we travel leads to the summit and we press on with joy.

By some Divine interior awareness, call it what we will, there is an intuition within man which pushes him forward. There is some spark which has never been entirely extinguished. The prayer of faith and belief, communion of the soul with its Source, fans this spark into a Divine blaze in whose light dark shadows no longer lurk. This is inspiration. This is illumination. This is the perception of wholeness.

Suppose a man were to prepare himself a mental diet garnished with spiritual realization, his meat the living word, his bread manna from heaven, his fruit the inspiration of hope, and his wine the essence of joy. And suppose in addition to this he should see this table spread before him in the wilderness and waited upon by the Law, the servant of God and man, would he not then realize that he is today in the Kingdom of Heaven, that today God is his Host, and would he not exclaim, "Oh, Wilderness were Paradise enow!"?

Bibles of the World

Fragments from the spiritual history of the race revealing fundamental UNITY of religious thought and experience

BUDDHISM—Be not concerned with other men's evil works or deeds or neglect of good. Look rather to thine own sins and negligence.

Though one should conquer in battle thousands and thousands of men, whoso shall conquer himself—he is the greatest of warriors. To overcome oneself is better truly than to overcome others.

CHRISTIANITY—Thou hypocrite, first cast out the beam out of thine own eye; and then shalt thou see clearly to cast out the mote out of thy brother's eye.

Wherefore let him that thinketh he standeth take heed lest he fall.

CONFUCIANISM—The good in you I will not dare to keep concealed. And for the evil in me I will not dare to forgive myself. I will examine these things in harmony with the mind of God.

Give repose to your mind. Examine your virtue. Send far forward your plans. And thus by your generous forbearance you will make people repose in what is good.

HINDUISM—The man of steady wisdom, having subdued all senses, becomes fixed in Me, the Supreme. His wisdom is well established.

To those men, ever controlled, who think on Me and worship Me with undivided hearts, I bring the power to gain and guard.

ZOROASTRIANISM—   May thy mind be master of its vow!
May thy soul be master of its vow!
And all the nights of thy life
Mayst thou live on in the joy of thy soul!

JAINISM—Prove constant to truth.

Right belief depends on the acquaintance with truth, or the devotion to those who know the truth.

Exert yourself in the truth. Knowing the truth, one should live up to it.

How Mind Creates
Office of the Dean

My Dear Friend,

You will find several references in this lesson to cross sections of our Textbook. They are of vital importance so please read them carefully. For what you are trying to discover is perhaps the greatest of all truths, which is that there is only One Mind in the Universe and you use It.

You and I do not have a mind separate from God any more than we have a law of nature that belongs to us individually. Here we are in the midst of nature and we can learn how to use her laws because the Mind of God is in us, telling us about these laws and how to use them. This is true of every scientific discovery and none the less true in the discovery of the Science of Mind and how to use it, for it is both an exact and an exacting science.

As our lesson says, we all use this Mind and live in this Divine Presence. Each individualizes It. God, the Divine Presence, is personal to you, and the Law of Mind is right where you are, ready to be used. It cannot refuse your approach because It is a Law.

In the article on *The Consciousness That Heals* we are trying more strongly to emphasize that there is a scientific method, a right way to use the Laws of Mind. The article on *Religion* deals with Spiritual Consciousness and shows the fundamental mental attitudes that we should assume.

You will realize that we do not criticize anyone's religion because we believe in all religions. We are trying to arrive at the essence of all religions, for when we strip them of non-essentials they all teach the same thing. This is why we are enclosing quotations from different religions of the world.

Sincerely,
Ernest Holmes

Lesson 6
Only One Mind, p.87, to Law, p.92

One of the most difficult things for us to realize is that there is but One Mind in the universe. We are accustomed to think of our individual minds and the Mind of God as though they were separate and divided from each other and yet in reality there is but One Mind which we all use.

If you turn to page 41 under the heading, *A Riddle of Simplicity*, and read through to the bottom of page 42, you will get a better understanding of the reality of this unity of Mind. You will notice at the bottom of page 41 these words: *The intelligence by and through which we perceive that there is a Spiritual Presence and an Infinite Mind . . . constitutes our receptivity to It.* That is, the very act of self-knowing which takes place in your thought is in reality this One Mind recognizing Itself.

As much of this One Mind is released through us into operation as we are able to embody. The action of this Mind through our thought creates the forms which appear in our experience. This should be kept in mind while reading on page 483, *The Law of Correspondents*. Each one of us is a law unto himself through his particular use of the Creative Law of the universe.

We need not seek other powers or other minds but we must clearly perceive that all the power there is has already been delivered unto us. All the good there is, is ours but we must consciously enter into this good. If we have not been experiencing as much good as we desire, we must make definite and conscious use of the Law with the direct end in mind of experiencing more good. We must really use our technique for conscious practice.

On page 458 you will find a description of a concrete method of practice under the heading, *A Formula for Effective Prayer*. Jesus told us that when we pray we are to believe that we have already received. This is not always easy and yet the greatest spiritual genius who ever lived gave us this formula, this method of approach, this conscious use of the Law of Spiritual Cause and Effect.

When we pray we must believe that we already possess the object of our desire. This calls for implicit trust; for complete faith. Until we believe that we already possess, we have not created the image of our desire and projected it into the Creative Medium so that it may attract to itself that which shall give it form.

We should believe that God wills everything good for us; that it would be impossible for God to will anything other than good. We should think of the Law as our obedient servant and the Spirit as our immediate friend. The Spirit ever inspires us, the Law ever obeys us.

This formula for prayer which Jesus laid down for our use certainly reaches the very rock-bottom of Spiritual Causation. *Blessed are they that have not seen and yet have believed*. For when we turn from the confusion of fear to the certainty of faith, we may be sure that the Universal will respond and that we shall demonstrate our desired good.

On page 88, the third paragraph, we are told that *the Body of the Universe is the result of the thought of Spirit operating through the medium of Soul*. You will find on page 633 a definition of the word *Soul* as we use it. The Soul represents the Creative Medium, the Universal Law, which is subject both to the Will of God and to the will of man.

Soul has been spoken of as the servant of the Spirit throughout the ages. Soul is Subjective Law. It has been referred to as the Womb of Nature because it has been thought of as the Feminine Principle of nature, which means the productive side—that Creative Medium which receives the images of thought, whether of God or of man and gives birth to corresponding form.

Under the heading, *The "Personalness" of God* (page 88), let us carefully consider that Spirit is more than an abstract principle. It must forever be to each one of us warm, colorful, but Infinite Personalness. As we read in the Glossary on page 618, under *Personalness*: *To think of God simply as an Infinite Principle would be to resolve the Divine Being into an Infinite IT*. The text states, also, that God is personal to all who believe in Him.

Let us carefully consider once more the dual unity of Spirit and Law and though we may seem to be continually referring to this topic, it tends to make us realize the necessity of coming to see definitely and having it fixed completely in our minds that there is a difference between Person and Principle. In working out Universal Principles we need never deny Universal Personalness.

We may and should retain all of the warmth and color, all of the responsiveness latent in the idea of Personalness. We need this if we are to have a true sense of our right relationship to the Spirit. I think this is an important thing for us to consider and we should give it a great deal of thought.

Read the Meditation on page 548 called *The Personality of God* and also the Meditation on page 549, *Unity*. After having read these meditations, combining the two as one, think carefully on the meaning of each word and phrase. Do this daily until finally there comes to you, as there will come, a sense of your unity with the Whole. You will discover an intimate relationship with the Universe which will enable you to use It even more effectively for definite purposes.

The question which so many people ask, in taking up the study of a metaphysical system of thought, is whether or not in so doing they will lose God. As a matter of fact, for the first time they will find the Real Divine. On page 419, the third paragraph you will read that all the mystics have recognized the unity of God and man. We can never be separated from that life of pure Spirit of which we are some part. Always this Essence is flowing into action through the imagination and the will. The Essence, the imagination, and the will are spontaneous; the action is mechanical.

Read page 447, *How to Approach the Spirit*. You will see that the consciousness of the Divine Presence is an inner experience. It would be very difficult and perhaps impossible, to give any dogmatic instruction or method of procedure which would be sure to enable us to become conscious of this inner Spirit. The Spirit is already here, and we must feel for It until we really feel It, or, as the mystic said, *Act as though I am and I will be*. We should daily practice this Presence of God.

In the first paragraph on page 91 we are told that the Soul, or the Subjective Medium, executes the will of the Spirit but has no self-choice. It merely reflects the images that the conscious Spirit holds before it or casts into it. This Principle that we have to demonstrate—that all objective form starts in a subjective idea—is the foundation of scientific mental work. As a practitioner you must use this Principle with deliberate intent and with specific purpose.

On page 435 we are told to pray believing that prayer should be direct and specific and should always be accompanied by positive recognition and receptivity. You will soon discover that mental and spiritual work is definite. When you give a treatment you know exactly what you are doing. There is never anything indefinite or vague about it.

A treatment is an active thing; this activity is mental recognition, and such mental recognition is usually put into the form of spoken words followed by a deep inner realization of the truth of those words. You will find the process simple and direct.

On page 415, the second paragraph, is the statement that we must realize our Divine Partnership, a partnership which exists between the visible world of effects and the invisible world of Causation. Man's place in the creative order is really that of a distributor of the Divine gifts. He uses the Law, which already exists, and gives form to the Substance, which already exists, and he does this because the impulsion of the Originating Spirit, the Parent Mind, is already operating through his imagination and will.

Our paragraph says, *The hope of destiny is latent in the slumbering thought, and genius lies buried until the attention is winged with love and reason.* The impulsion of Love, the sense of our Divine relationship to God and to each other, the resulting compassionate desire to help others, is the awakening of the soul to the high call of the Spirit. But since everything in the universe is reasonable, we shall never be called upon to do anything that contradicts an intelligent, law abiding universe.

In giving your treatments you should always feel the Divine Presence, but you should never forget the immutable Law. For in such degree as your word is in harmony with Truth, it must be power. Thus the Will of God is made manifest through the Law of Life, which returns to us exactly what we reflect into It.

We should ponder the deep meaning of this rather abstract but at the same time simple concept of the universe—that universal laws are always self-active. This means that when it comes to giving a treatment what you put into your treatment, as consciousness, will appear in physical form. Not only will it appear, but it must appear.

We are ready, then to consider the main paragraph on page 92, which is the description of the creative and reflective Law of Spirit. The Law says *Yes* when you say *Yes* and *No* when you say *No*. If you hold a triangle before a mirror, the image of the triangle is reflected in it. Just so, if you think poverty into the Law It reflects poverty back to you. It reflects fear for fear, faith for faith.

But because this Law reflects the exact image of thought that we think into It, and has no other choice in the matter, then it follows that no matter what the Law may be holding now as being true about us, through a new process of thinking we so completely change Its tendency as to alter the experience. If this were not true it would be useless for us to pursue these studies in the Science of Mind, but our study of this principle will enable us through practice to prove that the principle is correct.

On page 339, second paragraph, you will find a discussion of involution and evolution, the Law of Cause and Effect. Please note that evolution is the effect of Intelligence and not Its cause and that evolution follows involution. At the same time read the definition of *Evolution* on page 590, and *Involution* on page 603. Try in your imagination to see exactly how this works. Try to sense that the entire process of evolution, which is the passing of Spirit into form, is an effect of thought—that your entire experience is an effect and that you stand in the position of the conscious creator of that effect.

Therefore learn definitely and deliberately to create new images of thought that new and better conditions may be cast in the mold of your experience.

Summary

There is only One Mind and you use It. The individual mind is a center in this Mind and not separate from It. God wills only that which is good for us but our thought is creative and automatically brings to us the things we think about.

The Spirit is more than an abstract principle. It is a warm, living, colorful Presence personal to each one.

God can have no will for anyone other than the will of good, freedom, liberty, life, truth, love, and beauty.

The Spirit is at the center of your own being; if you believe It will reveal Itself to you, It will.

Spiritual mind treatment is always an active thing. It is the Law of Mind in Action. It is Mind doing something definite as It reacts to our thought.

A consciousness of Love and of the Divine Presence is the foundation for all use of the Law of Mind. We feel this Presence and we use this Law.

No matter what happened yesterday, we can change it today because the law reflects the images of our thoughts as we think them.

Because we can wipe out the old images of thought or their effects and create new ones, we are free. But even this freedom will do us no good unless we use it. Therefore we must definitely use the Law of Good at all times and for all purposes. Each must become the arbiter of his fate, and learn to mold his future more nearly after his heart's desire.

Questions

Brief answers to these questions should be written out by the student after studying the lesson and the answers compared with those which will be included in next week's lesson.

1. What is it within us that knows?
2. To what extent can we use the Mind of God?
3. What do we mean by being conscious of and embodying the Mind of God?
4. How much power and good do we have to use?
5. How do we make prayer effective?
6. What is the will of God for us?
7. How should we think of Spirit and the Law?
8. Is the Spirit personal to us?
9. Is the Law personal to us?
10. What is the difference between Spirit as Person, and Law as Principle?
11. In dealing with God as Infinite Mind, do we lose anything?
12. Is mental work a definite thing?

13. What is man's place in the creative order of the universe?
14. What gives power to our word?
15. How can we use the Law of Cause and Effect as a principle of freedom rather than bondage?

Answers to Questions on Lesson 5

1. By creation we mean the invisible world becoming visible. In the mental world, mind formulating ideas.
2. Endless creation means the Spirit eternally creating and taking form.
3. By resolving things into thoughts we mean uncovering the mental cause.
4. In mental science, resolving things into thoughts means making a mental diagnosis.
5. By mental diagnosis we mean uncovering discordant thought that it may be replaced by harmonious thought.
6. By mental correspondents we mean the images of thought behind objective experiences.
7. We use the Divine Creative Power every time we think.
8. By involution we mean placing an idea in mind as we would plant a seed in the ground.
9. By evolution we mean the act of thought taking form as the seed becomes the plant.
10. By reducing faith to science we mean understanding Spiritual Law and making conscious use of It.
11. By entering the closet and closing the door when we pray, we mean mentally turning from appearance and accepting the desired answer without the necessity of knowing how it is to be brought about.
12. Intelligence decrees and Law executes means that the Word of Spirit (and man is Spirit) decrees and the mental Law of Cause and Effect executes .
13. The unity of thought and imagination in treatment means both the intellect and feeling accept the treatment.
14. Man as a creative center of God consciousness means man is individualized Spirit and because God's thought is creative, man's thought is creative.
15. Abstract statements without specific realization and direction will not demonstrate because abstract statements are only a recognition of Law, while specific realization and direction gives instruction to the Law.
16. We must make conscious use of the Creative Power of Mind; otherwise we cannot direct It for definite purposes.
17. Both cause and effect are Spiritual because they are two ends of the same thing and because Spirit takes form, which is effect.
18. The secret of the power of Jesus was his realization of his unity with God.
19. Energy and intelligence moving as mathematical law means that laws of thought, like laws of physics, are exact.
20. We get better results from mental treatment on some days than on others because sometimes our thought is clearer and our realization of its power is greater.

The Temple of Truth

In his chapter on *The Building of the Temple*, Troward says that the Bible teaches that certain universal principles are at the root of everything, whether it be the World of Man or the Divine World. God, man, and the universe all have fundamental laws unifying and coordinating the inner relationship of the parts with the Whole. In this way each plane reproduces the one just below it on a higher level and the one just above it on a lower level; the same laws obtain on all planes or as Hermes said, *As above, so below*.

It was a realization that man in his real nature reflects or reproduces the Universal Spirit that caused Jesus to say, *Be ye therefore perfect, even as your Father which is in heaven is perfect*. And John to say, *Beloved, now are we the sons of God and it doth not yet appear what we shall be but we know that when he shall appear, we shall be like him; for we shall see him as he is*.

The Bible, in its many and varied illustrations, points to three central themes, God, Man, and the Universe. Troward states, *However deep the mysteries we may encounter, there is nothing unnatural anywhere. Everything has its place in the true order of the Great Whole*. Ignorance of the true order will not exempt us from suffering the results of a misuse of its laws; hence ignorance binds us until we become redeemed by the Truth. This is the meaning of sin and salvation. Since sin means making a mistake or missing the mark, salvation must stand for the correction of the mistake or hitting the mark. Both sin and salvation are potential in all of us since we are individuals.

The laws of nature never change and Troward tells us, *The only question is whether through our ignorance we shall use them in that inverted sense which sums them all up in the Law of Death, or true and harmonious order which sums them up in the Law of Life*. He also points out that Solomon's Temple symbolizes this Grand Order of the Universe. Before the Temple stood two pillars, Jachin and Boaz. These pillars were in no way connected with the Temple. Jachin stands for *The One*, while Boaz stands for *The Voice* or *The Word*. Jachin, then stands for the mathematical principle in the universe and Boaz for the Word which utilizes this principle or as Troward said, *The formulated Word is the expression of a definite Purpose and therefore stands for the action of Intelligent Volition*. He adds that we enter the Temple only by passing between these two pillars which symbolize the combined action of Law and volition. It is one of the purposes of the Bible, Troward states, to teach us how to pass between these two pillars and into the Temple that the inner secrets of the sanctuary may be open to us.

The Temple refers to man's mind, consciousness, or being. *Know ye not that ye are the temple of God and that the Spirit of God dwelleth in you? . . . the temple of God is holy, which temple ye are*. Emerson said, *God builds his Temple in the heart on the ruins of churches and religions*. And Seneca affirmed, *Temples are not to be built for God with stones piled on high; He is to be consecrated in the breast of each*. St. Augustine wrote, *A pure mind is a holy temple of God and a clean heart without sin is His best altar*.

Troward explains that Moses, Solomon, and Jesus are the three chief characters of the Bible, and that they are all builders of the Temple. His comparison between these three men is unique and interesting. He tells us *Moses erected the tabernacle, that portable temple which accompanied the Israelites in their journeyings*. It is evident that this tabernacle stands for an external and temporary representation of the Divine Creative Spirit. It is symbolic of the human body. In II Corinthians 5:1,2 we read*, For we know that if our earthly house of this tabernacle were dissolved, we have a building of God, an house not made with hands, eternal in the heavens. For in this we groan, earnestly desiring to be clothed upon with our house which is from heaven*. Does this not mean that the human body has a divine pattern in Heaven, a spiritual prototype? Since Jesus described Heaven as an interior state, we know that we are to be clothed upon, not by some force or power external to the Self, but by some creative agency already within the Self. Thus the tabernacle of Moses was called *the antitype of the True or Heavenly*.

Troward tells us, *Solomon reproduced it* (Moses' tabernacle) *in an edifice of wood and stone fixed firmly upon its rocky foundation*. Jesus, with a still deeper insight, perceived a Temple that could not decay— *Destroy this temple, and in three days I will raise it up*. Troward states that the three builders, each in his own way, proclaim the same all-embracing truth that God, Man, and the Universe—however varied may be the multiplicity of outward forms—are One. A conscious knowledge of this Divine Unity is the key which unlocks the Temple door through which we pass to the Secret Place of the Most High.

The building of the Temple is something which takes place through interior perception, through a recognition of one's true relationship with the Universal Wholeness. Not that man awakes to a recognition of the Universal Wholeness to the exclusion of his individual being, but that he as an individual is immersed in pure Spirit; he is an individualized *I* within the *I AM*, recognizing his greater Self to be the Universal Wholeness. It is this greater Self that Troward points out to us as the true Builder, because it is none other than the reproduction of the Infinite Creative Power of the Universe. It is the recognition that the Spirit of God is also the spirit of man, bringing us again to Emerson's concept of *one mind common to all individual men*.

Troward wishes us to realize that the key to a proper understanding of the scriptures is a realization that the Universal cannot, as such, initiate a course of action on the plane of the particular. Now this is not as difficult to understand as it appears to be. It means this: God can give us only what we take; what God does for us He must do through us. If we are to reproduce the Mind of God it can be done only by the Mind of God incarnating Itself in us. This is the only way that the apparent two can become One.

It is this unity with Life at the very root of our being which makes our thought creative. Thought is creative not by will, wishing, longing, prayer, or supplication but because it is its nature to be so. Man is a microcosm within the Macrocosm, a little world within the Big World. But because man is an individualized expression of God Consciousness he has the prerogative of apparent isolation. He must consciously enter the Temple; he must come into conscious union with the Spirit which indwells his soul. This is the Secret Place of the Most High that brings him under the shadow of the Almighty. That is, it brings him under the government of Good. And according to the Law of Cause and Effect, it is only when he recognizes his union with the First Cause that he can consciously partake of the harvest of such a union.

Since *harvest* symbolizes a gathering in of the fruits of wisdom, it follows that man with true wisdom must consciously unite himself with Good before he can become a conscious builder of the Temple. Troward tells us that when we enter this Temple, a Divine Interpreter will meet us on the threshold. *Threshold* is described as a symbol of higher planes of Mind which are the entrance to Spirit. Thus we see that being met on the threshold means entering into a conscious union with Reality.

Each individual is a Temple in himself. Within this Temple before the altar stands the high priest of the mind and the priest of speech. Before the altar stands the Mind which perceives and the Law which executes. The true priest is one who knows there is no gulf between God and man; that the Divine is forever pouring out Its beneficence. It is the business of the priest to become the mediator between this inward Principle and Its outward manifestation. It is written that there is no mediator save Christ, which means that there is no mediator save our own true nature.

No one can enter the Temple for us but ourselves. No one can offer the sacrifice but ourselves. No one can receive the blessing but ourselves. Thus ancient wisdom tells us that the altar, the sacrifice, the one who makes the sacrifice, and the one to whom it is made, are identical.

It was this same perception of unity which Whitman disclosed in his great poem to himself. It is only when a person recognizes that each must become his own priest that he truly stands before the altar; it is only when he has renounced all disunion that the proper sacrifice has been made, and it is only when this has been done in love that the sacrifice is acceptable. Thus one greater than Moses said that it is useless to lay our gift upon the altar while we have anything against our fellow man. This does not mean that God becomes angry with us; it is an affirmation of the Law of Cause and Effect. We can enter into the Nature of Reality only by first complying with such Nature. The giving up of everything which denies this Nature is the great sacrifice.

We must, as Troward suggests, give up everything that denies the creative power of thought; everything that finds itself bound only to external appearances and everything that denies the fundamental unity of God. If we wish to enter into a less limited experience we must sacrifice our limitations. If we wish greater love we must sacrifice our hate. It is impossible to do this, as Troward points out, while we persist in the belief that the truly originating causes of things are to be found anywhere but in our own mental attitude.

Again he states that we cannot do this unless we come to realize First Cause as that which acts independently of all conditions. It is self-evident that if we are dealing with Causation we are dealing with that which creates conditions and could not be limited by them. But because our images of thought are too often the mere reflections of our external environment, we automatically limit the gift of Spirit. Consciously we say that since we have never experienced very much happiness we probably never shall; unconsciously, we affirm that joy and prosperity do not belong to us; unconsciously we create our patterns of thought after those borrowed from others, not realizing that the act of thought is independent and that conditions flow from thought. Effect reflects cause.

When we learn to receive our visions of Reality as a result of having entered *the temple not made with hands*, then we shall truly become liberated. The tabernacle which Moses erected in the wilderness will have disappeared, the temple made of wood and stone which Solomon built will have crumbled. But the real Temple, the spiritual prototype of our external focus, will have become revealed.

What particular lesson are we to learn from this symbolic presentation? For it is certainly never wise to leave things in their symbolic state, at least it would not be practical. The lesson is this: The story of the building of the Temple does not in reality depict some ancient happening, nor yet some far off divine event; it is the story of every man's life as he lives it here and now. What is the dominant suggestion or belief in our consciousness? Are we looking merely at the external? Is our prayer one of the intellect only or have we passed between the pillars of Jachin and Boaz? Have we understood the meaning of the Law and of the Word and have we realized that these pillars must be arched by love and unity?

If so, we stand on the threshold of a greater Reality. The doorway to the Temple is open and we may advance, not with fear and trembling but with confidence, peace, and perfect trust. Petition has now become transmuted into communion, which is conscious unity with the Divine Creative Spirit. Hate, fear, and uncertainty have been left behind. The gift which we lay upon the altar of our faith is now acceptable because it unifies with Life. Hence our request will be answered.

We would miss the meaning of this chapter if we failed to realize that the true Temple is our own consciousness, and that the consciousness of good which we entertain is not different from or other than the essence of Goodness Itself. It is not separated from the Power which both creates and projects. Therefore Jesus said that because he always did the Will of God, because he lived in union with the Nature of Reality, his requests were always granted. He was not referring to the nature of a deity who withheld gifts from some while granting them to others but to Reality Itself, which cannot refuse to deliver Itself when we comply with Its nature. This is the gift made from the foundations of the world.

Our Temple is the Self; our altar the denial of evil and the affirmation of Good; our sacrifice a renouncing of the great negations; our gift, which is acceptable, the supreme affirmation: *I am that I AM, beside which there is none other*. This Universal *I AM* and this individual *I* are one and indivisible.

The Consciousness That Heals

In the fifth chapter of James we read: *And the prayer of faith shall save the sick, and the Lord shall raise him up*. When we analyze what the prayer of faith means we discover that it is a statement of belief in some power which is able, ready, and willing to do the healing. At first this may seem like rather a cold-blooded analysis, for to pick a prayer of faith apart seems to rob it of its sentimentality. Nevertheless if we would arrive at a state of consciousness that heals, we must be willing to analyze some of those things which seem so intimate and so holy that we dislike even to mention them.

The prayer of faith may be thought of as a petition, as a beseeching, or as an agonizing cry of the soul for deliverance, but whatever we term it and from whatever viewpoint we look at it, we discover that it still is an attitude of thought, a way of thinking, a movement in consciousness. If the prayer is one of faith, then this mental movement is one of acceptance, for *faith is an acceptance unqualified by denial*.

Complete faith is absolute and positive. Faith is the attitude of one who makes a complete mental surrender. It can arise only through a consciousness of complete abandonment. To the consciousness of faith there are no longer any arguments against its conviction. Faith has no opposites; it is an uncompromising mental attitude and this is exactly what the prayer of faith is. It is a prayer, a petition, or a beseeching stated in some form of mental acceptance, unqualified belief, unquestioned trust.

While the burden of petition and the necessity of faith rest on the one making the petition or having the faith, the response to this petition and this faith is made by some creative agency which has the power and the willingness to perform the act. It is God who raises him up.

What is this but a statement of *spiritual cause and effect*, for it plainly states that we have our part to play in creative faith, and that as a result of our belief some principle in nature responds by accomplishing the desired result. This result is obtained without further effort on our part. Another parallel statement to this is, *And ye shall know the truth and the truth shall make you free*, which implies that there is a truth which known, automatically becomes demonstrated.

Surely in these two statements—*The prayer of faith shall save the sick and the Lord shall raise him up* and *Ye shall know the truth and the truth shall make you free*—a definite principle is involved which all can understand and use. It is the understanding of principles with the ability to make conscious use of them that constitutes what is called the scientific method in any and all research into the secrets of nature.

There are several things which happen in the pursuit of this scientific method. First someone evolves the theory that a certain principle exists in the universe. Perhaps through observation, possibly by intuition, he conceives his theory. Having conceived this theory he begins to experiment with it, and if his theory is correct he discovers that there are certain laws involved. These laws flow out of this principle, so to speak.

Having discovered his principle he experiments with it until he learns more of the laws which govern it. Next he uses these laws for definite purposes. What has he done? He has uttered what might be called a prayer of faith. He has felt that certain things must be true, and he has had such faith in his belief that he has actually set about to discover the laws governing the theory. If his theory is correct, his faith is justified. He uncovers the natural laws of cause and effect relative to that theory. The scientific researcher always finds that there are no variations whatsoever from this result. When he uncovers a principle of nature it is changeless and invariable—he can always depend upon it.

Civilizations may come and go, empires may flourish and decay, time may pass, and change may deface all previous experience, but law is eternal. Thus the scientist learns to depend on law. His prayer of faith to his principle is a willingness to comply with the operation of its law. His cooperation and his understanding teach him how to use this law for specific purposes. We might say his prayer of faith enables him to use the principle intelligently and definitely. Thus his prayer of faith causes a response on the part of the law and the operation of the law accomplishes the desired result. What is this but another way of saying that the prayer of faith shall save the sick and God shall raise him up?

The two ideas are identical, but because we have been so accustomed to thinking of spiritual things in unnatural ways, and because we have been so used to divorcing natural things from the spiritual, we have believed in a dualistic universe and have failed to realize that Spiritual Causation is in reality the invisible end of every objective fact.

To whom does any principle of nature belong? We have never yet heard of a sane scientific man declaring that the principle of mathematics or chemistry belongs to him because he happens to be of some particular religious conviction.

Science knows no race, no particular generation of men, and no separate dispensation. The only revelation that science knows is that revelation which comes to the listening ear, the expectant thought, the intelligent uncovering of nature's laws. When a scientific principle is uncovered, it belongs not to the scientist who uncovered it, but to the God who gave it and to any individual who has sense enough to use it.

Let us take our scientific method and return to the thought that the prayer of faith shall save the sick and the Lord shall raise him up. The prayer of faith is a consciousness of acceptance, a mental conclusion in a person's mind, based on the belief that the Creative Spirit responds directly to him.

In the words of Jesus: *What things soever ye desire when ye pray, believe that ye receive them and ye shall have them*. When we bring the two words *soever* and *them* into bold relief, what do we have? We have what we might call a conscious specializing of the Law for definite purposes. The prayer of faith is a prayer which expresses faith about *some particular* thing. *What things soever* include our specific wants, our definite needs. If a man were praying for a home he would not be asking for an automobile. If he were praying that his neighbor be healed he would not be asking for money with which to take a trip.

When we return to our central thought that the prayer of faith shall save the sick and God shall raise him up, we must remember that the prayer of faith is definite—it is faith *in something* and *about something*. This type of prayer is not generalized but specific. It is conscious and definite.

This brings it into line with the scientific method, for the scientific use of any law is always conscious and always definite. The principle governing the law is universal, but the use of the law is always individual. It is this element of personality injected into the universal law which differentiates it when we use it for specific purposes. The consciousness that heals is definite and deliberate; it is a specializing of the Universal Law. In this Law we may have absolute and implicit confidence, but we must also remember that the Law can do *for* us only what it does *through* us. Its energy and creativeness must be interpreted through our belief and imagination.

We should add another proposition to our general statement, which is: *And as thou hast believed, so be it done unto thee*. We now have these words—*what things soever, them*, and *as*. This is but another way of saying that if we want the principle of electricity to light our living room, we must provide a fixture which makes it possible for the electricity to become a light. This is what is meant by the *as*. When we pray in faith we receive *what things soever* we pray for. If we believe that we shall receive them, we shall receive *them*.

There is a specific, definite thing we are to receive, but we are to receive it *as* we believe. Let us say that we are praying for supply. Because we are praying for supply we are to receive supply, according to the principle that what things soever we believe when we pray, we shall receive. If we are praying for supply we shall receive supply, but the supply will be measured *as* we believe. The quantity of the supply must take the mold of our mental equivalent of supply.

Since we know that this like all other principles must be subject to definite law, and since we now understand the law, let us again inquire into the consciousness that heals. It is recognition of the Principle, faith in the Principle, conviction that It will always respond, plus the knowledge that It can respond only by corresponding to our mental attitudes. This is the secret of the consciousness that heals.

Someone might ask whether or not we have left God, the warm, pulsating Divine Presence, out of this discussion. The answer is, "Certainly not." It is impossible to leave God out of anything, for do we not realize that God means the very Intelligence by which we understand this Law; the very consciousness by which we use It? Never forget that this Law, being the Law of Cause and Effect, is merely a mechanical force in the universe, though an intelligent one. When it comes to the Law of Mind, we must think of It this way, for this is the way to work.

God is not left out. The very inspiration which causes us to inquire into this Law is the ever-present Spirit of God forever seeking self-expression through us. Unless our use of this Law is impulsed by love and unity we shall be automatically shut out from the most effective use of It.

Let us once more remind ourselves that the universe is foolproof and that the Holy of Holies is entered only through the sanctuary of the heart, purified by love, directed by reason. The more feeling we put into our conviction, and the more faith we have in Divine Givingness, the more perfectly we shall be complying with the Law; hence we shall have greater power over It.

We should return, then, to our central theme with renewed hope and increased vigor and most certainly with exuberant enthusiasm; with something of the spirit of an adventurer or explorer who goes out to discover new countries. The untold good which the Creative Spirit has placed at our disposal waits the magic touch of our consciousness to spring into expression for us, filling the cup of our desire with Its manifold gifts. Who does not wish to be well, happy, and prosperous? Is there any normal person who desires to be inactive, impoverished, and in pain? Of course not! And is there not a voice within each of us forever proclaiming and insisting upon this Divine potentiality? This urge to express is natural.

Feeling unexpressed is frustration, but energy converted into action is accomplishment, and we can be certain that the Eternal is with us and never against us when we are never against anyone else. Moreover, we can be certain that the prayer of faith will save the sick and God will raise him up. Let each, then, in his own way, lift up the chalice of his expectancy for the outpouring of the Spirit, that he may receive from It all that his soul can contain.

What Is Religion?

Religion means our attitude toward God. This attitude is based on our concept of the relationship which exists between God the Universal Spirit and man the individual spirit. If we believe that God is some far-off Divine Being from whom we are isolated, we shall give up in despair or our entire endeavor will be in seeking a reconciliation and reunion with this Divine Being.

We are compelled to think of the Spirit as either apart from us or within us, and if God is apart from us rather than a part of us, our search will be to reunite ourselves with this Divine Source of our being. Moreover, in our search we shall be laboring under the difficulty imposed by not knowing where to go or how to get there. But if we can conceive of the Divine Being as already existing within us, no search is necessary. Instead of a search there is an unfoldment.

Again, if we conceive of the Divine Being as separated from us, any communication must be across the void which separates us. From this viewpoint prayers, petitions, or attempts at communication with the Infinite must bridge some gap, cross some chasm, travel in some unknown direction with no certainty that they will reach their goal. Communion with the Infinite is possible only on the supposition that the Infinite is omnipresent, and if omnipresent, at the center of our own being.

All religions are attempts to interpret man's relationship with this indwelling and overarching Infinite, with a Spirit which fills all nature, all time, and all space with Its Presence. The purer the religion, the more completely has it approached an attitude of unity, a complete oneness between God and man. Jesus boldly declared, *He that hath seen me hath seen the Father*. The purer the form of the religion, the more perfectly has it presented the idea of an indwelling Presence which directly responds to man's thought.

The recognition that the Spirit thinks through our thought and expresses Itself through our act must necessarily create an intimacy which makes Divine communion more real and more beneficial than would any concept based on the thought of God as separate from our lives.

A true religious concept is an indispensable aid in spiritual mind healing. The mental practitioner has a better chance of success when he believes in the indwelling Spirit, when he believes that God's work is already accomplished and perfect even though it is eternally unfolding. Moreover, his words will have more power when he believes that they are power, and he endows them with power in such degree as he senses the Divine Presence back of them.

This inner testimony of the soul is real and valid. Who could deny the artist the privilege of appreciating beauty? We all know that as a result of his sense of beauty he creates the beautiful, which is the object of art. We know that some artistic productions surpass others, and we recognize that back of them is a deep impression, a subjective feeling. We have not weighed or measured the reality which the artist contemplates, and yet we have evidence of it in his work.

The mental science practitioner whose mind is filled with spiritual awareness will speak a more powerful word than the one who rests his claim solely on the Law of Cause and Effect. The practitioner whose thought reaches the highest spiritual level will demonstrate that his word has the greatest power. The fact that the Law of Mind knows only how to obey and has no purpose of Its own to execute, demonstrates the proposition that a higher altitude of thought will find a corresponding higher level of manifestation, just as water will reach its own level by its own weight. It is in this sense that a true religious perspective is necessary to effective mental practice.

The Law, being a doer and not a knower, never acts of Itself; It merely reacts. The Word of Spirit is the enforcement of this Law. How can we expect a result to rise higher than its cause? It is self-evident that there is a coordinating Spirit and, as you will find continuously reaffirmed in these lessons, this coordinating Spirit must have within Itself a prototype or a perfect idea of every form.

A deep underlying sense of this spiritual universe is necessary to the most effective form of mind healing. To the technical work of the mental practitioner there should be added this deep spiritual sense of things. A subtle emanation of Spirit should flow through all the statements which he makes, for every statement must be based on the proposition of One God, One Man, and One Universe—a spiritual system which is complete, Divinely organized, spiritual not only in its origin but also in its manifestation.

The spiritual mind healer must learn to see God in his patient. His conviction of this indwelling Divinity must be more than intellectual. For there is a field of Reality higher than the intellect, and it uses the intellect as its instrument. We should not decry the intellect since it gives shape and form to this inner feeling, but without the feeling nothing comes into being. This has been referred to as the spirit and the letter of the Law and we have been told that the letter without the spirit does not quicken. Applied to mental healing this means that the words we speak must have a deep meaning to us, and we must sense that behind them there is a Power seeking expression.

This Power is infinitely greater than our intellect. The intellect does the best it can, but unless it is directed by the Spirit it finally succeeds in reaching only a gigantic negation, a complete denial of its own existence, a repudiation of the supreme fact of existence which is the act of directly experiencing Spirit.

You could not convince one who has had such an experience that it was an illusion or an hallucination, for this inner testimony of the soul is valid to the one who has it. It is just as much a part of him as is his thought, and the proof of its reality is evidenced by the results which it has produced in the lives of those who have been most deeply sensitive to love, truth, and beauty. To come into closer daily contact with this Supreme Source of wisdom and illumination should be the earnest desire of every worker in this field.

Appreciation of human experience will be quickened rather than retarded through unity with this indwelling Spirit. When a person learns to see God in everyone, he will become more spontaneous. He will feel a deep and abiding inner joy.

Our spiritual experiences reach higher levels at some times than at others, and we should seek to bring the inspiration of these moments of illumination into our everyday living. If the philosophy of Christianity were lived, wars would cease, unhappiness would cease, economic problems would be solved, poverty would be wiped from the face of the earth, and man's inhumanity to man would be transmuted into a spirit of mutual helpfulness.

This would not mean the reducing of all persons to one common level. We are individuals in a cosmic wholeness. Each is a unique representation of the one and only Mind and Spirit, and since this Mind and Spirit is Infinite, Its capacity to individualize must likewise be without limit. Each may remain himself while seeing God in the other.

The spiritual mind practitioner should always have a sense of this fundamental unity and should realize that it is continuously differentiating Itself through each one of us. Every man becomes a unique manifestation of the Whole, a microcosm within the Macrocosm; rooted in the Infinite he personifies It. Some part of It, inseparable from It, remaining in It, he is still an individual. The paradox of the many and the one is explained not on the basis of a God apart from man, but on the basis of a God incarnated in man.

The religion of the spiritual mind healer must be one of unity and law. He must feel that he is one with the Spirit. Being one with this Self-existent Spirit, he must sense that he uses the Law. There is nothing arrogant about this, for he knows that should such use be exercised in behalf of duality, he himself must experience the effect of that very dualism which he attempts to project. The universe is foolproof, and the profane do not enter the Holy of Holies.

Humility, reverence, and adoration are not to be confused with self-obliteration. We are not called upon to consider ourselves unholy; we are neither conceived in sin nor shapen in iniquity. Man's place in the creative order is as a dispenser of the Divine gifts, a husbandman of the indwelling Lord.

The morbidity which has come with the sense of isolation and separation from God must be healed if joy and laughter are to take the place of sorrow and tears. How can we believe in a weeping universe, or a sad God, or a melancholy First Cause? Such concepts would contradict the fundamental necessity of Reality, that God is a synonym for wholeness.

Negation does not belong to the Infinite, and being undivided It is never separated from Its own good. We must arrive at an abiding sense of our unity with Good. Much that we have believed must be discarded, for we can never avoid the conclusion that with what judgment we have judged, by that same judgment we must ourselves be judged.

The approach to Reality should be simple, direct, and spontaneous. The Secret Place of the Most High is neither in the holy mountain of Samaria nor at Jerusalem; *for, behold, the kingdom of God is within you.* This Kingdom is finished, complete, and perfect from eternity to eternity, but the manifestation of this Kingdom is the eternal activity of right ideas, law, order, truth, and beauty. Man is given dominion in this Kingdom by a fundamental necessity of his nature. It is impossible that this dominion should be withheld from him.

There is no deific power which either withdraws from man or advances toward man. No more of God is in one place than in another, and in the place where man is, God is, and where man recognizes the Divine Presence, there the Divine Presence responds—not some of It but all of It.

The communion of the soul with this Over-Presence is a natural act. To feel that a Presence greater than we are is guiding us is normal. To trust this Presence is sanity. To desire that the Divine Eternal shall project Itself through our thought is to be receptive to that greater side of our nature which lies open to the upper reaches of thought. This is religion.

Bibles of the World

Fragments from the spiritual history of the race revealing fundamental UNITY of religious thought and experience

JUDAISM and CHRISTIANITY—But to us there is but One God, the Father, of whom are all things, and we in Him.

And thou shalt love the Lord thy God with all thy heart, and with all thy soul, and with all thy might.

HINDUISM—He is the Creator, He the Disposer. He Himself is one, single, one only.

How many gods are there?
One! I know that Person, the Last Source of every soul.

ISLAM—Your God is One God.

He is the Lord of the East. He is the Lord of the West.

SIKHISM—The True One was in the beginning.

The True One is now. The True One also shall be.

TAOISM—There is a Being wondrous and complete. Before heaven and earth It was. How calm It is! How spiritual!

Alone It standeth; and It changeth not. Around It moveth; and It suffereth not. Yet therefore can It be called the World's Mother.

SHINTOISM—When the sky is clear, and the wind hums in the fir trees, 'tis the heart of God Who thus reveals Himself.

CONFUCIANISM—Heaven will give great blessing.

Meditation

I know there is but One Power in the universe, and this Power is God. This Power manifests in and through all form, all people, all conditions, and is at the very center of 69my being.

This God-Power I AM

This Power is Life Itself and Its nature is Love. It contains all Wisdom, Peace, Strength. At the center of my being I feel this Perfection in me. I know It is all around me. Everywhere I turn I behold It. It is my whole being. Every cell and atom of my being, my every thought and feeling, my every act is an expression of this God Power.

The Intelligence within me is constantly guiding me. Clearly I see the right thing for me to do; I know the right thing for me to say in every circumstance. This God Intelligence within me deals with every situation harmoniously. I find life thrilling, stimulating.

I know that Love protects Its own. I know that Love now makes clear the way before me, eliminating every seeming obstruction. I am guided into an ever widening unfoldment of being, and I rest in perfect peace.

One with all Life, my every need is now fulfilled.

Subjective Creative Medium
Office of the Dean

My Dear Friend,

Perhaps by this time you are wondering why we put so much stress on the Law of Mind in Action and why we so often repeat the same thoughts. The answer is that this whole series of lessons deals with but a few fundamental principles which must be stated over and over again in order that they may be kept at the point of your attention. There is no other way to teach a science.

Every science has a fundamental principle governing it. Our basic principle is Universal Mind, the use of which we call the Law of Mind in Action. We set this Mind Principle in motion through our thinking, whether or not we know it. The Law and the Word is what we deal with, and our word becomes the law of our experience.

Our word uses the Law, and we are not responsible for Its action any more than an electrician is responsible for the action of electric energy in ringing a doorbell. He uses a law for his purposes and the law responds. The law is a doer but not a knower. The electrician is the knower.

So in using the Law of Mind in Action you are the knower, the Law is the doer. You are not responsible for the operation of the Law, but you are responsible for the way you use It. Therefore be certain that you use It definitely and consistently, and in such a way that you will be glad to experience Its action.

Sincerely,
Ernest Holmes

Lesson 7
Law, p.92 through p.97

This lesson further explains that the creative medium of Spirit, which is the Universal Soul or Subjective Mind, is the mental Law of the Universe. A law that is subjective must of necessity be subject to the intelligence which uses it. Page 403 explains that *the Law of Mind is not selective.*

Of Itself the Law has nothing to say about the ideas that are put into It. It knows how to create them into form and must do so mathematically, but It has no selectivity. Like electricity which has no conscious knowledge as to whether or not it is to become light or heat, the Law of Mind has no self-conscious determination. The self-conscious determination is in the Spirit which uses the Law, and man is Spirit.

It is this understanding that will enable you to use the Law for other people. When you say to yourself, "This word which I am now speaking is for John Smith, who lives at 108 West Seventh Street, New York City," you are conscious that you are using the Law for this particular John Smith who lives at this specific address, and you are conscious that the Law is operating on your thought for him. It has no selectivity of Itself—you are choosing what It shall do. You are the knower; the Law is the doer. It knows how to create without knowing why It is creating and without having any choice whatsoever.

The first three paragraphs on page 347 explain further the meaning of Subjective Mind. Particularly seek a clear realization of the meaning of the words in italics. For it is only when we see that what we call *our* subjective mind is merely our individual use of the Creative Law of the Universe, that we shall be able to have a real scientific approach to the subject, and only when we have a scientific approach can we expect to make conscious and definite use of the Creative Law.

As a practitioner you must always know what you are doing and why you are doing it, as well as how to do it. As a result of the word you have spoken, you must have implicit confidence that your decree in the Law will produce a definite physical manifestation in whatever direction you turn your attention.

Law is defined as *Mind in Action* (page 605). Study the entire definition. While there is no limit to the Law, there appears to be a limit to man's use of It. This means that even though the Law of Creativity is Infinite, we shall draw from It only as much good as our measure will hold, no more, no less. This brings us back to the central theme of our entire course of study—the Universal Creative Spirit of God creates by self-knowing or contemplation. Man, being the image and likeness of the Universal Creative Spirit, must act in accordance with his nature, that is, he creates by contemplation or self-knowingness. This is the explanation of the great saying of Jesus: *And ye shall know the truth, and the truth shall make you free.*

It is evident that if the knowing of something can produce freedom, there must be a law which automatically reacts to our knowing. It is of utmost importance that the Laws of Mind and Spirit be understood. When you treat for a physical or a financial betterment in some other person's experience you must be conscious that his good is now made manifest and in such degree as you are aware of that good it will appear in his experience.

Becoming aware of his good is an interior awareness. It is something the mind does to itself, and as a result of this self-recognition, self-knowingness, or state of consciousness as it is often called, the Law which automatically reacts to this self-knowingness produces an objective form, a physical condition which exactly balances and equals the self-knowingness, just as water reaches its own level by its own weight.

Spirit and Law were never created. They coexist; they are a part of the Eternal Reality. The Law which man uses, the Mind which he uses, and the Spirit which he is, are all One. Again let us consider the fact that there is no such thing as *your* mind, *my* mind, *his* mind, *her* mind. Mind is an Eternal Principle in the universe, and when we think, we are making use of It, and as we think, we are individualizing It. This individualization of It we speak of as *myself*.

Just as all physical nature is made up of One Ultimate Stuff, which includes our physical bodies, and just as each body is a peculiar individualization of that Stuff, so all individual mentalities emerge from one Universal Mind. We should think of ourselves as being in such complete unity with this Mind that there are no longer two—only One. As we think inside our own being, we think upon the only Being.

The next great step which the psychologist will be compelled to take will be the recognition of the unity of mind. But this unity of mind will never contradict a diversity of thought; hence there is no real restriction in this idea; indeed it is the only guarantee we could have of a complete freedom.

If you will carefully study the fourth and fifth paragraphs on page 93, you will realize the significance of the idea that every time we think, we are using this Universal Creative Medium. In the first paragraph on page 406, Spirit is referred to as being present in Its entirety at all times. It follows that all of Spirit is wherever we center our thought. Therefore the Truth in Its entirety is ever with us, ever available. Spiritual inspiration always awaits our recognition, and Divine guidance waits on our consent. The Spirit flows through us as an outlet for Its own Self-expression.

Mind is the realm of causes. Conditions are in the realm of effects . . . New thoughts create new conditions (page 406, last paragraph). The new condition will be created in such degree as the subjective state of our thought becomes clarified. The subjective state of our thought becomes clarified as we consciously determine to think only what we wish to have happen.

This is not always easy, but we must realize that the Law of God is one of liberty (read page 488). Freedom already exists, like truth and beauty, but it exists in an abstract and formless state. It can take only the form which thought gives it; therefore you will see that the thought of limitation creates the very limitation conceived by that thought. Freedom and bondage are merely two ways of expressing a limitless possibility.

If we wish freedom, we must be conscious of freedom, and since the idea of God as a symbol of spiritual liberty gives us the greatest concept of freedom, it follows that the more completely we spiritualize our thought, the freer we shall become. To dwell upon lack is to create it; to think of disease is to perpetuate it; to remain unhappy is to attract unhappy situations. There is no other way to objectify that which we desire than to turn deliberately and definitely from that which hurts.

But we all, with open face beholding as in a glass the glory of the Lord, are changed into the same image from glory to glory, even as by the Spirit of the Lord (page 489). There is already a spiritual realm within the mind which knows these things; hence we must turn to this great within, and with uplifted thought become receptive to this Divine Influx. This is the meaning of the paragraph at the top of page 480. It is really the unfoldment of Spirit through our own consciousness and in our own act.

At the top of page 94 we find that we cannot expect one thought to be creative while another kind of thought remains unproductive. We may as well set it down as a law that all thought must be creative, but since the Universe is not a duality but a unity, thoughts of good destroy thoughts of evil just as the light overcomes the darkness. It does this without argument and without contention. As this paragraph states, when we declare the Truth about anyone, the speaking of his name directs the Law for him in a specific and definite way, in an individual and personal way.

It is not always easy to see that this mental work is done at the center of our own being; that is, that the practitioner treats himself in order to help his patient. But we are sure that by now you will understand how this Principle operates. Man's consciousness is a point in the Infinite. Therefore man's consciousness is the Infinite, not limited, but taking the form of this thought.

It does not limit the Infinite to take a particular form any more than we could say that a flea has less life than an elephant because it is smaller. Life in Its entirety and in Its intensity exists at any and every point, and each man is a point in the consciousness of the Universe. Hence when he thinks within himself he thinks upon It, and when he directs his thought within himself, he directs his thought within It. That is how his word becomes law.

If you will read the paragraph under *Mind and Ether* (page 94), you will see that the laws of attraction and repulsion, gravitation, adhesion and cohesion, etc. (which from the standpoint of physical science operate through the ethers or upon the ethers) must be an exact physical correspondent of the more subtle mental law which says that thought operates upon Mind. From this viewpoint—and we believe it to be a true one—attraction and repulsion, adhesion and cohesion, are primarily mental concepts. This we know to be true, that the law of attraction is a mental thing.

Turn to page 534, to the Meditation called *My Atmosphere*. In reading these words carefully and thoughtfully, over and over again, as you say each one, let them stimulate your imagination to an active belief that you are a Divine Center of Spiritual Causation. As the consciousness or realization of your own true being dawns in your thought, realize that you have arrived at a place of Spiritual Power.

The next step is to use this Power for a definite purpose, to treat specifically for yourself or someone else. Sense the Power back of your words but do not try to put any power into them. We need conviction, not power—power already is, while conviction may be lacking. Do not practice any method of concentration or the holding of thoughts; merely be still, but definitely know in the silence of your own soul that some desired good is taking place. In this way you are certain to demonstrate.

On page 499, under the heading, *Doers of the Word*, we find: *What we know we can do*. We are told to be doers of the word, and not hearers only. As our spiritual comprehension increases, we should be able to make better and better demonstrations, both for ourselves and for others. This will call for a calm, persistent, insistent determination to believe and to mentally act on that belief. Whatever stimulates our faith, whatever inspires us, will be an aid in this demonstration.

What is it that we wish to demonstrate? We wish to demonstrate that spiritual thought forms or spiritual consciousness actually overcomes physical conditions; that each one of us has the power to control his destiny, to help and to heal others, and that there is a place at the center of every man's being where the Infinite and Almighty is eternally enthroned. *The will of God is always toward that which expresses life and happiness* (page 412, third paragraph).

We need not be afraid of using our Divine Power, nor need we fear that we are usurping the throne of God. This *is* the throne of God. Please read paragraphs 2, 3 and 4, page 404, which will explain to you the result of fear—how it blocks the givingness of the Spirit, how it produces a sense of limitation because it is a denial of the Divine Givingness. God never withholds any good from His creation. And as we more completely realize this, we shall change bondage for freedom and sadness for happiness.

You will find a very helpful suggestion for the practice of this Divine Consciousness on page 358, second paragraph, where it speaks of providing the mental equivalents of life, creating a spiritual consciousness in our own thought which is equivalent to our desires. It is both reasonable and rational to desire the good, the beautiful, and the true.

There is nothing wrong in our desire to be free from pain and lack, sickness, want, and limitation, any more than there is anything wrong in desiring the end of war or pestilence, famine or poverty in the world. As a matter of fact the more completely the righteous prove that God is all there is, the sooner wars and human contention will cease. *For all they that take the sword shall perish with the sword*.

On page 95 the question is asked, *How can Spirit create?* Well, we shall never be able to answer this question. That is the miracle of Life Itself. Remember, the Truth is that which is—birthless, deathless, and changeless. How are you going to explain your own life? By experience and through faith we accept life and the laws of nature. So accept your own Divinity, accept the Power that is within you, but use this Power definitely and for specific purposes.

At the bottom of page 95 we are told that we must be careful not to divide Mind against Itself when we speak of the subjective, the subconscious, and the conscious. There will be no danger here if you are always careful to realize that the Spirit is the conscious, and that which we call the subconscious mind is merely the Law of Mind in Action.

From this viewpoint (see page 97) the subjective mind is never an entity. *Each person in his* objective *state is a distinct and individualized center in Universal Mind, but in his* subjective *state . . . each is Universal* (page 352).

Summary

The Law of Mind is not selective; It is reactive only. The creative soil in your garden does not care whether you are planting tomatoes or cucumbers. When you say tomatoes, it answers by producing tomatoes as though it also said tomatoes; and when you say cucumbers, it responds by saying cucumbers or producing the cucumbers. It has no self-determination. All laws are like this, and the Law of Mind is no exception to the general rule. Therefore as a practitioner you must know what you are doing and why.

There is no limit to the Law Itself. Any limitation is in the way we use It. Neither the Spirit nor the Law was ever created. They are coexistent and coeternal. They are a part of what is.

Since the Spirit is One and Undivided, all of It is wherever we center our thought. We do not go anywhere to find It. It is right where we are. Freedom already exists. Freedom and bondage are the same thing in that they are but two ways of using One Principle. Abundance, success, and happiness are in our own thinking.

We sense the Power back of our word but make no attempt to put any Power into it. Conviction, faith, and acceptance take power out of the word. The way we use the Law decides what It is going to do for us.

Each one individualizes the Universal Spirit. We are what the ancients called a microcosm within a Macrocosm—a little world within a Big World.

The Creative Power which is at the center of everything is discovered in our own consciousness.

Questions

Brief answers to these questions should be written out by the student after studying the lesson and the answers compared with those which will be included in next week's lesson.

1. What is meant by the creative medium of Spirit?
2. In speaking of the Creative Law of Mind, what do we mean by *intelligent but subjective*?
3. Why is it that you can direct the mental law for others?
4. What is our subjective mind?
5. How should a practitioner feel about his word?
6. What is meant by the Self-contemplation of Spirit?
7. Does the Self-contemplation and Self-knowingness of Spirit have the same meaning as the Word of God?
8. What is the next great step which psychology must take?
9. When do we use the Creative Principle?
10. Why is it that new thoughts create new conditions?
11. How do we change our thought patterns in order to create more desirable conditions?
12. Are negative thoughts such as bondage, poverty, fear, sickness, etc., equal in creative power to the positive thoughts of freedom, abundance, faith, wholeness, etc.?
13. What do we mean by declaring the Truth about someone?
14. Where does spiritual or mental treatment take place?
15. How can a treatment which is given in the thought of the practitioner affect his patient?
16. What place has power and conviction in mental treatment?
17. In the Science of Mind what do we seek to demonstrate?
18. Can we explain the Creative Power within us?
19. Is our philosophy weak because we cannot explain the Creative Power within us?
20. Do we divide Mind against Itself when we speak of the conscious, subconscious, subjective, etc.?

Answers to Questions on Lesson 6

1. It is the Mind of God within us that knows.
2. We use as much of the Mind of God as we are conscious of and accept.
3. By being conscious of and embodying the Mind of God, we mean an inner faith, a spiritual awareness, and a mental conviction in our thought.
4. We have all the Power and all the Good that there is to use.
5. We make prayer effective by believing that it is effective.
6. The will of God for us is harmony, good, peace, joy, and life.
7. We should think of the Spirit as our friend and the Law as our servant.
8. The Spirit is infinite and personal to everyone because It is in everyone.

9. The Law is not personal to us. It is merely a mechanical force of nature.

10. The Spirit as Person has warmth, color, and responsiveness. The Law as Principle also responds to us, but merely as a mechanical force.

11. In dealing with God as Infinite Mind we gain, since God being omnipresent is in us and personal to us.

12. Scientific mental treatment, in order to be effective and produce desired results, must be conscious, definite, and active.

13. Man's place in the creative order is to make use of and distribute the life, love, and substance of God.

14. A feeling of the Divine Presence, coupled with the knowledge that the Law must respond, gives power to our word.

15. If we wish to use the Law of Cause and Effect for freedom rather than bondage we must change the image of our thought from bondage to freedom.

The Name of the Unknown

In his chapter, *The Sacred Name*, Troward informs us that according to ancient tradition, *the knowledge of the secret Name of God enables him who possesses it to perform the most stupendous miracles*. He suggests that it is the office of the name of anything to convey to us the idea of its whole nature; accordingly the correct Name of God should be a concise statement of the Divine Nature as the Source of all Life, Wisdom, and Goodness, and the Origin of all manifested being.

The Secret Name, therefore, suggests the nature of Reality Itself. The realization of this Reality opens up the wellsprings of our Being and enables us to drink from that perennial fountain of life which Jesus referred to when he said that if one drinks from this fount he shall never thirst again.

Troward makes plain that while the Bible refers to Reality under a variety of terms and names, each of them has practically the same meaning, *since each suggests some particular aspect of THAT which is the all-embracing UNIT*. This is also true of other sacred literature. *Realize that thou art "That" Brahman, which is the cessation of all differentiation . . . eternally unconditioned and undivided*. What is this but a statement of the Nameless One? *The Tao, considered as unchanging, has no name,* and from Hermes: *Immovable God alone, and rightly alone; for He Himself is in Himself, and by Himself, and round Himself*. . . . This means that the Infinite Creative Cause, being all that is, makes things out of Itself by Itself becoming the thing which It makes.

In Job we find this statement: *Canst thou by searching find out God? canst thou find out the Almighty unto perfection?* God is not found in the stone and yet God is the stone. By searching outwardly we do not discover the Nameless One but when we stop searching, become still and know, the Name of the Nameless proclaims Itself through us. The Upanishads say, *Not in the sight abides his form, none beholds him by the eye. Those who know him dwelling in the heart and mind become immortal*. From the Gita: *But verily thou art not able to behold Me with these thine eyes; the divine eye I give unto thee*. This has also been referred to in mythology as the All-seeing Eye. One instantly recognizes that all these presentations refer to That Something in the universe which is Absolute Cause, That which being Formless gives birth to form; Timeless, It projects all time; without Itself moving, everything moves within It. It is the One Unit within which all differentiation takes place.

Troward tells us that the name Jehovah signifies *Unity passing into manifestation as the Multiplicity of all individual beings*. This Unity includes both the active and passive factors; both the masculine and the feminine natures, the Father Principle and the Mother Principle. The Father Principle represents Absolute Being but since Absolute Being must have an object of Its being, that is, since cause must be cause to something in order to exist as cause, the Creative Cause must have a Son. Or, as Hippolytus stated, *For He (God) was . . . all love; but love is not love unless there be an object of love*. This means that the Divine Creative Cause must become Father to something in order that It may experience Its own Being. And that to which It gives birth must be born out of law and order; hence the Divine Mother Principle so often referred to in antiquity, particularly in ancient Hindu symbols. For as the Divine Father Principle represents the impregnating Principle of Self-assertion, so the Divine Mother Principle represents the feminine or receptive aspect of the manifesting Spirit which brings forth the forms of creation. Thus in one of the ancient writings we find this: *Like a mother to her subjects, intent on their welfare . . . She (referring to the Mother Principle) was the most eminent of Goddesses to the whole world*.

Implied in the Sacred Name we have a combination of that which projects and that which gives form. Not as though they were two principles in nature but two aspects of One Principle, a dual unity. It is the union of this masculine and feminine which gives birth to all form. In our terminology we say that thought operating through the creative field of Mind produces condition. From this standpoint the conscious projection of thought represents the Creative Principle in Its masculine aspect, while the Law of Mind represents the Creative Principle in Its feminine or productive aspect. It is the union of the Word with the Law which gives birth to creation.

The Nameless One is that Reality which ancient scriptures refer to as something which was not born and cannot die. *There is no beginning or end to the Tao. There is but one Brahma which is Truth's Self, it is from ignorance of that one that Godheads have been conceived as diverse . . .* (Mahabharata). This means that Reality is One, but being confused over multiplicity we have given many names to this One. These names are diverse and they largely contradict each other. We do not understand that Cause and Effect are but two ends of the same thing. We are confused when we view only the effect.

We are of a like nature with Reality Itself but since we have become confused by looking upon the multiplicity of effects which rise in One Reality, we have come to believe in a multiplicity of causes. The Upanishads say, *. . . so over rules the All Glorious, Adorable God; One alone, all that exists is likeness with its cause*. And from Hermes: *The Oneness, being Source and Root of all, is in all things as Root and Source. Without (this) Source is naught; whereas the Source (Itself) is from naught but Itself*. The Gita tells us, *When he (anyone) perceiveth a diversified existence of beings as rooted in One, and spreading forth from It, then he reacheth the eternal*. In Revelation we read, *I am Alpha and Omega, the beginning and the end. . . .* And in Psalms we have a poetical description of this Unity of all life: *Whither shall I go from thy spirit? or whither shall I flee from thy presence? If I ascend up into heaven, thou art there . . . If I* *take the wings of the morning and dwell in the uttermost parts of the sea; Even there shall thy hand lead me. . . .*

The Sacred Name contains everything that is implied in the meaning of cause, medium, and effect; God, man, and creation. It implies a complete and absolute unity of all life. Troward sums up his findings by stating that the name Jehovah contains in itself the Three Fundamental Principles of the Universe—the Unity, the Duality, and the Trinity, and by their inclusion in a single word affirms that there is no contradiction between them, but that they are all necessary phases of the Universal Truth which is only ONE.

Next Troward takes up a study of the Lost Word, which word is a symbol of the Life Principle as It expresses on each and all planes. In the *Egyptian Book of the Dead* we find this statement: *I concur by this most mighty word . . . and "I Am" brings to my remembrance in Him what I had forgotten*. This is a definite reference to the word of power which is a symbol of the higher qualities and of wisdom. Troward tells us that the Lost Word, or Word of Power, is also the Sacred Name, and he refers us to Deuteronomy 30:14 where it says, *But the word is very nigh unto thee, in thy mouth and in thy heart. . .* The Sacred Name is *I AM*. Troward tells us that this is the Divine Name revealed to Moses at the burning bush and is the Word enshrined in the name Jehovah. Thus he said, *The Word of Power is close at hand to every one and it continues to be the Lost Word only because of our ignorance. . . .*

Jesus prayed, *Our Father which art in heaven, Hallowed be thy name*. Since he had located the Kingdom of Heaven within, was he not then addressing the Divine Being at the center of his and of every man's soul? And the Text of Taoism states: *The Tao does not exhaust Itself in what is greatest, nor is It ever absent from what is least; and therefore it is to be found complete and diffused in all things*. In the Gita it says, *I, the Father of this universe, the Mother, the Supporter, the Grandsire, the Holy One to be known, the Word of Power*. This refers to the *Father which art in heaven*, in everything. And the Father, and Heaven, man, his world, creation, all are One. Or as we find in I John 5:7, *For there are three that bear record in heaven, the Father, the Word, and the Holy Ghost: and these three are one*.

The word of power is *I AM*, signifying the essence of being. In the *Egyptian Book of the Dead* we read, *For "I Am" is my rest in His seasons*. The *I AM* is the true individuality and has been called The First Born. The *I AM*, as we have already discussed is Universal as God and individual as man. Again from the *Egyptian Book of the Dead*: *For "I Am" is that God even . . . the Lord of hosts . . . .*In Yogi philosophy we read, *The ego is beyond all disease, not within the reach of comprehension, free from all imagination, and all pervading*. Also a quotation from the Apocrypha: *And I appointed him as ruler on earth, to have wisdom and there was no one like him. . . .* In Hebrews: *Thou madest him a little lower than the angels; thou crownest him with glory and honor . . . Thou hast put all things in subjection under his feet*. And from Hermes: *The soul however, is not forever in a mortal body, for it can be without a body*. Jesus referred to the *I AM* as the Way, the Truth, and the Life. He also said, *I am the resurrection and the life*.

Resurrection means passing from a lower to a higher place, from a lesser to a greater comprehension of life. *I am the resurrection* refers to the God Principle in us that Jesus talked so much about. The Power and Intelligence through which we expand our consciousness is this Living Spirit within. God the Eternal *I AM* is in everything; God the individualized *I* is at the very center of our being.

Unless we believe in and embody the Spiritual Principle within us we shall continue in our mistakes. The purifying principle of experience, suffering, etc., which purges us from our mistakes, has been likened to Purgatory, Hades, the Regions of Darkness. It has also been likened to Sheol, a place for the burning of garbage. It is generally considered that all such figures of speech are symbolic of the lower planes which have been called mental, astral, etheric, and physical. These planes become purged in the all-consuming fire of Spirit which burns out the dross of human experience, leaving nothing but the incarnation of the Eternal *I AM*, the Ego.

Troward tells us that the true recognition of the *I AM* is the recognition of the Self. This true Self is always one with the Infinite. Next he refers to the Mystical Marriage, the union of the soul with its source. This refers to the conscious union of the Word of Spirit with the creative Principle of Mind. In Meade's comments on Hermes we read, *But the chief of all mysteries for Philo was apparently the Sacred Marriage, the mystic union of the soul as female, with God as male.* The Mystical Marriage like the New Birth is something which is forever taking place. The resurrection from the lower to the higher or the lesser to the greater, is a process of eternal evolution or expansion. What is this other than a discovery that, as Troward says, the whole principle of being is in ourselves?

It is evident that until we understand our relationship with the Eternal we continue to perish in our mistakes. That is, we continue to transgress the Law of rightness or righteousness. Since ignorance of the law excuses no one from its consequences, we suffer until the lesson is learned. It does not necessarily follow that this is because of viciousness, but more largely because of ignorance.

One of the most interesting illustrations Troward draws is that the Bible is the picture book of the evolution of man. In referring to the burning bush he tells us that *bush* represents wood or matter or the material universe and *burning* represents Spirit. Hence the burning bush signifies the union of Spirit and matter into a single whole. The bush is not consumed but burns with a Celestial light, with the Light Eternal which is in and through everything. Thus all creation proclaims the luminous *I AM*.

Troward next explains that just as there is a sacred Name for all nature, there is a sacred Name for man, and we all remember that it is written that there is no other Name whereby we can become saved. Here again we must realize that salvation is not from a power of darkness but rather from the darkness of ignorance.

The name Jesus was commonly used, as it is today in most Latin countries. Jesus represents the son of man; Christ represents the hidden or true Man whose kingdom is not of this world. Jesus, the son of man, the son of a lowly carpenter, becomes Christ, the Son of God. Isaiah refers to this when he speaks of the son of the virgin as named Emmanuel, which means God-with-us. The blood that flows from Emmanuel's veins is symbolic of the life-giving energy of Spirit pouring Itself from the Christ Principle, which is the Son of God, into the Jesus Principle, which is the son of man. This is why we are told *And whatsoever ye do in word or deed, do all in the name of the Lord Jesus, giving thanks to God and the Father by him.*

This reference to the name of the Lord Jesus is not merely to a historic character, howsoever benign; it also refers to the indwelling Principle which Jesus located at the center of every man's being. In this way the name of God becomes the name of Man, since it is Emmanuel or God-with-us, God immanent in us. It is the discovery that *unto us a child is born*. This child is the Son of God referred to in the New Testament in this passage: *The Spirit itself beareth witness with our spirit that we are the children of God.*

The birth of Christ is symbolic of the higher nature impregnating the human soul. It is as Campbell suggests, . . . *the discovery and exercise of our highest faculties*, sometimes referred to in the East as the Atma-buddhi energizing on the higher plane. The First Adam is of the earth, earthy and liable to death; the Second is from Heaven and triumphant over death. In Luke 21:27,28 we read, *And then shall they see the Son of man coming in a cloud with power and great glory . . . then look up and lift up your heads; for your redemption draweth nigh.* This is symbolic of the incarnation consciously recognized as the living essence of one's own being. This deific birth into the soul, coming from the clouds, means the descent of Spirit into the lower mind.

Phillips Brooks said, *It may be that the clouds that for us mortals haunt that land of righteousness and truth, may long hang so thick and low that living close to Him the soul may still fail to see Him, but some day certainly the fog shall rise, and the clouds shall scatter, and in perfect enlightenment of the other life, the soul shall see its Lord. . . .* Lord is symbolic of the higher self. The Wonderful Child which appears when we look up through the clouds is the Eternal *I AM* reflecting and incarnating Itself in us. *And it is the Spirit that beareth witness, because the Spirit is truth* (John 5:6).

In the *Egyptian Book of the Dead* we find this remarkable concept: *"We will not let thee enter into us,"* say the bolts of this door, *"Unless thou tellest our names."* And it goes on to reveal that the names are Right and Truth. We must look through the clouds of obscurity to Right, to Truth, to the very Source of Life Itself. *For with thee is the fountain of life: in thy light shall we see light* (Psalm 36:9). It is light that dissipates the clouds. It is Truth that dissipates error.

It is evident that as the name of God is *I AM*, so the name of the son or the child which is born into the consciousness of sonship is also *I AM*. Troward tells us the individual is illuminated through realizing that he himself is a personification of the Universal Spirit. Thus the Eternal *I AM* is at the root of our individualized being. The proverb of Solon, the Athenian lawgiver, *Know Thyself*, is an admonition to discover the nature of our own being and to realize that the name of the Father and the name of the son are One. It is from a recognition of the union of the Father with the son that knowledge is found and salvation gained.

In St. John 1:12 it is written, *But as many as received him, to them gave he power to become the sons of God, even to them that believe on his name.* When we recognize our union with good and live in compliance with this recognition, spiritual power is automatically delivered to us. The Sacred Name must of necessity be the word of power, for it is nothing less than the original creative Spirit operating through our own minds.

It would be impossible to suppose a greater union than that which is inherent in the nature of our own being. The God Principle wIthin us constitutes the whole Reality of our being. Living in conformity with this Principle, in conjunction with Its Divine Will, we are automatically given as much power as we can conceive. But this power is never one of disunion, since the Principle of Reality can never be divided against Itself. Thus the Apostle James tells us that we ask and receive not because we ask amiss; we ask contrary to the Divine Nature, which is Love, Truth, Beauty, and Wisdom.

No doubt the entire search of humanity has been, consciously or unconsciously, a search for Divine Wisdom, for somehow or other we feel that there is a wisdom from which power must flow. This is an intuitive perception; thus it comes from the highest faculty in man, the true Atma, Christ, or High Counselor within us. We desire wisdom and power because there is an incessant urge toward self-expression within all. We wish more completely to enter into the joy of living. We wish certainty for uncertainty, faith for fear, life for death. This is not only natural but right, and a wisdom greater than our own impels this search toward Reality.

How wonderful it would be to discover the Sacred Name embosomed in our own being; that the Child who is called Wonderful is already in our soul; that salvation is from within through the recognition of the Divine at the center of our own being. To *be still and know that I am God* means to be alone in our own consciousness with the realization that all power is delivered to the uses of goodness.

As we meditate in the silence of our consciousness, thinking deeply upon the meaning of the Name hidden in the soul, shall not the New Birth take place through us as it does forever in all creation? Shall not the waste places of our lives, like the burning bush of old, leap into flames radiating a warmth and glow which brings wholeness and peace?

The Principle of Mind at Work

Unless the one studying spiritual mind healing practices this Principle he will neither understand its nature nor appreciate its value. Therefore its practical application becomes of prime importance, and each of us should become a practitioner even if he himself is his only patient.

Like any other principle in nature, we must use this consciously and deliberately. The practitioner resolves things into thoughts, for it stands to reason that only thought can reach that which is the result of thought. We do not expect thought to reach some physical condition independent of mind. If there is such a thing as mental healing it must be based on the supposition that all form is a manifestation of mind and that mind controls its manifestation.

From the standpoint of the mental practitioner, disease must be seen as primarily a thing of thought, and the diseased condition as a mental declaration of discord, an argument of confusion, or a mental experience of negation. It is the wrong kind of manifestation, and whether or not we believe that it originates in mind, the mental practitioner must confine his work to the operation of thought, for this is his field.

The mental practitioner resolves things into thoughts and proceeds to untangle the wrong thought through the recognition of the omnipresence of God or Truth. Mind can never operate outside of consciousness, and if the practitioner believes that disease or conditions are external to consciousness and treats them as if they were, he will soon discover that he is trying to bombard them from without. He is trying to make mind reach something which is not mental, or trying to make thought reach something which is outside of mind. He is doomed to failure.

When he realizes that everything is either mind in an absolute state, or mind in a concrete form, he has no difficulty in rearranging thought positively instead of negatively. This is exactly what a spiritual mind practitioner does. He does this deliberately and consciously. The name of a disease signifies to him merely the thought about the disease, whether a person believes it to be curable or incurable, whether he believes it will take a long time or a short time to heal, and it signifies the mental reaction of the race consciousness. This is the only significance the name can have to the practitioner, for in this field he cannot treat one disease as organic and another disease as functional, since from the standpoint of our practice all disease is a negative statement in mind.

Now I am fully aware that the thought that all disease is a negative statement in mind is a rather difficult one to understand, and is likely to produce considerable confusion in the minds of those who hear it for the first time. But let us remember that this field is entirely different from other fields. Here we have a practitioner who treats through the instrument of thought alone. He is not antagonizing any other form or method of practice; he is not refusing his patient the right to have any other form of practice even while he is being treated mentally.

He is a spiritual mind practitioner, and from his viewpoint, no matter what the condition is and no matter what it has been pronounced to be, it must remain a thing of thought, for as already stated, if it is not thought, how is thought going to reach it? And the practitioner is thoroughly convinced that thought does reach it, that pure Mind exists everywhere, and that pure Mind is at the very center of the diseased condition.

The practitioner must conceive of pure Mind as being in a state of harmony. Instead of feeling that he is treating some terrible disease he feels that he is explaining why this negative condition need not be. His explanation is to himself about his patient; it is never to his patient. Therefore he is not trying to convey a mental suggestion. What, then, is he doing? He is clearing up his own consciousness, and in order to do this he must resolve the disease into a thing of thought.

The practitioner uses any statement about a particular case which will untie the mental knots in his own consciousness about his patient. Generally he is confronted with the idea of fear, and he should begin his treatment by removing all sense of fear. He must know that there is nothing of which to be afraid and he must make a definite statement not only that there is nothing of which to be afraid, but that there is no one to be afraid. He must say this for his patient, not *to* his patient but *about* him. When giving a treatment he never addresses the patient by name nor speaks to him personally in mind; he merely identifies his treatment with his patient by saying, "This treatment is for so-and-so," and then he forgets all about his patient objectively and gives the treatment within his own consciousness.

If God is all in all there is nothing of which to be afraid, for perfect love casts out fear; where love is, fear cannot enter. The practitioner knows that fear cannot operate through his patient or through anyone around him. Man is a spiritual entity; therefore he has no disease, nothing which is opposed to life assails him, nothing is operating through him which can produce death, since there is no death.

If he is using the argumentative method of treating, he brings an array of arguments to support his position that God is all in all and to reject the belief that it is necessary for his patient to suffer from this particular disease or any other. The form of the argument and the power of the argument is merely to produce realization. Argument itself is not realization any more than musical technique is harmony. The argument merely gives form, definite intention, specific direction to the treatment. Argument leads toward a realization of the allness of Good. Probably more people are helped through argument than by any other method, although in every instance one should seek a growing conviction and an increasing realization of the meaning of one's argument.

The Life Principle Itself is the healer, or if one chooses to put it this way, God is the healer. The patient is a spiritual entity and there is nothing about a spiritual entity that needs to be healed. Disease of itself is neither person, place, nor thing and has no location. It did not begin in time, it has no duration in time, it does not end anywhere in time. It is no longer being experienced in the consciousness of the one who has been affected by it. These are merely suggested arguments for the purpose of clearing up the mind of the practitioner, for his thought is the only thought that he can heal in this practice.

The practitioner assumes that the Body of God is perfect, including every manifestation of Itself. Man is the Body of God. For instance, the idea of vision, of speech, or of any other faculty or organ of the body is an eternal idea, an infinite idea, and an omnipresent idea.

The practitioner treats to know that there is only one perfect pattern of lung or heart; there is only one idea of lung or heart, because there is only one Spirit, one Absolute *I AM*, one Eternal God, or one everlasting Reality. The heart God made is a perfect heart, the lung God made is a perfect lung. It may help to realize this better when one knows that the physical vibration of heart or lung is the same wherever the manifestation of heart or lung takes place, whether it is in an animal, a bird, or a man. It shows the universality of the idea of heart or lung and helps him to realize that when he declares for the oneness of any Divine idea, he is declaring the Truth about that idea.

The practitioner, then, treats of the oneness of manifestation, and it is about this oneness that he makes his declaration, always declaring that this oneness is true about his patient. It would not be enough to say the Heart of God is perfect and there is only One Heart, but he must complete this statement by saying, "This Heart of God is the heart of this patient. Nothing ever happened to it, it didn't enlarge; there was never any tension around it, there was never any pain in it; it never caused pain and there never was any emotional state that caused it to pain. It was never repressed, depressed or suppressed. It was never tired nor worn out, it never broke down, and the whole circulatory system, being a part of the Divine Life Impulse, never was impaired."

Heart is a Divine Idea and the Heart of Reality is the heart of this particular person whom you are treating. The Divine Reality must be considered as perfect, complete, ever-present, always active, ever available, and the negation of this must be reversed in the mind of the practitioner, that is, the denial of it must be understood to have no power.

Thus the spiritual practitioner converts things into thoughts. He can think not only of *our Father which art in heaven,* but also of our perfect body and perfect organism which are in the Kingdom of Reality now, and to the practitioner this must be an intense reality. He must believe what he says. He must understand that the Kingdom of Heaven is at hand. He cannot do this unless he contradicts much that is experienced. Mentally he never deals with a material condition nor a diseased condition, but he knows that since Spirit is the only power there is, there is no mind which has been hypnotized into believing that there is or can be any opposite to Spirit.

The practitioner must know that Creative Mind hears and answers his thought because Creative Mind is ever present. He knows that right idea is the operation of true Principle, whether it be in the science of mathematics or the Science of Mind. The Principle cannot help hearing. The mind which makes the request is the mind which fulfills the desire, since there is but One Mind. If the practitioner can bear in mind that what he is destroying is belief, he will do well.

Now right here the uninstructed will say, "Do you mean to tell me that I do not experience discord or disease?" We do not deny that man experiences discord or disease. What we affirm is that the experience is the belief in form and that the disintegration of the belief will produce a corresponding disintegration of the form. That is why we so continuously say: *Turn things into thoughts and heal the thought.* In mental practice the practitioner must deal with belief or with thought, and he must deal with form as though it were belief and thought, else, as we have already stated, how can he conceive that thought can reach that which is not of the nature of mind, thought, or thinking?

For instance, if someone should draw a picture of a horse on a blackboard, and others seeing it should believe it to be a horse, it still would be nothing other than a picture. Now you come along and take an eraser and rub out the picture. Where is the horse? It was never a thing in itself; it only appeared to be an entity. Your knowledge that it could be rubbed out and your act of rubbing it out were but two ends of the same thing. So the mental practitioner must realize that his argument or his realization rubs out the argument of negation which projects discord. He cannot do this unless he understands that the projection of the discord is just as much a thing of thought as what he calls the thought behind such projection.

It is perhaps a little difficult to make this clear, but it means that the practitioner works in a field of mind and thought alone, and all he has to neutralize is thought, never things. It is one of the most subtle parts of this entire system of practice, one to which we should pay the most careful attention. For the root of all evil is in mental conviction, not in evil itself. The axe of Truth has to be laid at the root of evil and the false condition chopped away, so to speak. Therefore spiritual enlightenment in the mind heals the body because the body is mind in form and because spiritual enlightenment changes the form of thought in mind.

If this is true there is no adversary, no opponent, no opposition. When in the mental argument a practitioner reaches the place where he perceives or understands the Truth of his argument, his argument ceases as argument and begins as realization. It has passed from analysis into conclusion. It is this realization which is the creative power in treatment. And what is it that is to be realized? The perfection of the patient, the perfection of all people, the harmony of the condition. Furthermore, whether one is treating to heal physical disorders or treating to heal financial disorders, or any other disorders, the operation of the Principle is identical.

Substance is supply. There is but one Substance; this Substance is omnipresent, It is right where the need appears to be, and It meets the need according to the acceptance of the one who experiences the need. It could do neither more nor less than this. One must accept supply if Substance is to interpret Itself as supply in one's experience. The practitioner realizes the omnipresence of Substance, hence the ever availability of supply.

This in no way turns Spirit into matter, nor does it materialize Spirit. It merely gives form to Substance. As the physical universe has been likened to the meditation of God, so our individual experiences may be likened to our meditations of life. And our meditations of life are our awareness, our realization—an inner feeling and conviction which transcends the experience taking place in an objective world. From the standpoint of practice, there is but one Substance, but this Substance is forever active as supply. Just as there is but one Heart, which is forever active as perfect circulation and perfect impulsion, so there is one Substance forever operating as supply.

The practitioner does not necessarily need to treat his patient for specific things. He realizes the activity of Substance in the experience of his patient, and that whatever mental equivalent his patient has automatically will be filled. It is well that we understand this because it is self-evident that the patient brings his bowl of acceptance with him. In other words, he has thoughts and desires which he wishes to have fulfilled, which are personal to him and individual with him. The practitioner pours his realization of abundance over the entire situation, and wherever there is a mold it is automatically filled, for since Substance is omnipresent It can fill all molds without depleting Itself.

So the practitioner declares that there is but one Substance and his patient's need is supplied out of this Substance today—whatever his patient needs, everything he needs, and all that he needs is amply supplied. The limitless activity of the Infinite now manifests in form in this man's experience. His activity always produces good results; it always produces abundance because Infinite Substance is limitless supply.

Now this Substance cannot be depleted. It remains exactly what it is and its nature is forever to flow. Therefore, wherever there is an acceptance there is a manifestation. Wherever there is a belief which inhibits manifestation, the manifestation is limited to the acceptance. That is, through unbelief we still believe in a limited form of that which we deny. The practitioner treats the form of lack as a belief in lack. He heals the belief. He works to know that Substance is omnipresent, is forever flowing into the experience of his patient as supply, as right action.

The patient himself brings the mold of money or house, of automobile or a suit of clothes, of position or environment. The practitioner does not have to supply the mold for his patient. To assume that he has to do so would be to assume that he must take control of his patient's thought, which would be an attempt to hypnotize his patient. Naturally, he would be unsuccessful.

The practitioner does not supply the mold of thought for his patient in any instance. He merely realizes that the mold which his patient supplies is filled by the Substance which forever flows into form. Therefore the practitioner has no personal responsibility. It is his business to realize the flow of Substance; it is the privilege of the patient to receive that Substance in the form of his own desire.

Bibles of the World

Fragments from the spiritual history of the race revealing fundamental UNITY of religious thought and experience

JUDAISM and CHRISTIANITY—Canst thou by searching find out God? canst thou find out the Almighty unto perfection? It is as high as heaven . . . The measure thereof is larger than the earth, and broader than the sea.

As for God, his way is perfect; the word of the Lord is tried; he is a buckler to all those that trust in him.

One God and Father of all, who is above all, and through all, and in you all.

TAOISM—There is no end or beginning to the Tao.

As soon as it proceeds to action, it has a name. When it once has a name, (men) can know to rest in it. When they know to rest in it, they can be free from all risk of failure and error.

ZOROASTRIAMISM—Demand of me, thou upright one! Of me, who am the Maker, the best of all beings, the most knowing, the most pleased in answering what is asked of me; demand of me, that thou mayst be the better, that thou mayst be the happier.

To Atar—the God who is a full source of Glory, the God who is a full source of healing.

MITHRA-RELIGION—For from the Paternal Source naught that's imperfect spins (or wheels).

For the Self-begotten One, the Father-Mind, perceiving His own works, sowed into all Love's Bond . . . so that all might continue loving on for endless time, and that these weavings of the Father's Gnostic Light might never fail. With this Love, too, it is the Elements of Cosmos keep running.

ISLAM—And he had no host to help him instead of God, neither was he able to help himself. Protection in such a case is of God—the Truth: He is the best rewarder, and He bringeth to the best issue.

But God will bring untruth to naught, and will make good the truth by His word; for He knoweth the very secrets of the breast.

Individual and Universal Subjective
Office of the Dean

My Dear Friend,

This lesson deals with unity and multiplicity. It sounds simple but is one of the most profound thoughts the human mind ever has entertained. It is necessary for us to realize that there is unity at the center of everything and multiplicity and variety at the circumference. There are many people but only One Person. We are people; God or Spirit is the One Person. There are many manifestations of life, but only One Cause back of all.

Because this is true, freedom and bondage are at the center of our own consciousness, since freedom and bondage are made of the same thing. We must always keep in mind that the Original Creative Cause is at the center of our own being. That is where we use It. We are mediums between Absolute First Cause and relative experience; between the Power that makes all things and the things that It makes for us. The original meaning of the word *husbandman* so often referred to in the Bible, is *a distributor of the Divine Gifts, one who distributes them.*

As you study this lesson try more fully to realize that you are not dealing with two powers but with the varied operations of One Power. You are not dealing with two minds but with different ideas in the Mind Principle. We know that this thought will interest you, as it does all who have entertained it.

And again may we ask if you are daily following our suggestions and actually working for yourself and someone else?

May all good be with you.

Sincerely,
Ernest Holmes

Lesson 8
p.98 to *Unity and Multiplicity,* p.102

In the Science of Mind we learn theoretically to substitute ideas for objects. The objective body, whether we think of it as a planet or as our own physical being, is an effect. This does not mean that we deny the physical body. Rather, we affirm a Spiritual Principle which projects the physical body.

To deny the reality of the physical body would be to affirm that we live in a world of illusion. We do not believe that the illusion is in the object, as though the object were unreal; we believe that if there is any illusion it is in our interpretation of the object.

On page 599 under the heading *Illusion* you will find this thought: *Nature is the great no-thing, yet it is not exactly nothing.* This saying from the teachings of Plotinus, one of the greatest spiritual thinkers of all ages, who lived and taught about A.D. 150, does not deny the objective world; it merely affirms that the physical world is not a self-knowing entity. For instance, the tree does not know that it is a tree, the mountain does not know that it is a mountain, the lake does not know that it is a lake.

The physical world has an actual existence but it is not a thing in itself. It is a definite form within a comprehending Mind. Because you and I live in the Mind which projects the physical world we are able to perceive what this Mind, which is also within us, has projected into form. How could you and I recognize each other unless there were one common medium of Mind or Intelligence between us? It is upon this Principle of the Universality of Mind and Intelligence that our entire science rests.

As we have stated, the illusion is not in the thing but in our interpretation of it. To say that the body is unreal would be a mistake, but it would be equally as great a mistake to say that the body is a thing in itself. We must become accustomed to the thought that there is a projector as well as a form projected. The form is real, but it is real only as a form. Further interpretation of this point will be found on page 594 under *Form: First in the chain of Causation is the Word, and this Word is conscious of Itself*. Then there follows an explanation of how this Word takes form. This should be carefully thought out.

On page 594 read the definitions of *Formless* and *Formless Substance*. They explain how Creative Mind gives form to the ideas with which it is impregnated. You will readily see that form is temporary but Mind is eternal. The body or any physical form is as real as it is supposed to be, but it is never a thing in itself. The physical body exists that the soul may function on this plane, and when by reason of any experience it is no longer possible for it to function in this plane, then the spirit severs itself from this particular form and passes to a new one.

Our definition of *Body*, page 577, says, *The entire manifestation of Spirit, both visible and invisible, is the Body of God*. The manifestation of Spirit in form is what we mean by body, whether that form is the human body or any other physical manifestation. It seems probable that the human body is an objective counterpart of an ethereal body.

Under the heading *Immortal Clothing*, page 491, you will find a more extensive explanation of the idea that there is a body within a body, and that we are not unclothed but *clothed upon*. We are to know no man after the flesh but only after the Spirit, which means that we are to realize that the real man is made of the essence of pure Spirit, is some part of God. The real man has consciousness. To be conscious he must be conscious of something; hence he must be clothed in form. Therefore upon whatever plane he may be functioning, he must have a body. This body is an outward manifestation of his inner realization of life. Turn to page 492 for an explanation of *The Inner Man* and his relation to the world of effect or body.

Body means more than mere physical form and more than just invisible essence. It means the invisible essence taking form. From this viewpoint, consciousness is not confined to the body, while the body is confined to consciousness. Consciousness or the Indwelling Spirit is more than any particular body. It is interesting to note the theory now accepted by some, that our physical bodies change in their entirety at least once a year. From this standpoint no living person has a bodily form which is even a year old.

We must not confuse this thought with a denial of the body, for we are not living in a world of illusion but of realities. We need never deny fact in order to affirm faith. To think of the physical world as a picture is probably correct, but the picture is real as such. It is projected, however, upon the screen of experience through some interior and invisible process of thought, of consciousness, of will, of imagination, and of feeling.

We are now ready to discuss that which changes (page 100). Since Spirit cannot change, as we have already affirmed, and since we are living in an objective world which continuously changes, we are compelled to draw the conclusion that it is only the effect that changes. If you turn to the top of page 588 you will find the statement that effect is that which follows cause and that Causation is pure Spirit and absolute Intelligence; hence both cause and effect are in reality spiritual; they are two ends of the same thing.

If we can comprehend the meaning of spiritual ideas, such as peace or joy, we shall certainly be able to demonstrate peace and joy in our experience through a conscious use of the Law of Cause and Effect. To say that the Law of Cause and Effect works in a mental medium is correct. You as an individual are the one who uses this Law of Cause and Effect, imparting to Its impersonal but creative nature the inspiration of your thought. When this inspiration is definitely directed toward specific purposes its creativeness is unlimited and can solve all human problems.

The purpose of the study of the Science of Mind is to impart a conscious knowledge of mental principles and a definite technique for practicing them. The greatest good that can come to any person is to know that he can help himself and others without attempting to go outside himself. The eternal activity of the Spirit produces an eternal creation, ever-changing forms within the Formless.

In the last two lines on page 100 you will find this statement: *Form comes and goes but it is not self-knowing*. Since all forms are as real as they are supposed to be, even the form of disease or discord need not be considered an illusion, but the result of a wrong conclusion about life. When we come to see that discord and disease are a result of wrong thinking, would it not follow that to change the thought would result in automatically projecting a new effect?

A further development of this idea is found in the second paragraph on page 416—the chief characteristic of subjective Law. A new contemplation will produce a new form. The question is not can a new form be projected, but can a better idea be conceived—an idea of harmony, of truth, and of beauty. The problem lies in our consciousness and not in the Law Itself.

We must not think of any particular form as evil because it brings pain instead of pleasure, for the mind within us must be expressed; this is its nature and we can never beat Nature at her own game. The question is, what form shall we express? Upon what idea shall we meditate? How much good can we conceive? Do we really believe that love overcomes hate? Have we a complete acceptance that peace heals confusion or that faith casts out fear? If we have, then we take our place as beneficent agents in the Divine Creative Order.

It seems impossible for us to arrive at a very great use of spiritual power unless we first arrive at the highest concept of good. It seems necessary that Nature be protected from any seriously wrong use of her laws. Therefore we should expect the destructive use of these laws to destroy their instrument, temporarily at least, until through experience one learns the lesson of Cause and Effect, that *whatsoever a man soweth, that shall he also reap.*

Just as form is never a thing in itself, so time is never a thing of itself. Both form and time are creations of the imagination projected upon the screen of experience. In the Cosmos the entire physical manifestation, which we call the Body of God, is a projection of the dynamic thought of the Infinite Thinker.

Let us consider anew the idea of Cause and Effect as found on page 101. All effect is subjective to its cause. These simple but meaningful words explain why it is possible for us to demonstrate health, happiness, and success. All effect is subjective to its cause. In other words, nothing in our external world projects itself.

Our individual world is projected by the mind that conceived it. When this mind withdraws its contemplation from any object, that object begins to disintegrate, whether it is the physical body when the soul has deserted it, or the body of our affairs when the Creative Mind no longer thinks them into existence, or holds them in the form which Its thought has already given to them.

From this viewpoint every man carries his destiny in his own mind, so to speak, but he does not know it, and most people would not believe it if one were to tell them. We can speak only to those who are willing to believe. It is written: *But as many as received him, to them gave he power to become the sons of God, even to them that believe on his name* (John 1:12). The philosophy that Jesus taught was one which necessitates belief in an invisible Principle. Recall how he said, *Do you believe?* or, *Believe and it shall be done.*

Jesus certainly implied that there is a Power which can, does, and must act, but Its action for us is limited to our belief. That is, the effect is subjective to its cause. If we have thought poverty until everywhere we look we see it, we have surrounded ourselves with an atmosphere and an environment of impoverishment. It seems as though we were caught by an inexorable foe, but we are not. It is written: *A man's foes shall be they of his own household.* You will find a more complete explanation of this subject on page 431 under the heading, *The Secret of Prayer.*

Nothing can happen to us unless it happens through us. This sounds simple enough, and yet it penetrates the very depths of Creative Causation. Nothing can happen to us unless it happens through us, since every effect is subject to its cause. It may not be easy to sense a happy environment when we are in the midst of unhappiness, but this is what we shall be called upon to do. We may be certain that the Law of the Universe is for us, and that there is nothing against us but ourselves. We must reverse the order in which we have been using the Creative Principle.

Again let us realize that the Creator is greater than His creation. Always the artist is greater than his art. Always the thinker is more than his thought. If he were not, his thought would engulf him, so to speak, and there would be no thinker left. It is a wonderful relief to know that we do have the power to turn within and meet the Creative Cause, even though we do not use this Power to the fullest extent of Its ability to accomplish for us. The creator is always greater than his creation, and if thought creates, by the same process it can re-create. To know that, that which molds can remold, that which projects can withdraw, that which integrates form can disintegrate it, is to know the way to freedom.

Now let us consider that in the idea with which we impregnate the Creative Mind there is involved everything necessary to produce the desired results. Moreover, once the process of involution is set in motion, evolution is certain. What does this mean? It means, for instance, that if an author is writing a play and he declares that he wants a certain character to form in his mind, by his declaration he actually creates the character which now must project itself on the screen of his imagination. It is a mental creation.

When an idea makes a demand upon Mind we are dealing with the principle of involution; we are invoking the Divine Creative Mind for a specific purpose. The Law being plastic, impersonal but creative, It must at once begin to create a form like the idea involved, and through a process of evolution It presents the form to us. Thus our ideas come back to us in form, for what the Spirit involves must evolve. In our system of thought we never deny the principle of evolution. We merely say that evolution is an effect of involution. We believe that evolution and involution are the two great Principles of the Universe; that one balances the other.

In practical work this means that when you give a treatment there is already contained within it a picture of the form which is to be projected, and that the projection of the form is in the nature of an effect. The effect must follow the cause, mathematically. Evolution must follow involution mechanically. Man is a principle of involution, and we might say he is some part of all The Principle of evolution. It is impossible for him to think without creating some form, and if he wishes to consciously control his destiny he must control his thoughts, mental states, states of consciousness, which of course are largely subjective.

Subjective thought is the only medium between the Absolute and the relative. On the subjective side of life we are always projecting forms into the invisible, and this invisible Creative Medium is always returning some condition to us. We call the condition good or bad, big or little, better or best, but it is always some form of thought.

If thought could not be controlled, then the Universe would be caught in its own trap. Then would the potter become subjective to his clay. Then would the Creator have been lost in His creation. Happily such is not the case. That which molds can remold, that which forms can re-form, that which creates can re-create. Let us learn to create after the pattern of harmony, peace, wholeness, and abundance.

Summary
Everything we see objectively is an effect of a subjective and spiritual cause. We do not deny the varied effects; we do affirm a unitary cause.

We are not living in a world of illusion but of evolution, and in a certain sense everything is as real as we make it. We never deny the physical body or the physical environment. We merely affirm that we have this physical body and experience this physical environment because we are one with the Mind that projects both.

All created things come and go, for this is the play of Life upon Itself, but the Mind that projects them is constant and changeless.

One of the great secrets of this science and the thing that should perhaps appeal to our imagination more than anything else is the thought that when we treat the physical body or work to change our environment we never go outside ourselves. The *Secret Place of the Most High* is within.

Within you is something that observes the change of Life, but the thing within you that observes the change is changeless.

Since the Law of Mind is not an entity in Itself, that is, It is a doer and not a knower, and since It responds to your thinking, the answer to all problems is in consciousness.

All causation is subjective; it is within and beneath the surface in which all objective forms are rooted. It is because of this that we have the possibility of freedom. And because these things are so, and because the Law responds to us at the level of our own inward awareness and affirmation, it follows that we must believe not only in the Spirit and the Law but in our own ability to imbibe the Spirit and use the Law.

Questions

Brief answers to these questions should be written out by the student after studying the lesson, and the answers compared with those which will be included in next week's lesson.

1. What do we mean when we say we substitute ideas for objects?
2. Do we deny the physical body or physical universe?
3. What do we affirm about the physical body and physical universe?
4. How can we be conscious of physical facts and their invisible causes?
5. Why do we have physical bodies?
6. Why is some type of form or creation necessary to consciousness?
7. How is our world of experience projected?
8. What do we mean when we say only effect changes?
9. (a) How shall we consciously use the great Law of Cause and Effect? (b) Where do we contact this Law of Cause and Effect?
10. Does disease, lack, unhappiness, limitation, or any other created form have self-consciousness or self-determination?
11. How do we change undesirable forms such as sickness, poverty, unhappiness, etc., into desirable forms, such as health, abundance, happiness, etc.?
12. (a) What do we mean by the use of Spiritual Power? (b) How do we arrive at the greatest use of this Power?

13. Is it right to use Spiritual Power to satisfy personal needs and desires?
14. Why is it necessary to believe in the Invisible Principle of Mind in order to consciously prove It?
15. Why is the Creative Principle limited to our belief when It operates for us?
16. What do we mean by a subjective state of thought?
17. What do we mean by the Absolute and the relative?
18. Why is our subjective state of thought the medium between the Absolute and relative in our lives?

Answers to Questions on Lesson 7

1. By the creative medium of Spirit we mean the intelligent but subjective creative Law of Mind.
2. When we use the words *intelligent but subjective* we mean that the Law of Mind which acts upon our word is creative but not selective.
3. You can direct the mental Law for others because It is everywhere present. It is a doer and not a knower; hence It must follow your direction.
4. Our subjective mind is the place where we use the Universal Law of Mind, which is subjective.
5. A practitioner should have confidence that his word acting through Law will do what it is supposed to do.
6. The Self-contemplation of Spirit means the Self-knowingness of God.
7. The Self-contemplation or the Self-knowingness of Spirit has an identical meaning with the Word of God.
8. The next great step which psychology must take will be the recognition that Mind is an Eternal Principle which man individualizes.
9. We use the Creative Principle every time we think.
10. New thoughts create new conditions because thought is creative, while conditions are in the realm of effect.
11. We change conditions by reversing our thought patterns, i.e., turning in thought from the undesirable, and steadfastly contemplating that which we desire.
12. Since the Universe is a Unity and not a duality, positive thoughts of good always overcome negative beliefs in evil, such as lack, limitation, etc.
13. When we declare the Truth about someone we affirm his Spiritual nature, his unity with Good, his wholeness in Spirit, mind, body, and affairs.
14. A spiritual or mental treatment takes place in the thought of the one giving it.
15. The treatment given in the thought of the practitioner affects his patient because each lives in the One Mind.
16. The power of a treatment is in the conviction that the power is already there and does not have to be concentrated but merely recognized and used.
17. In the Science of Mind we seek to demonstrate that the spiritual thought force in us can overcome all forms of limitation.

18. We cannot explain the Creative Power within us, but we can recognize, accept, and make use of It.

19. Our inability to explain the Creative Power within us in no way weakens our position. No scientist will ever attempt to explain first principles; he merely accepts them.

20. The conscious, subconscious, subjective, etc., are all phases of the One Mind; hence we do not divide Mind against Itself when we use these expressions.

The Great Negation

Evil is never a thing in itself, and yet we could hardly deny its existence in human experience. While we know that two and two can never make five, we are aware that many mistakes are made in dealing with the principle of mathematics.

In his chapters, *The Devil*, and *The Spirit of Antichrist*, Troward explains that our Divine Sonship, carrying with it as it must the prerogative of self-choice, makes possible the experience of limitation. Perhaps the most difficult thing to realize in dealing with the laws of thought is the absolute neutrality of the Principle of Mind. We recognize the characteristic of neutrality in all other laws of nature, but fail to realize that mental laws are also natural laws; that there must be a Universal Creative Medium which corresponds to our thought exactly as we think it, thus making evil appear to be a thing in itself.

Troward tells us that . . . *since God alone is, the Devil is not. Since God is Being, the Devil is Not-Being.* It is a paradox to speak of nonexistence producing anything, and yet in a certain sense this is what evil is. It arises from a misunderstanding of Reality, and thus a failure to comply with Its true nature. But because our thought is creative and as Troward says, *owing to the impossibility of ever divesting our Thought of its Creative Power, our conception of the Negative as something having a substantive existence of its own becomes a very real power indeed . . .*

The Bible likens the power of evil to Satan, to the Devil, and to the serpent which tempted Eve. Eve stands for the feminine or Mother Principle in nature: *And Adam called his wife's name Eve because she was the mother of all living*. The serpent is the Life Principle, and this Life Principle presents Itself to us in the form of our own experience; otherwise we could not be individuals.

The problem of evil, then, is not a problem of something which is a reality in itself, but rather a problem of coming to understand the nature of Reality. In the Text of Taoism we read, *But how can the Tao be so obscured that there should be "a true" and "a false" in it? . . . Tao becomes obscured through the small comprehension (of the mind).* And from the Buddhistic: *For the cause of the karma which conducts to unhappy states of existence is ignorance.* From the Talmud: *Not God, but ye yourselves are the creators and supporters of moral evils. When a field is covered by weeds, shall a farmer complain of God?*

Perhaps one of the most illuminating passages of all referring to evil comes from the Gospel of John: *Ye are of your father the devil, and the lusts of your father ye will do. He was a murderer from the beginning, and abode not in truth, because there is no truth in him. When he speaketh a lie, he speaketh of his own: for he is a liar and the father of it.* And in II Corinthians: *. . . for what fellowship hath righteousness with unrighteousness? and what communion hath light with darkness?*

The nature of Reality is such that the Law of Mind presents us with experiences which reflect the images of our thought. The Law which executes our conscious and unconscious will is neither good nor bad. It is a neutral law. When our will, choice, decision, and action emanate from goodness, then there is no evil. When our thought operates from a destructive motivation we create the evil we experience. This evil or devil is the one referred to as the *Not-Self which is opposed to the True Self . . . the one bending downward to matter, the other bending upward to God.* Swedenborg tells us: *Sin and the devil are one and the same.* And Bishop Wilberforce said, *The true devil against whom we have to be sober and vigilant is within man . . . the power within ourselves that makes for unrighteousness.* Campbell said, *Evil is a negative . . . it denotes the absence rather than the presence of something . . . Evil is not a principle at war with good. Good is Being and evil is Not Being.*

The spiritual and intellectual minds of the ages have sensed that evil is not a thing in itself, but is a self-created experience through which the soul passes on its evolutionary journey. This journey is not so much toward perfection as it is toward the recognition and realization of perfection. For instance, in spiritual mind healing we say that sickness, pain, poverty, impoverishment, want, fear, doubt, uncertainty, or any other type of negation is not a thing in itself, but a result of false belief and action.

The successful demonstration of spiritual science is based on the supposition that evil is the great No-Thing and that the knowledge of its nothingness, together with the recognition of the Allness of God, is what really heals. In a verse of antiquity we find this:

> *We praise Thee, O Father;*
> *We give Thanks to Thee, O Light;*
> *In Whom Darkness dwells not!*

And in Habakkuk 1:13: *Thou art of purer eyes than to behold evil, and canst not look on iniquity.* We also have this enlightening message from the Koran: *Whatever good betideth thee is from God and whatever betideth thee of evil is from thyself.*

The answer to the problem of evil is individuality and freedom. We are not dealing with an entity but an illusion; an illusion that is more than mere imagination. It has been an experience so universally suffered that it seems like a solid fact. It is self-evident, as Troward says, that the Infinite could not be evil, because if it were it would not be a creative agency. It is impossible that Life can produce death or that That Which Is can be neutralized by that which is not.

If, as Troward suggests, God stands for everything that is good, then the devil stands for everything that is opposed to good. But since there can be no real final opposition to good because God is One and Perfect, the power which seems opposed to good is suppositional only. Thus the devil is not only called "a liar" but "the father of lies in whom dwells no truth at all." Troward points out with remarkable clarity of thought that we must differentiate between God the Living Spirit, and the laws of nature which have no volition of their own. For instance, would the fact that fire can burn us prove that the nature of Reality is, or contains, evil? All laws of nature are subject to two kinds of use. The wrong use of any of these laws produces suffering, which we call evil, until through suffering we come to righteousness. Hence even though evil is not a thing in itself, the wrong use of the Law which automatically causes us to suffer becomes, as the Apostle suggested, *the schoolmaster to bring us unto Christ*, that is, to a true understanding of our sonship.

Troward tells us that *the Power of the Negative . . . has its root in our denial of the Affirmative.* This does not mean that illusion is created out of Reality but that the mirror of life will reflect those conditions and situations which we continuously affirm to be true. In this way evil becomes a denial of good; the opposite of true sonship.

It does not follow that what we call the material universe is evil, for nothing is evil in itself. It is the use of things which makes them evil. We certainly will make a limited use of things until we acquire a less limited idea of Life and of our relationship to the Supreme Spirit. We are brought back to the proposition that we must recognize Life as the Supreme Good, the supreme evil, or a mixture of each. We cannot serve God and mammon. If we would come to the Spirit for healing we must turn from everything which denies the Divine Presence. *Let him eschew evil and do good; let him seek peace and ensue it . . . He who knoweth me, unborn, beginningless, the great Lord of the world, he, among mortals without delusion, is liberated from all sin.* These passages taken from the Gita are not unlike those found in our own New Testament: *Finally, brethren, whatsoever things are true, whatsoever things are honest, whatsoever things are just, whatsoever things are pure, whatsoever things are lovely, whatsoever things are of good report; if there be any virtue, and if there be any praise, think on these things* (Philippians 4:8).

Troward tells us . . . *the whole question of the power of evil turns on the two fundamental Laws . . . the Law of Suggestion and the Law of the Creative Power of Thought.* He means by this that evil is not a thing in itself; neither "the devil" nor "a devil" are entities. Evil or devil stands for everything which acts or poses as a suppositional opposite to good. Consequently Troward informs us that our whole mental concept should be built upon a realization of the Wholeness of Spirit; upon a conscious perception of Its life-givingness. We should recognize It as Love as well as Life. In Romans 8:31 we read, *If God be for us, who can be against us?* All of which is summed up as the Spirit of Christ which the Bible sets before us as the Divine Ideal of Sonship, the Universal Norm.

If living in harmony with the Creative Law of the Universe, and consciously seeking to adjust ourselves to Its love and Its divine beneficence, constitutes the Spirit of Christ, then Its suppositional opposite would constitute what has been referred to as the spirit of Antichrist, that which is in opposition to good. Not that there is any real opposite to good, but that the very creative power of our false belief makes it appear as though there were such an opposite.

The Bible clearly states that Christ is within everyone. Riley says that *this Christ idea, like the germ or tiny seed, lies beneath the crust of materialism . . . the Divine Germ will . . . gradually unfold.* Robert Browning refers to this Christ in his great poem "Saul" where he says, *A Hand like this hand shall throw open the gates of new life to thee! See the Christ stand!*

It is written in John 3:6,7, *That which is born of the flesh is flesh . . . Ye must be born again.* Symbolically, this new birth takes place through the crucifixion and death of the lower qualities, transforming and transmuting the lower into the Higher Self. This is putting off the old man and putting on the new man which is Christ. This is what is meant in Isaiah 9:6: *For unto us a child is born, unto us a son is given . . . .* It is what Jesus meant when he said, *I am the way, the truth, and the life.* And when he said, *I am the light of the world; he that followeth me shall not walk in darkness . . .* Again: *For as the Father hath life in himself; so hath he given to the Son to have life in himself.* Jesus tells us that as we arrive at a correct understanding we pass from death into life. In *Echoes from the Gnosis*, the Hymn of Jesus, we read:

I am a lamp to thee who seest Me.

Amen!
I am a mirror to thee who understandest Me.
Amen!
I am a door to thee who knockest at Me.
Amen!
I am a way to thee a wayfarer.
Amen!

The spirit of Antichrist is a suppositional opposite to all this. It is a denial of God as peace, joy, union, love; an affirmation of power as hate, unhappiness, disunion, and any and every other name that stands for the incarnation of evil. The Bible sums up this whole category of negation under the name Antichrist, which is a symbol of the adversary of the Higher Self. The Great Negation consists in making evil equal with good, and particularly in seeking to use spiritual power for evil purposes. One is the supreme affirmation and the other the supreme denial. One builds up while the other tears down.

Human experience teaches us that the more definite our knowledge of the laws of nature, the more destructive we may become unless Divine Wisdom attends such knowledge. There is a vast difference between knowledge and wisdom, for knowledge pertains to the nature of laws; wisdom to their proper uses. For example, if the money spent in destructive purposes in the last quarter of a century had been spent instead for constructive ends, it would have eliminated any necessity for poverty throughout the world.

Again we might ask ourselves why the Divine and Beneficent Spirit, or God, permits such destruction? And again we come back to the answer given us from the enlightened throughout the ages, and which Jesus so plainly symbolized in the story of the Prodigal Son. Man is let alone to discover his own nature and to suffer the experience of any misuse of that nature. From the *Cup of Monad* we gather this saying: *God's image hath been sketched for thee . . . if thou wilt attentively dwell on it . . . that image shall become thy guide.* In II Corinthians 3:18: *But we all, with open face beholding as in a glass the glory of the Lord, are changed into the same image from glory to glory . . .* Even God cannot give us what we refuse to accept. Thus we create evil through the mistaken conception that Good is divided against Itself. This is the Great Negation.

Reference to the spirit of Antichrist does not mean that there is a real Antichrist. It refers only to the wrong use of the laws of our being and the consequent suffering which such wrong use imposes upon us. Troward tells us, *The temple which is profaned (by the wrong use of the law) is the innermost sanctuary of our own heart.* And, *. . . it is of the utmost importance who is enthroned there.*

Are we enthroning Love, Wisdom, Truth, and Beauty? Is the altar of our faith erected before the one true and only God, and Christ, the one true and only Son, already within us? Or is it erected before that which denies this eternal unity of good and which affirms that each man is for himself; that power alone is worthwhile? Power uncontrolled by love is chaos. Is our altar erected to chaos in the midst of our own confusion? Or do we believe in an All Supreme Wisdom and permit It to govern us?

In no way would this belittle or render futile our individuality. We should merely be using it for righteous or right purposes. The Law would still be our servant but our use of It would be on the side of right. Troward states, *The greater the power you put into anyone's hands, the more mischief will result if through ignorance of its true uses he misapplies it.* Therefore the sacred scriptures of the ages warn us that the gateway to Reality is narrow and the road is straight. *On this (road) proceeds he who knows Brahma; he has been a doer of the good whose nature is like light.* This quotation taken from the Upanishads is not unlike one from Proverbs*: But the path of the just is as the shining light, that shineth more and more unto the perfect day.*

It is interesting that in warning us against the uses of evil the ancient scriptures have never assumed that evil is a thing in itself. It has always been called the great No-Thing. That is, the great Nothing in Itself, the illusion, because the deep thinkers of all times have perceived that Reality must be One, even though this One manifests in multiplicity.

Jesus sums up the whole spirit of worship in the simple phrase that it should be done in Spirit and in Truth. Troward tells us, *The essence and not the form is what counts, because the whole thing is a question of mental attitude.* We are to realize that there is but one infinite creative agency in the universe; it is God, the Living Spirit Almighty. There is also a Law in the universe which obeys the will of God and of man. The Spirit is the very essence of Truth and Goodness; the Law is the actor. The Spirit is Love; the Law is power. The Law of Mind, like the law of electricity or any other law in nature, is entirely neutral and impersonal, just as the creative soil is entirely neutral and impersonal. We personify It through the use we make of It. This use may be what we call evil, but from the standpoint of Reality Itself the only final use we could make of this Law would be the use of goodness, since any other use of It would merely destroy its own embodiment. This is the only power evil has.

Back of the Law is the spirit of goodness, the spirit of inspiration, Divine Guidance, etc. Both Christ and Antichrist are ways of using the Law of Cause and Effect. The Spirit of Christ is the spirit of one who uses It in Divine Love and Wisdom. Thus power, obeying love and wisdom, produces happiness, peace, and joy without harm to anyone. But the use of power uncontrolled by love and wisdom produces transitory discord. Whether or not we choose to call this an illusion makes no difference; it is most certainly a human experience.

We must not hesitate to use the Law of Mind for fear of suffering a negative consequence, for always we shall be using It constructively if there is nothing in our use of It which denies good. The most simple-minded can differentiate between the two. It is never right to use the Law of Mind to influence anyone, to control anyone, to suggest anything to anyone. It is always right to use It to help, to uplift, to heal, to make happy, to bless.

Troward tells us that the Law of Mind which has been called Anima Mundi is not the originating Principle, but is the avenue through which this Principle works. Medieval writers referred to It as the Universal Medium, esoterically called Water, just as they spoke of Animus Dei, signifying the Divine Spirit, and they were careful to discriminate between the two. Troward simplifies such expressions by calling the Universal Creative Medium the subconscious Mind of the Universe, which by Its nature affords a matrix for the germination of the seeds of thought that are planted in It.

Mental Technique for Spiritual Treatment

Unless there were a definite method of procedure in spiritual mind healing it could not be considered scientific. Unless a definite technique could be delivered there would be no intelligent approach to the subject. Unless one could learn this technique and consciously apply it, it would not be universally applicable. But the Science of Mind is just as definitely scientific and just as positively based on an actual principle as is any other science.

The fact that we are dealing with invisible forces makes them no more intangible than any other force of nature with which we deal. All life is invisible, all energy is invisible, all causation is invisible. The Principle of Mind is invisible and Its practice is invisible, but Its results are the word made flesh.

Since the modern approach to mental science has developed simultaneously along both the psychological and metaphysical fronts it is well to analyze our position and determine where we agree with the psychological method and where we depart somewhat from it. For whether or not we are conscious of the fact, we more or less combine both methods.

Unfortunately, many people in the metaphysical field do not understand this and in their ignorance of the subject deny psychology a place in their system and just as unfortunately many psychologists do not understand the metaphysical viewpoint, and in their ignorance deny its place in their field. With the broader understanding of both fields there will be a more conscious cooperation, for each in its own way is seeking to help and to be helped.

The approach of psychology to mental healing has already passed through several distinct stages. Starting with mesmerism it developed into hypnotism; next into mental suggestion and finally into mental explanation, which is the method employed by most psychologists, that is if we reduce their methods to the simplest interpretations.

Neither psychiatry nor analytical psychology is hypnotic, nor do they practice mental suggestion. Their entire field is one of explanation. In analytical psychology the explanation is drawn from the patient's consciousness in such a way that he self-sees his trouble and by this self-seeing the difficulty is supposed to be dissipated.

In the earliest stages of analytical psychology it was thought necessary that the analyst should draw out of the consciousness of his patient every trivial incident which might have led to his mental and physical undoing. This has made of analysis one of the most subtle of arts, as well as one of the most difficult practices. If one expects to draw out of the consciousness of one's patient the most trivial incidents of his life, the method becomes painstaking, laborious, more or less cumbersome, and generally the treatment must cover a long period of time.

There is a tendency today among many practicing analysts and psychiatrists to shortcut this method somewhat, and to drain more quickly the psychic confusion from the unconscious memory of the patient, thus producing a quicker response.

In spiritual mind healing we do not have to uncover every unconscious cause of mental confusion with its attendant physical distress. We know that broad, generalized statements often effect a healing of disease without either the practitioner or the patient having any specific knowledge of its cause. We know that the clearer one's consciousness is and the more definitely certain one is that Spirit is the Absolute Cause of all, and that Good alone governs, the more quickly will healing take place. We know that silent recognition and realization elevates the consciousness to a place of greater power and makes possible a more immediate manifestation. Jesus did not analyze; he announced.

In actual practice we combine analysis with realization. Sometimes we use one and sometimes the other, but more often we combine the two. It is probably safe to say that, in most practice, the combination of these two methods has been more effective than the use of one to the exclusion of the other. No one appears to be in a continual state of conscious spiritual power, but we all have the capacity to give scientific mental treatments. We must resort to our definite technique for practice and through mental statements arrive at a spiritual conclusion, a consciousness of the Allness of God and the ever-present availability of Good.

We claim to have a science which can be delivered to all intelligent persons, and we claim that the average person can effectively use this science provided he complies with its Principle and Law.

It is therefore necessary to deliver a definite technique and a conscious method for procedure. That is why we start with the proposition of Perfect God, Perfect Man, and Perfect Being. This is the spiritual Principle which the mind, through right ideas, seeks to demonstrate, and in so doing it will probably combine argument with realization. Just what do we mean by argument in mental treatment? We mean the phases of thought through which the mind goes to arrive at a conclusion. The following example may help to clarify this point:

A person suddenly finds himself feeling greatly discouraged and mentally depressed. He knows that God is neither discouraged nor depressed. He knows that nothing has happened to the Divine Reality. He might, by sitting in quiet contemplation for a few moments, so fill himself with this Spirit of Reality that his negation would disappear as mist before the sun. This of course would be the ideal way. But suppose in contemplating this he fails. His next step is to resort to his mental technique. He begins to make definite statements, similar to the following:

> *God is neither sad nor depressed. There is no life apart from God; therefore my life is God. Consequently I am neither sad nor depressed. God is not afraid of anything. My mind and the Mind of God are One Mind; therefore my mind cannot entertain fear.*

At this place in treatment, the image of fear or some memory of fear may arise. Immediately he would say,

> *This fear is neither person, place, nor thing. It has no law to support it, no power to uphold it, no consciousness to conceive it, no law to enforce it, no person to express it.*

He would be repudiating the negation and would follow such repudiation by the affirmation:

> *My mind is the Mind of God—calm and peaceful, unafraid and certain. All presence, all power, all peace and joy are mine today. I am not afraid of anything because I now see that there is nothing to be afraid of. The images of fear cannot operate through me. I am completely separated from any belief in fear. I do not remember anything in the past of which I was afraid. I do not anticipate anything in the future of which I shall be afraid, and I am not conscious of anything going on today of which I am afraid.*
>
> *There is no discouragement. I am protected by the only Power there is. I live in the only Presence there is. This word completely neutralizes, obliterates, casts out, expels every thought of fear and every belief that there is anything to be afraid of.*

A person making statements similar to these would probably find himself gradually lifted up mentally to the place in thought where he would begin to feel at ease. The images of doubt would no longer assail him. Calm and peace would accumulate in his thought. In such degree as he embodied the meaning of the words which he had just spoken, a sense of realization would fill his consciousness with peace. This sense of realization he should mentally hold in his consciousness for a period of time and finally it would become permanent.

One thing, however, we must be careful to avoid, and that is fooling ourselves. Our work rests upon demonstration, and whatever method we use, how much argument we employ, or whatever state of realization we may reach, we must prove our position. We must actually demonstrate that thought manifests in form, in actual conditions, in objective life. If thought is not manifesting in this way in our experience, we must work with ourselves until it does. We must never take *No* for an answer. To do so would be to repudiate the Principle in which we believe, and wreck our faith in It.

Therefore we must persist in our effort until the purpose we have in mind is accomplished in actual fact and not merely in fancy. We must always remember that proper use of the Science of Mind is not a practice through which we fall into a mental reverie as an escape from objective life. Our work is not done properly unless something happens as a result of it.

This something that happens we can always weigh and measure objectively. For instance, if we are treating someone who has high blood pressure our work is not accomplished until the patient can go to a physician for proper and thorough physical examination and receive the verdict that the blood pressure is normal.

Treatment is not for the purpose of helping us either to avoid reality or endure unhappy situations. It is for the express purpose of changing situations, and unless situations or conditions are changed as a result of the treatment, we have missed the mark. Always we must insist that we demonstrate our proposition, for our motto is *To do is to know, and to know is to do.*

Bibles of the World
Fragments from the spiritual history of the race revealing fundamental UNITY of religious thought and experience

BUDDHISM—If you see a wise man, like a guide to treasure-trove, pointing out your faults and failings, follow him. Such company brings prosperity, not woe.

CONFUCIANISM—Heaven protects and establishes us so that in everything we may prosper.

When you find wealth within your reach, do not try to get it by improper means; do not seek for more than your proper share.

HINDUISM—Thou, Lord of wealth, art Master of all treasures.

JUDAISM and CHRISTIANITY—But the fruit of the Spirit is love, joy, peace, long-suffering, gentleness, goodness, faith, meekness, temperance; against such there is no law.

Wherefore, if God so clothe the grass of the field, which today is, and tomorrow is cast into the oven, shall he not much more clothe you, O ye of little faith?

But let him ask in faith, nothing wavering. For he that wavereth is like a wave of the sea, driven with the wind and tossed.

ISLAM—It is God Who hath created the heavens and the earth and Who hath sent down the waters from the heaven, and so bringeth forth the fruits for your food.

SIKHISM—At the beginning and the end God is ever our Helper.

God is immortal, undecaying, imperishable, and of changeless purpose, Creator of all, the Remover of sickness, sorrow, and sin.

Meditation
I know that the Power of Good is an underlying Principle of the Universe. It is a manifestation of God. I know that God is All-Good. I know that Good underlies all manifestations of thought and form because Good is all there is. Good is at the root of all manifestation, regardless of its seeming absence.

I know that this Good is the basic principle of my existence. That which I Am is Good. I know that Good is the Law of my being. It is the vital, living Force that supports my every harmonious thought and deed. There is no other power, for God is Good and there cannot be God and something else. God is in all; God is all, and God is Good.

I know there is nothing in me that could possibly obstruct or withhold the Divine Circuit of Life and Love, which Good is. My word dissolves every negative thought or impulse that could throw a shadow over my perfection.

Good flows through me to all. Good shines through my thoughts and actions. Good harmonizes my body so that it is revitalized and manifests perfection in every cell, in every organ, in every function. Good harmonizes my mind so that Love sings joyously in my heart, and I am completely conscious of All-Good in me, around me, and in all that is.

I am in complete unity with my Good.

Mind and Matter
Office of the Dean

My Dear Friend,

I hope you are deriving great benefit from these lessons and that you are taking time every day to prove that this science is practical and workable. For what good is a lot of information unless we use it? To say that we believe in the principle of a science is quite different from using that principle.

It is not enough merely to believe in the Principle of Mind. We must understand that the Law of Mind in Action is something that we can use. Reduced to its greatest simplicity this means that we must realize that definite thoughts, mental statements, affirmations, and denials produce a corresponding action in the universal ether of Mind that receives the impress of our thought and acts upon it.

This Mind Principle acts exactly like a mirror. Your statements are reflected in it as though they were pictures, and the reflection comes back to you as conditions. When you want to change things in a mirror you never try to rub out the reflection; you change the image in front of it. The new reflection is automatic. It cannot contradict the image which you hold before it.

You as the image maker must be certain that you are imagining only what is good for yourself and everyone else. Within this good is contained everything necessary to happiness, health, success, and mental and spiritual well-being.

May all your endeavors be successful.

Sincerely,
Ernest Holmes

Lesson 9
Unity and Multiplicity, p.102, to Freedom or Bondage, p.108

In this lesson we shall consider once more the meaning of unity and multiplicity. All physical forms are made from one etheric substance. The lesson to be learned from this is that since all physical forms are condensations of energy into unique types, there must be some intelligence weaving the patterns, as it were, for these types. The design must have a designer, for apparently it has no self-determination. The tapestry is never conscious of the pattern that is woven into it; it merely takes on the pattern which is woven into it.

If we have One Substance taking innumerable forms there must be a multiplicity of patterns, and if the forms are not self-determining it follows that the pattern is the determining factor. And if the pattern itself is the result of some creative thought it also follows that the thinker is the creator of the pattern, while the pattern is the creator of the form. (Read the meaning of *Creator* on page 583.)

The Creator thinks—the thought takes form. This is a play of Life upon Itself. If you will turn to page 578 under the definition of *The Changeless* you will find it referred to as the One Cause back of all, which has nothing to change into but Itself. All forms are different variations of One Substance.

We should arrive at the most intense realization as we contemplate this most significant of all truths, that nothing changes but form. There is a reality and a stability to our nature. There is a place of calm at the center of our own soul which is never disturbed; a place from which we may say to the turbulent waves which toss and moan around us: "Be still and know that I am God." Thus the changeless thing within us is always expressed in the varying changes around us. Chance and change, objective forms and conditions and situations are all subject to this immutable Presence, this eternal Stability which is at the very center of our own being. All of the negative conditions which surround us we shall some day discover to be self-inflicted.

Read page 336, next to the last paragraph, to and including the first paragraph on page 337. You will find a discussion of the difference between believing that evil is an entity and thinking of it as merely a passing experience of the soul. If evil were a real entity we could not overcome it, but if it is merely one of the patterns which we are weaving, then we can change the pattern. Our text says that there cannot be any law which demands lack or limitation. Neither can there be any final salvation outside our conscious cooperation with the Creative Principle within us and the God around us.

On page 407, the third paragraph, we read that cause and effect are but two ends of one unity. To understand this would be to solve the mystery of life, to answer the problem of evil, to replace lack with abundance, and to find *the garment of praise for the spirit of heaviness*. But the arbitrary control of man's destiny must stop just as soon as the principle of evolution brings man to a place where he is self-conscious (page 342, last paragraph). Having arrived at self-consciousness, man could not possibly be free unless he had self-choice, and unless his self-choice had the power to bring about at least a temporary manifestation of the thing chosen he would remain in a dream world, his life would be an hallucination, an illusion, and not a reality.

It so happens that God's world is a world of reality. Even the most trivial fact is true enough, but when we place it in its right relationship it may or may not be significant. The compulsory process of evolution certainly stopped when man rose on his feet and said, "I am." From that time his entire history has been one of self-discovery. It should not seem strange that he may be entering into a new era of self-discovery. Just as we have discovered physical laws, we are now discovering mental, spiritual, and psychical laws, which will do infinitely more for us than our knowledge of physical laws has done.

On page 498 under the heading, *Evil Is Created by Man*, you will find the idea that we make our own mistakes, suffer from our own foolishness, and must make the return journey into righteousness ourselves. Since Truth never changes, the only thing that we can do is change our attitude toward It. No doubt we shall soon discover that bondage and freedom are two ways of using one power.

Power Itself is never limited, any more than a rope is limited because it is tied around someone's neck. It could just as well be tied around the trunk of a tree or straightened out; of itself it has no personal ambition or desire. So the Law of Life is subject to a dual use, but the Law Itself is never duality.

Experience will finally teach us to return to the Father's house where we shall discover that nothing has happened so far as Reality is concerned.

One of the good things that will happen to us when we realize this, is that we need place no limit on the Creative Principle which we have the privilege of using. Big and little are in our own minds, not in It. It merely reflects what we think into It. Absolute Causation is at work in our experience at all times, and multiplicity is rooted in unity. Hence we should not separate Life from living, Spirit from matter, Divine Principle from universal creation. God is All in All.

Whatever scientific research we may be pursuing, we shall soon discover that all roads lead to Rome. The inductive research through which any science leads us is back to the invisible, to intelligence, to law, to order, and to manifestation. So our own thought leads us back to the center of our consciousness which is God, and which is ever able to project new pictures upon the screen of our personal experience.

The Almighty goes forth into creation through every living soul. Our text says, *So close is the union of creation with the Creator that it is impossible to say where one begins and the other leaves off* (page 103). There is but One—One Infinite Substance, One Immutable Law, One Infinite Person. We are in this Infinite Person and He is manifest through us. No closer union could possibly be imagined (page 323).

On page 366 you will find this thought expressed in blank verse—*Thou art the center and circumference of my life*. God is our whole being; there is nothing else. We begin by saying, "In the beginning God"—Spirit plus nothing leaves nothing but Spirit; Causation plus nothing leaves nothing but Causation; God plus nothing leaves nothing but God. Within this Divine Unity is included all action and all reaction. Cause and effect are merely two ends of one sequence.

On page 443 under the heading, *The Real Father and Son*, this idea is still more completely developed through the concept of Jesus, as in the exaltation of his mind he comprehended the mystic union of his soul with the Oversoul. Therefore we should never attempt to separate Life from living, nor Principle from creation. God is in everything and through everything, and when we learn to recognize the God-essence in people and things they will respond to us harmoniously, happily, and with power.

This is the secret of all our studies—to know ourselves and each other, to understand creation, to so unify with the invisible Cause that at will we shall be able to draw to ourselves, into our personal experiences, for our own benefit and for the help and benefit of others, anything and everything we need to make life happy and abundant.

God is not apart from His creation, but is in it; yet God is always more than His creation. That is, God is both immanent and transcendent. Turn again and read the definition of *Immanent* (page 600) and *Transcendent* (page 638). *How, then, can we doubt that the very mind which we now use is the Intelligent Principle from which all life draws its power to be and its intelligence to express?* (page 104).

On page 394, the fourth paragraph, we read that *man's mind is the Mind of God functioning at the level of man's understanding of his place in the Universe*. Study this entire paragraph and meditate deeply upon its meaning, for here is a Power which can do anything and everything for us. It is undoubtedly the

Power that Jesus used. He must have had complete access to It by reason of the fact that he was always in harmony with the Spirit back of the Law. We draw as much power out of the Universe as we are able to perceive acting for us.

It is a most remarkable thing to realize that there is an interior process of thought which can produce an actual physical manifestation in our objective experience; to realize that there is a creative power which we may direct for the benefit of others. What greater good could we ask? And yet how little we use this power, consciously. I suppose we are using it unconsciously all the time; indeed we must be. From now on let us seek to use it consciously and for definite purposes, and realize that *whosoever will may come.*

Turn back to page 393, third paragraph, for a description of Substance as being energy plus intelligence. The creative Law which is at our disposal is substance and energy, and It is a substance and an energy which has the intelligence to respond to us, but having no volition of Its own, It is not conscious; that is, It is not self-conscious of the way in which It is responding. We could not ask for a more fitting servant. Here is really the perfect servant waiting for our recognition. How well Jesus must have understood this when he said, *The words that I speak unto you, they are spirit, and they are life.*

Is it clear that the Law can never say "I will not," but can act only as instructed? (page 105) Again let us caution you not to be confused by misunderstanding the terms *the Law* and *the Spirit.* Turn again to the definitions of *Spirit* on page 633 and *Law* on page 605. A misunderstanding of these terms has brought confusion into the thought of many persons. You will never be a scientific practitioner until you understand the significance of Law and Spirit and your place in the creative order.

The Law can never say "I will not"; It can only say "I will." For our "Yes" It says "Yes"; for our "No" It says "No." But since the Law of the Lord is perfect, that is since It is immutable, whatever we set in motion in It will tend to take form. Hence Intelligence or Spirit is the ultimate creative agency of the universe.

Notice under the heading, *Man Re-enacts the Nature of God* (page 106), that *whatever is true of the Universe as a Whole must also be true of man as some part of this Whole.* For God and man are one and not two; God in the Infinite World, man in the finite world. How marvelous to conceive the possibility of such freedom. How greatly we all desire to express this possibility in terms of joy and more abundant life for ourselves and others. And here the power is, resident in each one of us. *Behold, I stand at the door and knock.* The creative Life Principle, ever ready to be individualized through us, must wait our recognition of It.

We should be able to see now why there must come a change of thought before there can come a permanent betterment in conditions. We can never get away from the creative power of our thought. There is no use trying. We would do well to begin immediately to use this Law for definite purposes. We should use our imagination, will, and emotion to the end that we may have freedom instead of bondage, joy instead of unhappiness, peace in the place of confusion.

The world has learned all it should through suffering (page 107). We should like to make this thought come true. We do not say that we have learned all we ever shall through suffering; we affirm that we should not have to suffer in order to evolve. Limitation is the only sin there is; knowledge and enlightenment the only salvation.

If we would come consciously to the Father who seeth in secret we should follow the instructions at the bottom of page 430 and at the top of page 431; we should turn to the Indwelling Spirit who lives in the secret place of our own lives. There is no other way. We must seek the center and the cause which can be found nowhere except within. For we are individuals in a universe of limitless possibility, using powers which are so stupendous that they stagger the imagination. Until now we have been using these powers in ignorance; let us begin today to use them with intelligence.

Summary

There are many patterns but only One Tapestry of Life. You are the weaver. The Tapestry cannot refuse the pattern given it.

Evil is never a thing in itself but we do not deny its existence as a condition in human experience. But if it were real we could not change it. If it had an actual universal law supporting it, then it would be a part of God. We can change only that which has no life nor intelligence within itself. We are the life and intelligence of that which we experience. We do not deny the experience as though it were an illusion, but we affirm that it need not be this particular kind of an experience.

Every person lives under the law of his own soul whether he knows it or not, because the One Law of all Life is ever responding to him. The Law of Itself cannot be changed but our use of It can. The limitations we suffer are not inherent in the Law; they are the result of our own ignorance.

We return to the Father's house when we come into conscious union with the all-sustaining Beauty, Presence, and Power of the Living Spirit. There is no place where we begin and God leaves off, or where God begins and we leave off. Every man is a point of consciousness in the One Mind, the One Presence, and the One Power.

We should never try to separate ourselves from Life or the joy of living, but rather bring the joy of living into everything we do. We should unify with all the people we meet and harmoniously enter into every legitimate activity. God is not separate from His creation but is in it, yet always more than it.

Questions

Brief answers to these questions should be written out by the student after studying the lesson, and the answers compared with those which will be included in next week's lesson.

1. What do we mean by *Unity and Multiplicity*?
2. What is the determining factor in shaping the innumerable forms of creation?
3. What is meant by Creation as the play of Life upon Itself?
4. What do we mean by negative conditions being self-inflicted?
5. Is evil an entity?
6. Why is it man cannot be free, unless he has self-choice?
7. What is meant by the compulsory process of evolution?

8. What is bondage and freedom?

9. Are we limited in our use of the Creative Principle?

10. What is inductive research?

11. What is the meaning of One Substance, One Law, and One Person?

12. Explain the meaning of *We should never separate Life from living.*

13. Explain *God Immanent* and *God Transcendent.*

14. What is man's mind?

15. What is the power that Jesus used?

16. Can we use the same power that Jesus used?

17. Does the Law say "I will" or "I will not"?

18. What do we mean by God in the Infinite World and man in the finite world?

19. Can we escape the creative power of our thought?

20. What do we mean by the Father who seeth in secret?

Answers to Questions on Lesson 8

1. In mental treatment, when we substitute ideas for objects we are recognizing that all facts have a mental origin.

2. In the Science of Mind we deny neither the physical body nor the physical universe.

3. We affirm that the physical body and the physical universe are manifestations of the Mind of God. Hence the real Truth about them is Wholeness, Harmony, and Perfection.

4. We perceive physical facts and their invisible causes because we live in and are one with the Mind which conceives all ideas and projects all facts. This Mind is the Mind of God and man.

5. We have physical bodies because they are necessary for self-expression on the physical plane.

6. Form or creation is necessary to consciousness; otherwise Mind would remain unexpressed.

7. We project our world of experience through the invisible process of thought, will, imagination, and feeling.

8. When we say that effects alone change, we mean that while the world of facts, experiences, created forms, etc., changes, the Cause back of it which is God, Mind, Spirit, or the Creative Principle, remains permanent.

9. (a) We consciously use the Law of Cause and Effect by definitely impressing our desires upon It. (b) We contact the Law of Cause and Effect at the center of our own being.

10. Since all created forms are but effects of the Mind Principle, they of themselves can have no self-determination.

11. We change the undesirable form into a more desirable one by consciously and definitely letting go of the idea behind the one, and mentally contemplating and accepting the idea back of the other.

12. (a) By the use of Spiritual Power we mean the most effective use of Creative Mind. (b) We arrive at the greatest use of this Power when our thought is most completely unified with Its nature, i.e., when our thought is constructive, harmonious, and life-giving.

13. It is right to use Spiritual Power for any purpose, provided such purpose is life-giving and harms no one.

14. It is necessary to believe in the Invisible Principle of Mind in order to demonstrate, because we are living in a mental and spiritual universe and because that which the mind believes in and accepts, it experiences.

15. The Creative Principle can operate for us only by operating through our belief. Hence we limit Its operation to such belief.

16. A subjective state of thought means any habitual thought pattern in a person's mind.

17. By the Absolute we mean the invisible Cause; and by the relative we mean the visible effect which depends upon this invisible Cause.

18. Our subjective state of thought is the medium between the Absolute and relative, because it contains our habitual thought patterns which are continually projecting themselves into mind.

Freedom

Someone has said that frequently a symbol which has spiritual significance for the wise has been worshipped as an idol by the ignorant. It is the idea back of the symbol, not the symbol itself, which is to be reverenced. When Jesus said, *I am the door*, he meant, to use the words of R. J. Campbell, *There is in every man's heart an open door toward the eternal, and through that open door the messages of God can come.*

In ancient times it was said that Christ represented the highest nature of man. Hence Christ, or the Universal *I AM* in us, becomes an entrance for the Buddhic or enlightened virtues, represented by sheep. *I am the door: by me if any man enter in, he shall be saved, and shall go in and out, and find pasture* (John 10:9).

Let us not forget that salvation is from the lower to the higher self, and not the salvation of a lost soul, for nothing can be lost in the eternal Oneness and Unity of all Life. To be saved means to become redeemed from the limitation of the lower nature. It is then that we are able to *go in and out*, which means passing from the contemplation of pure Spirit in the inner life to our external or objective actions in everyday life.

Jesus said that when we pray we should shut the door. We should close out external images of limitation and conflict. Thus the doorway to Reality becomes narrow and straight. Evelyn Underhill states, *At the apex of your Spirit there is a little door so high up that only by hard climbing can you reach it . . . hence come . . . faint echoes from the Truth hammering at your gates . . .* Gate is used to represent the higher and the lower mind. As a symbol of the higher it represents an entrance through which consciousness rises to a heavenly state. As a symbol of the lower mind it represents the passage of Spirit or the Ego into lower planes. In the Twenty-fourth Psalm David sings, *Lift up your heads, O ye gates . . . and the King of glory shall come in. Who is this King of glory? The Lord of hosts, he is the King of glory.* He refers to the Spiritual Principle within us which the mind must lift up, that the gates to the heavenly state may ever stand ajar.

It is interesting that in numerous passages taken from different scriptures of the ages we find so many references to an inner principle of Reality, which acting as a symbolic door or gate must be open that the Eternal Light may flood the consciousness with its effulgent glory.

In Chapter IX, *The Law of Liberty*, Troward tells us, *The whole object of the Bible is to teach us to be ourselves and yet more ourselves*. He says that the Bible deals with two extreme ends in the universal scale of Being, that is, . . . *the Universal Mind and the Individual Mind*. When we learn to establish a right relationship between these two principles we shall have discovered the Law of Liberty.

We are not to think of these two apparent ends of nature as separated from each other, for the whole Law of Life is a Law of Unity. We are to think of the individual as an individualized center of God-Consciousness in a cosmic whole, or as Jesus said, *I and my Father are one*. The Father is the Parent Mind or Universal Spirit individualized, personified, and incarnated in us. Hence the Law of Liberty is the Law of Oneness and Unity, establishing not only the consciousness of One Power but the recognition of One Law forever emanating from this Power.

Troward, with the clarity of a well-poised judicial mind, tells us that we should look for no spiritual authority other than that of coming to realize *the Divine orderings can only be known by the Divine workings*. In this he is cautioning us to beware of false revelations. Anyone who is at all familiar with the field of psychism must realize upon what a sound foundation his warning is based. Things as they appear in the psychic world are not always to be relied upon, and we should be careful to differentiate between truth and error.

We may draw a good example from our psychological knowledge relative to the interpretation of dreams. It is generally considered that the chief character or symbol appearing in a dream is an unconscious projection of the dreamer. It represents the dreamer himself fantastically pictured in the form of a subconscious symbol. The true interpretation of a dream rests entirely on a correct understanding of what the symbol means. All dreams rise out of the subconscious, and most so-called revelation rises from the same source.

Many of the ancients understood this. They warned people against having familiar spirits, and told them to test the spirits to see whether or not they be of God; to speak not with confusion but with understanding. We should not believe everything we are told, but should test all so-called revelations and see if they are consistent with what the nature of Reality must be like. We should not be confused by tradition, nor by any other form of dogmatic certainty.

It is fundamental to a true perception of Reality that God is One. Since this is true and since God is changeless, Reality cannot change. Hence when varying beliefs in different ages proclaim revelations which fundamentally contradict each other, we may be certain that the fault is not with Reality but arises from this passage: *The mortal form doth change with every day. 'Tis turned by time to growth and waning, as being an untrue thing*. From another source of wisdom we inherit this splendid paragraph: *All products of Brahm, which is reality, are themselves also real; and there is nothing different from it. Whoever says that there is (anything different), is not free from illusion but is like a man walking in his sleep*. The Gita tells us, *The unreal hath no beginning; the real never ceaseth to be*. And the Upanishads: *All is the effect of . . . One Universal Essence*.

Troward says that both the teachings of Moses and Jesus are true, and because they are, one cannot contradict the other. Moses taught a universal Law of Cause and Effect. Without in any way seeking to destroy this Law, Jesus taught the relationship of the individual to this universal Principle. Moses taught that God is One—*Hear, O Israel: The Lord our God is one Lord*. Jesus added to this that man is an individualized center of God-Consciousness within this Eternal One. Thus he did not refute the teachings of Moses. He said, *I am not come to destroy, but to fulfill*.

If God were One when the Old Testament was written, then God was One when the Gospels were written. Troward tells us, *The Bible is the spiritual Natural History Book of Man*. He says it is the story of the evolution of individual life from the dim period before the advent of personal consciousness to the point where man recognizes himself. Up to this point the Law has done all It can arbitrarily. From now on man must . . . *wake up to the fact that he is what he is by reason of the Law inherent in himself* . . . He must not only discover that the Law is inherent within his own nature, but that his true nature is unified with the Original Creative Cause. He is an expression of It.

The teachings of Jesus infer at all times that what God is in the Universal, man is in the particular. Hence man reproduces the whole Cosmos on a miniature scale. And since the Cosmos Itself is the essence of goodness, truth, and beauty; of life, wisdom, and love; of freedom, joy, and self-expression, then the true and perfect Law, as St. James points out, is one of liberty. But there could be no real liberty if there were an actual power of evil. If Reality were limitation, the very knowledge of truth would create bondage. Such a conception of Reality is both absurd and impossible.

Again we are brought back to the truism that a house divided against itself cannot stand. The real Law is not only a law of liberty, but equally a law of goodness. We are centers of God's Creative Activity. In expressing God we are expressing ourselves, and in expressing the true Self we are giving self-expression to God. In the *Egyptian Book of the Dead* we find this statement: *I go forth into heaven . . . Indefinite time, without beginning and without end, hath been given to me; I inherit eternity and everlastingness hath been bestowed upon me*. We are told in I John 3:24: *And hereby we know that he abideth in us, by the Spirit which he hath given us*. The Talmud says, *The greatest wisdom is to know thyself*. Perhaps one of the most beautiful passages of all those inherited from the wisdom of the ages is this from the Text of Taoism: *If you keep your body as it should be, and look only at the one thing, the Harmony of Heaven will come to you. Call in your knowledge and make your measures uniform, and the spiritual (belonging to you) will come and lodge with you; the Attributes (of the Tao) will be your beauty, and the Tao (itself) will be your dwelling-place*. And from Ephesians 3:16: *That he would grant you, according to the riches of his glory, to be strengthened with might by his Spirit in the inner man*.

Since we are of the Spirit of God, the All-Creative Wisdom and Power, and since our individuality is the Universal Spirit acting on the plane of the particular, it follows that our spiritual individuality is never limited by anything which has gone before. The Creative Spirit is everywhere projecting Itself through us in a new and unique manner. The true Law is freedom and not bondage.

Troward tells us that real liberty must be according to law. There must be a coordinating unity, a universal norm; or to state it in other terms, there must be a Universal Principle which never denies Its own nature. Troward tells us that the Law of Liberty is not a law by which people contend, *to get their own way at somebody else's expense*. The pathway to freedom is not by the destruction of others, but through a unique expression of the Self. No two persons are alike, nor do any two think alike. Since thought deals with the Infinite Medium there is no limit to the scope of its possible manifestation; there is good enough to go around. Not until this becomes universally realized will wars cease, poverty be healed, and people learn to live together as human and divine beings.

Troward draws attention to the fact that the Bible continually repeats statements relative to the creative power of thought. It is a commentary, he says, on the text that man is of like spiritual nature with God. . . . *he is a reproduction in individuality of that which God is in universality*. If we always bear this in mind the Bible becomes simplified, since it states this proposition in innumerable ways, using many illustrations to drive home its point. But if we deny this fundamental proposition of the unity of God and man, then our interpretation of the Bible must be based upon a dualism which becomes self-destructive. It naturally follows that since these things are true, man will reach a new period in his evolution when he comes to realize the intimate relationship which he has with the Divine Presence; the dynamic power he may exercise over the Universal Law which has no choice other than to obey the will of the Spirit.

If one's whole thought is based on love, wisdom, unity, and goodness, there can be no danger in one's use of the Law. All misuse of the Law automatically punishes until the lesson of compensation is learned. Troward tells us . . .*the very Law which places creative power at our disposal necessarily provides punishment for Its misuse and reward for its right employment*. But since the true Law is one of liberty and since spiritually we are all perfect, even as the *Father in heaven (that is within us) is perfect*, then by dwelling upon this Divine Perfection and consciously seeking to breathe Its nature into our acts we shall not only be exercising freedom, but we shall be doing it in such a way that the fruits of our actions must result in good to ourselves and to others.

The fruit of action is a result of the karmic Law of Cause and Effect operating upon our ideas, thoughts, and desires. *An act either mental, verbal, or corporeal, bears good or evil fruit. . .*(Laws of Manu). Phillips Brooks tells us, *There is a mighty image of God standing in the center of all things and all things have to touch Him. And as all things touch Him, according to their characters, He becomes to them blessing or curse*. The fruits of our action are an objective manifestation of our internal states of consciousness. If we wish these fruits to be harmonious, always happy, never destructive, and ever increasing, we must remember with Jesus that as we are in God, so God is in us and we in each other: *That they all may be one; as thou, Father, art in me, and I in thee, that they also may be one in us . . .*

Troward truthfully states, *We can never get beyond the Law that the effect must be of the same nature as the cause*. Jesus laid great stress on the necessity of arriving at the consciousness that the Kingdom of Heaven is at hand.

The Law that sets us free, the true Law of Liberty, consists in being true to the wholeness of our real nature, which nature is God. Since God is All-in-All, over all, and through all, and since the Law is limitless, it follows that each one of us reproduces the Creative Liberty at the level of our present capacity to understand Reality. Emerson tells us that imitation is suicide, but that if each man will listen greatly to himself he shall uncover within himself that fountain of life to which Jesus referred when he said, *But whosoever drinketh of the water that I shall give him shall never thirst.*

The way to freedom is through an understanding that the Universal manifests Itself directly through us in a unique way. Complying with the nature of the Divine Being we automatically use the Law constructively; there can be no limit to Its use since we are dealing with Infinity. It is logical to inquire what method will best demonstrate this liberty which we feel is inherent at the very center of our own being. The answer is simple. If we wish greater freedom and if we are certain that we have already complied with wisdom, love, truth, then we must begin to think about greater freedom. But in order to think about greater freedom we must begin to cast out all thoughts of doubt or fear. As perfect love casts out fear, so mental identification with success casts out failure. This law we did not create, but as individuals are compelled to use.

If we would enjoy greater friendship we must recognize the One Infinite Being in all persons; the God in us meets the God in them and flows into Itself without effort. This is not a process of influencing people. Instead of being hypnotic it has the reverse effect. Truth tends to dehypnotize, to unmesmerize, to awaken rather than to anesthetize. Thus we are told to awake from our sleep that Christ may give us light. The process of awakening to friendship is opposite to the concept of influencing people.

There is but One Person, which is God; each personifies this One, and wherever we recognize this, the fruits of our recognition must ripen in the garden of our experience. Life is a mirror reflecting back to us the fruits of our action, even as we reflect the Divine Glory.

It would be untrue to say that a statement of a principle is equal to the use of it. Perhaps this is one of the places where we most completely fail to demonstrate spiritual power. Strange as it may seem, we do not make this mistake in using other laws in nature. We know that it is not enough to affirm that electricity is. This is a statement of our conviction; it is also a statement of truth. We cause electricity to appear in one place as a light, in another as heat, and in another as motive power. The Creative Principle of Mind must be used like other laws in nature if we would have a practical key to the Principle of Freedom. The saying that *Nature unaided fails,* attributed to Hermes, is a veiled statement of the principle that the laws of nature must become individualized, consciously used, if we are to derive a specialized benefit from them. And so it is with the laws of mind.

This is the purpose of mental and spiritual treatment—that the mind shall become aware of the gifts of the Spirit, shall accept them and specialize them in the experience of the individual life. The good that we desire we must take. The definite promises which we hope to see fulfilled in our lives must be accepted, and since we cannot accept what we reject or what we refuse to believe in, we must first come to believe and follow such belief with definite, concrete acceptance.

Jesus frequently asked people if they believed he could heal them, and if they answered in the affirmative he would reply, "According to your faith be it unto you." Do we really believe there is a Creative Power which can do it unto us? Has longing passed from the period of daydreaming into one of unqualified acceptance and faith? These are questions we must ask of the mind, of the imagination, and of the intellect. Is it possible for us to look away from the appearance to the Reality; to judge not according to the condition but to judge from the standpoint that new appearances can take the place of old ones? Have we the insight and the conviction to lay our yesterdays upon the altar of a faith which is steadfast and unwavering, and turning from despair look upon the face of hope whose eyes see not the past blurred with tears, but a future bright with promise?

Specializing the Mental Law of Cause and Effect

You are already familiar with the Mental Law of Cause and Effect, with the idea that Mind in Action is Law, and with the Principle upon which all mental practice is based; that we are surrounded by a Universal Creative Mind which receives the impress of our thought and acts upon it. This Mind is entirely impersonal, neutral, and plastic. It is subjective or subconscious to our thought, which means that It must receive the impress of our thought as we think it, and must, because of Its nature, tend to create after the pattern of that thought.

This Universal Subjectivity, once it is set in motion, continues to work until the tendency set in motion in It is neutralized. But we cannot neutralize the Law Itself. Laws are eternal, changeless, and immutable. We cannot neutralize the Law but we can reverse our position in It. We cannot change Its nature but we can specialize that nature.

Law as specialized by personality is represented by the two pillars that stood in front of the Temple of Solomon—Jachin and Boaz, one meaning the Law, the impersonal creative medium, and the other the Word, or personal element. Here we have personality and law combined, and it is through these two pillars that we must enter the Temple, which symbolizes the nature of Reality and our innermost life.

The Word of personality and the Law of impersonality, symbolized by these two pillars, is the great Mental Law of Cause and Effect which Emerson called the High Chancellor of God, and to which the Bible refers when it says, *Whatsoever a man soweth, that shall he also reap*.

We should not forget that this Law is a doer and not a knower. It has no choice of Its own, nor does It have any desire of Its own. It is a blind, intelligent force, creative but not directive. The personality dominates the Law. Both Law and personality are necessary to the universe of self-expression. The understanding of how best to balance these two, the personal and the impersonal elements, is what constitutes a correct knowledge of our relationship to the invisible. From our use of this relationship we reap either bondage or freedom.

We should not confuse the Law as an Impersonal Force, with God the Universal Spirit. God is Infinite Person individualized in each one of us, making our nature like God's and giving us the same dominion in our field of action that the Universal Spirit has in Its field.

The Law is the servant of the spirit of man even as It is the servant of the Spirit of God, and our word moves upon the face of the deep just as truly as the originating Creative Word moved. Refer again to the first chapter of this series, *In the Beginning God*, and refresh your memory with the idea that *in the beginning* means the eternal process of creation.

We are always specializing this Creative Law, but generally in ignorance. Ignorance of the Law excuses no one from Its effects, for that which we call good or evil, abundance or lack, are but two ways that one fundamental Principle operates. It neither lacks nor is It limited, nor can we say that It is less in a small form or greater in a large form, since our idea of size is entirely relative.

For example, if the physical plane upon which we are living were suddenly reduced to a mile in diameter, and everything else were reduced correspondingly, we should never realize that anything had happened. If, on the other hand, it suddenly expanded to an infinite diameter, and everything else expanded correspondingly, we should never know that this had happened.

But we know big and little, or think we do. Hence we set the Law in motion for the creation of what we conceive, and we say that bigness expands our experience and littleness contracts it. Therefore the experience is contracted or expanded according to our concept. This is the personal element working upon the impersonal, and it is just this possibility which guarantees our freedom.

When we know how this Law works and how to use It we can specialize It for a new purpose. We can use the power which has bound us to create the freedom we desire. We wish joy instead of tears, gladness instead of sorrow, peace instead of disturbance, success instead of failure, life instead of death. We cannot change the nature of the Law, nor can we change the nature of our being, but we can think and act differently, and the Law, being subjective to our thought, must change Its tendency toward us. In no way do we neutralize the Law of Cause and Effect; we merely use It in a different way.

The Law having no purpose of Its own, having no intention of Its own about us, is compelled to take the color of our dominant thought and create after that pattern. We, being persons, can change our thought and thereby remold our conditions. Indeed this is the great realization of freedom and to understand this is to understand how we may become released from bondage. Not to understand this compels us to remain in bondage until enlightenment comes.

The Law, undirected, does nothing. It is merely a natural energy in a spiritual world or a spiritual energy in a natural world. Whichever way we think of It, It is the Law of Cause and Effect and we are using It every moment of our lives. Of course our greatest use of It is through the subjective channels of our thought. Hence these subjective channels must be clarified and reorganized. The unconscious mental reaction must be redirected, for it is this subjective side of the individual which at all times reflects itself into the Universal Creative Law and the Law in Its turn molds the image into form and passes it back to us as an actual everyday experience.

It seems self-evident that the Law knows us as the sum total of what we believe ourselves to be and when we add to this the fact that what we know ourselves to be, or think ourselves to be, is largely subjective or subconscious, we realize that the Law knows each individual from the viewpoint of what the race thought proclaims to be true about all individuals. That is, about each individual as one of a class, plus what the individual has learned to believe about himself.

We should think this over carefully and come to a definite understanding of what it means, for it is of the utmost importance that we come to see that, as individuals, we have not really thought ourselves into limitation. What has happened is that the belief in limitation has operated through us and our *agreement* with this belief has tended to vitalize it.

We must reverse the whole process definitely and deliberately. This is exactly what Jesus meant when he said that it is done unto us *as* we believe. The new patterns of belief must be found in a higher consciousness and a deeper realization of man's position in the creative order as dispenser of the Divine Gifts and as the recipient of the Infinite Will and Willingness.

We need to repudiate the belief that we are bound. We need to know that the Spirit within us is now free, complete, and perfect. There is not a person living who cannot change his thought, at least somewhat. We can all improve and broaden our mental reaction right where we are, and with each new and better mental outlook there will come a corresponding reaction in our objective world.

In actual practice we must be definite. One of the main troubles with us is that we fail to realize that abstractions are not all that are necessary. The study of philosophy, no matter how spiritual it may be, will avail us but little from a practical viewpoint unless we definitely use the knowledge which we have acquired. To understand the working of the Law is knowledge, but to use It constructively is wisdom.

Daily we must consciously reverse our position in the Law knowing that we are no longer subject to the race suggestion of lack, limitation, want, or fear; knowing that the Spirit is with us and for us and operating through us; knowing that all good is ours, and specifically declaring that the particular good we desire is now made manifest.

A person who has everything which he desires in life except friendship should accept the good he already has and add friendship to this good. The individual who may be enjoying all good friendships, but who lacks supply, should accept these friendships and add to his idea of life a belief in the presence of supply. The one who may have friendship and supply but lacks physical well-being, should accept friendship and supply but continue to specialize the Law for physical healing. There is nothing too great and nothing too small; whatever the need is, we should seek to meet it through specializing the Law.

In teaching others to do this for themselves, be careful to explain to them that they should not accept this philosophy as merely a scientific belief or a beautiful system of thought, or as a new attitude toward religion. All of these things it is, but the fact that it is all of these things will never cause it to do anything in particular for anyone. They must use it.

When the pioneer settlers discovered the prairies it would not have been enough for them to have exclaimed, "What fertile soil! What wonderful harvests it will bring forth! How bountiful is nature! How beautiful the scenery! How marvelous is its vastness and how good is God to have led us here!" All such exclamations would have been true, but they would never have produced a harvest.

We have followed the old patterns of thought so long that transformation from the old to the new position is generally rather slow, and the mental ascent into the consciousness of completion seems beset by many obstructions; hence faith and expectancy are necessary, and above all, a great inner flexibility.

If you are teaching these principles you should insist that those to whom they are taught must use them and must never take No for an answer. The Law knows only to agree. It reaffirms our negation and presents us with bondage as easily as with freedom. But is not the knowledge that we can change bondage into freedom one of the greatest joys we can contemplate?

Bibles of the World

Fragments from the spiritual history of the race revealing fundamental UNITY of religious thought and experience

JUDAISM and CHRISTIANITY—Trust in him at all times: ye people, pour out your heart before him: God is a refuge for us.

For I will restore health unto thee, and I will heal thee of thy wounds, saith the Lord.

Acquaint now thyself with him, and be at peace: thereby good shall come unto thee.

TAOISM—In the Way of Heaven, there is no partiality of love; it is always on the side of the good man.

ISLAM—And never, Lord have I prayed to thee with ill success.

Man prayeth for evil as he prayeth for good; for man is hasty.

The Lord of the world, Who hath created me, and guided me, Who giveth me food and drink; and when I am sick, he healeth me.

HINDUISM—They rise upwards who are settled in Harmony.

HELLENISM—The good law of the mighty (One) is the good law.

This, then is truer than all truth, and plainer than what the mind perceives:—that from that Universal God of Universal Nature all other things for evermore have found, and had bestowed on them, the mystery of bringing forth; in which there is innate the sweetest Charity (and) Joy, and Merriment, Longing and Love Divine.

SIKHISM—The One God is known by him whose soul and body are thoroughly imbued with His love.

Let one love the omnipresent God. Then his heart shall be pure.

Meditation

At the center of my being is Peace, the Peace that is felt in the coolness of early evening after men have turned from their labor and the first star shines in the soft light of the sky.

There is a freshness, a vitality, a power underlying this Peace. It broods over the earth quietly, tenderly, as a mother watches over her sleeping child.

In this Peace that holds me so gently I feel strength and protection from fear and anxiety. It is the Peace of God, and within it I feel the Love of a Holy Presence.

As I become more conscious of this Love, all fear slips away as mist fades in the morning sunshine. I am one with deep abiding Peace. I know that all is well.

I permit this Peace to flow through my entire being, through my mind and heart, until every problem is released. The way is made clear before me. It is filled with joy and harmony.

I AM Peace.

I AM Love.

I AM Power.

I AM vitality and strength and all good.

Freedom vs. Bondage
Office of the Dean

My Dear Friend,

We might think it strange if someone were to tell us that everything is ours for the asking or the taking; that even bondage is a certain way we are using freedom. And yet if this were not true we could never be free. This is the meaning of our lesson.

Right here we want to make it clear to you that you must avoid the mistake of saying you are free if you are experiencing bondage. Never say "Peace" when there is no peace. Never say you are well and happy if you feel miserable and lonesome, unless when you make such statements you actually change the wrong conditions. This is what you are learning to do.

In actual practice you deny everything that does not belong and affirm everything that ought to be. If you accept this teaching and do your work according to the instructions you have received, success is bound to follow. We all must awake from the mesmeric sleep into which humanity seems to have fallen, to a realization of the One Power, the One Presence, and the One Law.

Keep up your practice according to the instructions in your first lesson and you will so completely prove this Principle and your ability to use It that there will never again be a question in your mind as to whether you can change bondage into freedom, fear into faith, sorrow into happiness, and lack into abundance.

I know that your honest endeavor will bring wonderful results.

Sincerely,
Ernest Holmes

Lesson 10
Freedom or Bondage, p.108 through p.112

Bondage is an experience. It is not a reality of itself any more than the drawing of a small circle on a blackboard denies the possibility of drawing a larger one. Here we approach the problem of the ages: *Why is there any limitation?* Again and again this question will rise in our contemplation of the nature of Reality and of human experience. Until we realize that we have created our own bondage we shall not understand how we can be made free.

Bondage of itself is neither person, place, nor thing. It is not an entity. It is neither past, present, nor future. As an absolute reality it has no existence. It is, however, a human experience and an individual experience. We would not say to a person who is sick, "Rest assured, nothing ails you," or to one who is poor, "Be assured that you are affluent." How can we say to a man who is walking on crutches, "Walk without them," unless first we have gained the spiritual ability to free him from his bondage? To do so would be sheer nonsense. Jesus was right when he said, . . . *first cast out the beam out of thine own eye; and then shalt thou see clearly to cast out the mote out of thy brother's eye*.

Our Glossary defines *Reality* as *the truth about anything* (page 624), and bondage is the result of an ignorance of Reality. Bondage is the exact opposite of Reality. If we consider that we are living in a spiritual universe governed by mental laws, the way to free ourselves from bondage must be to recognize Reality.

Carefully consider the definition of *Realization* on page 625 in the Glossary. This realization is of our oneness with God. It is a sense that for every apparent wrong there is an opposite right. Moreover, the act of realization proves that wherever good is recognized it instantly appears, for good is permanent while evil is temporary. *Truth crushed to earth shall rise again*. But since we comprehend the Infinite only to the degree that It expresses through us, we pass from one degree of bondage to a lesser degree as our sense of Reality increases.

Oliver Wendell Holmes says in *The Chambered Nautilus, Let each new temple, nobler than the last, Shut thee from Heaven with a dome more vast, Till thou at length art free*. This means that one experience gives birth to another. What is good today, being the best we understand, will become better tomorrow as our understanding evolves. Thus *Being*, which you will find defined on page 577, passes into Becoming; the essence of life takes new form as our realization grows.

In spiritual mind healing this is exactly what you try to do. You try to sense that your patient is a manifestation of spiritual ideas; that the very center of these ideas is the Real Man, the Christ of perfection, the Immanuel or God-with-us. Realizing that every manifestation of discord has a counterpart in mind, through the right action of your thought you seek to destroy the belief in this false counterpart, knowing that as the new concept takes form it will objectify in more harmonious conditions. This is the very essence of spiritual mind healing; this is what meditations are for. This is *why* you give treatments, so that you may understand and comprehend more, that you may realize more.

Turn to page 542, the Meditation called *Thy Strength is Sufficient*. Say this over and over to yourself. Try to realize its meaning. See if you do not gradually sense a new realization of the Divine Presence, and out of the Spiritual Power generated in this realization speak your word directly for the physical healing of someone whom you seek to help or for some condition which you wish to benefit. Have implicit trust and confidence in the power of your word and you will be certain to be rewarded.

If you wish to free yourself from fear turn to the Meditation on page 528, *As Love Enters, Fear Departs*. Let the mind dwell on the idea of love and protection until finally the images of fear are dissipated. Speak your word directly, believing. When you are giving treatments you must believe that what you say is true. You must have no doubt about the truth of your statements.

Turn to page 487, *The Great Awakening: Now it is high time to awake out of sleep*. Paul, in his Epistle to the Romans, was inferring that we are asleep to the greater realization. The belief in a life apart from good is a dream. We must arouse from this apathetic state, this mental drowsiness and claim our Divine Birthright to be one of freedom. This is not merely wishing or hoping, or even longing—all of which we have done—this is *knowing*. What is it that we are to know? That there is but One Power and but One Presence, One Perfect Law, One Divine Destiny and as Jesus said, *If ye abide in me, and my words abide in you, ye shall ask what ye will, and it shall be done unto you* (page 481).

When we ask in the name of Reality we are abiding in the Truth, and when we abide in the Truth we have All Power. Truth and Power mean the same thing. To abide in the Truth means to trust, to have faith and confidence, to believe, and whenever any doubt arises, to reaffirm this Divine assurance. We must cancel doubt by denying its existence. From this standpoint a mental denial is a scientific thing. It is a part of correct technique in mental treatment.

Treatment, as defined on page 638, is an art, an act, and a science. It is an art since there is feeling in it. It is an act since it is a moving thing in thought. It is a science since the movement of thought acts as law. Therefore as a practitioner you are an artist, an actor, and a scientist.

Never doubt the power of your own word, for when you abide in the Truth (read definition of *Truth* on page 639), you abide in that which is the Reason, the Cause, and the Power in everything and through everything. It is the Alpha and Omega of every creative series—the cause and effect. To abide in the Truth is to abide in the Spirit.

To turn back again to our illustration (page 481), *true liberty comes only through true harmony; true harmony only through true unity*. Of course we are always unified with good, but this refers to a conscious unity, or a unity of which we may become conscious. This unity always existed, but we must become conscious of it. The Truth never changes, but our idea of It does change.

It will readily be seen that bondage is a way we use freedom. *To assert our individuality is to rise above the law of averages into that more highly specialized use of the Law which brings freedom rather than bondage* (page 417).

Freedom is defined on page 595 as meaning *liberty but not license*; we are free to use the Law but never to abuse It. The abuse of the Law carries its own punishment with it, *for whatsoever a man soweth, that shall he also reap*.

The Law is foolproof. The Universe is foolproof. Sooner or later every man must learn this great lesson of life that while the Universe is for him and never against him, still, as Emerson says, *Nature forevermore screens herself from the profane*. This means that if in our use of the Law there is no element of hurt, then we may use It to the limit.

Freedom and bondage are tied up with our concept of good and evil. We must realize that we are not bound today by any previous mistakes which we have made, for the Universe holds nothing against us. Bondage has no history. The All-Good is ours in such degree as we imbibe the Spirit of the All-Good. In order to free yourself or someone else from the belief in mistakes, turn to page 561 and use the treatment which you will find there.

We must free ourselves from the belief in a past. You will find under the heading, *Divine Forgiveness*, (page 457), the idea of Jesus relative to forgiveness; the blotting out of all previous negations which are to be remembered no more against us forever. A deliberate act of the mind in spiritual treatment is to blot out all morbid reactions to the past and to sever the mental chain of cause and effect which pushes a negative past into our future to be endlessly repeated. What an emancipation when we realize that the Universe holds nothing against us. Forgiveness is both available and eternal, dissipating the feeling of guilt as light dissipates darkness. The light is eternal and available; the darkness is but a condition.

All evil, lack, want, and fear are denials of God as being the Essence of love, beauty and truth. We must decide which God we shall serve, for it is impossible to serve two masters. In other words, whenever in our imagination we attempt to divide the Truth against Itself we shall be creating confusion. We are dealing with the Allness of God. We are dealing with the Truth.

If you have any doubt of your ability to do this, turn to page 401, last paragraph, and again reassure yourself that it is not you but the Spirit within you which does the work. Read also the last paragraph on page 403 where attention is called to the fact that thoughts of lack manifest as limitation, while thoughts of abundance manifest as success and happiness.

Definitely and deliberately, but with flexibility, the will and the imagination should blend with conscious desires, for when this blending takes place we shall have a right combination between that within us which chooses and that within us which is creative. You will find on page 409, second and third paragraphs, a method for doing this. These references should not be read casually. They are concise statements which you must study. You may be certain that we lay no claim to having originated them. They are a result of the thought of the ages. We are inheriting these thoughts from countless thousands of individuals' hopes, aspirations, and realizations. Let us enter into our inheritance with a sense of gratitude and joy.

At the top of page 109 is the statement, *Freedom under compulsion would amount to the worst kind of bondage*. If there had been any way whereby God could have made man free without letting him alone to discover his freedom, then God would have made him free. I think you will realize that this is self-evident, for if man is an individual he must be a free agent; he must be free to express himself individually within the restrictions of the Universal Law of Cause and Effect. *Behold, I stand at the door, and knock*. The Divine Creative Wisdom must await man's recognition of It and his conscious cooperation with It.

Man must free himself through his right use of the Law of Liberty. Always remember that while there is a law of bondage, the real Law is one of liberty. The very power that binds you can free you if you reverse the way of using it. Does not the same wind blow the ship upon the rocks or safely into the harbor? *'Tis the set of the sail and not the gale, that determines the way we go*. Our winds of chance must become winds of certainty. We must know in Whom we have believed. We must have implicit confidence in the Law. We must definitely use It every day.

We are on the way to self-discovery, and our sufferings are the result of a misuse of the Law of Cause and Effect, through which in our ignorance we have brought upon ourselves the very bondage which we experience. In the midst of bondage is the agency of freedom operating in reverse, so to speak. We must shift the mental gear, deliberately take our place at the wheel, and learn to control our own destiny through that God-given Power in all men—the Creative Power of thought, will, imagination, and right action.

As our lesson states, it surely is a great comfort to understand that *human limitation has no existence from the standpoint of Divinity*. To know that even bondage is but a certain way of using the Law, is to discover how to create freedom instead of bondage. It is made out of the same stuff. The very fact that there is lack and want and limitation proves this.

Unless we could experience the result of our thought we should not be free (page 110). We discover that punishment and reward are inevitable results of thinking, and necessary to the immutable working of the Law of Cause and Effect. Read the definition of *Reward* on page 630, and of *Punishment* on page 623. I like this definition: *There is no sin but a mistake and no punishment but a consequence*. We do not say that we never make mistakes. We say that the punishment for those mistakes is not the act of an angry God but is eternal justice asserting itself. That is the meaning of the saying *Vengeance is mine; I will repay, saith the Lord*. Sin is its own punishment while righteousness is its own reward. A more complete justice than this could not be conceived.

Bondage is a misuse of the Law of Freedom. The Law punishes us automatically until through experience we learn what is right and just, and then we are immediately forgiven. The Universe holds nothing against us. How wonderful is this concept and how perfectly it fits our needs!

Read the paragraph, *How God Forgives* (page 431), and you will note that God can forgive us only as we forgive each other and ourselves, for is not self-forgiveness the way through which the Divine Spirit works to cleanse us from our wrongdoing? Love alone forgives and heals, and love is God. The spiritual man needs no healing. *What the healer does is to mentally uncover and reveal the Truth of Being* (page 418, paragraph 3).

Now turn to page 332 under *Individuality* and read through to the last paragraph of the following page. You will learn that it would be impossible for the Divine to give more than It does or to do so in a better way. Everything the Universe has is ours.

We must learn how to receive the Divine Gift, how to convert evil into good, how to change our belief in lack until it becomes a consciousness of abundance, until the human body takes on the warmth and color of our realization, and all evil, lack, and limitation is converted into peace and perfection. This is spiritual healing.

We do not say that man cannot sin; we say that since he is free he can make mistakes, but what a comfort to know that he will not always continue to make them and that today he can awake from his dream.

As stated in the second paragraph of Page 388, *With all these facts confronting us, we should learn to trust life*. The Divine Bounty is ever ours, and the God who cares for the birds who do not *gather into barns*, will likewise care for us through that Law of Liberty which is perfect. On page 432, under the heading, *The Divine Bounty*, you will find a discussion of the complete reliance Jesus placed upon God.

We, too, must have such confidence. We may learn to overcome the misery which we all suffer through the burdens imposed by our yesterdays and the bitter prospects of our tomorrows. Let us consider evil as a mistaken use of the Law of Freedom.

The remaining portion of pages 111 and 112 will be perfectly clear to you. I should like, however, to enlarge a little more on the thought that the conscious mind is the Spiritual Mind, since there cannot be two minds. As an aid to this discussion read again the definitions of *Conscious Mind* and *Consciousness* on page 580; the definition of *Positive and Negative Thought* on page 620; also the last paragraph on page 407 and the second and third paragraphs on page 408.

Man's consciousness of God constitutes his real and immortal self. That which we call our objective mind, since it is the part of our thought which is conscious and the only thing which has self-consciousness, must of necessity be our Spiritual Mind. It could not be otherwise since it is the only phase of thought which possesses freedom. Everything else reacts to it, and the whole Spirit is focused right here. This is the true way to the Absolute, to that Spirit which animates us at all times. When we learn to consciously control our everyday thinking we shall have discovered perpetual freedom and eternal joy.

Summary

Bondage may be an experience but it is not a spiritual reality. We do not deny the experience but we do deny the reality. Reality means the truth about anything.

The greatest reality in our lives is our Oneness with God.

To be conscious of the Divine Presence in and around you generates a spiritual power which you can speak into actual experience through conscious affirmations of the mind. In order to do this effectively you must believe that you can.

You must have confidence in yourself. This confidence you can have because you know that you are dealing with the creative Law of Cause and Effect.

To abide in the Truth means to have continual confidence and faith in yourself and in your own word, which is your treatment, meditation, or affirmative prayer, in a Law that responds to it, and in a Divine Presence that flows through everything.

Treatment is an art, an act, and a science, since it is a combination of feeling, action, and Law.

If we use this Law in the wrong way we suffer, not because the Law imposes suffering upon us but because we impose wrong action on the Law.

No evil can come from a consciousness of good; therefore we need not fear to use the Law provided we are doing so constructively. The past has no reality today. The Universe holds nothing against us. Our tomorrows will be projected by the thoughts we have today.

Questions

Brief answers to these questions should be written out by the student after studying the lesson, and the answers compared with those which will be included in next week's lesson.

1. How does the Science of Mind explain evil, which is the great philosophic problem of the ages?
2. If bondage and sin are the result of ignorance how shall we experience salvation and freedom?
3. Are bondage and evil ever things of themselves?
4. Why should we never say to those who are poor, sick, and unhappy, "Nothing ails you"?
5. What do we mean by a Spiritual Universe governed by mental laws?
6. Why is it that a recognition of good destroys evil?
7. What is meant by the phrase, *Being passing into becoming*, in our individual experience?
8. Name several steps essential in a mental and spiritual treatment as mentioned at the beginning of this lesson.
9. In mental treatment why should we have an attitude of knowing rather than wishing, hoping, or longing?
10. What does it mean to abide in the Truth?
11. How do we cancel the effect of doubt?
12. What do we mean by the law of averages?
13. Is Divine forgivingness a principle in nature?
14. What do we mean when we say that there is a law of bondage?
15. Do we deny that man sins and is punished for his transgressions of the Law of God?
16. Why is it that God can forgive us only as we forgive each other?
17. In summing up the whole problem of evil and limitation of any nature, what might one state?

Answers to Questions on Lesson 9

1. By *Unity* we mean that God, Universal Mind, Spirit, is one undivided Life Principle consisting of Infinite Person and Infinite Law and Order. By *multiplicity* we mean that this one Life Principle creates innumerable forms.
2. The determining factor in shaping creations is the Self-contemplation of Spirit or thought, idea, will, imagination, and desire, all of which are attributes of the Creative Mind.
3. Creation as the play of Life upon Itself means that the Creative Spirit thinks within Itself and produces form out of Itself. Creation is thought in form.
4. By self-inflicted negative conditions we mean that somewhere—through ignorance—our own thought or the race thought has created the limited conditions which surround us.
5. Evil is not an entity, not a thing of itself, but only a temporary negative experience.
6. Without self-choice man would be a mechanism, an automaton; he would not be an individual entity.

7. By compulsory process of evolution we mean that when man has evolved to a place of self-choice, his future evolution must be through conscious cooperation with the Spirit and the laws of nature.

8. Bondage and freedom are two ways of using one Power.

9. Our use of the Creative Principle is limited only by our imperfect cooperation with the Spirit, and our ignorance of the Law. Thus ignorance is the only limitation.

10. Inductive research means going from effect back to the nature of cause.

11. One Substance, One Law, and One Person means that Substance is the invisible stuff from which all creation is made; that the Law of Cause and Effect governs all creation; and that Spirit is Infinite Person, everywhere present, within, around, and through us.

12. When we use the expression, *We should never separate Life from living*, we mean that the Spirit is expressed in us, through us, and around us in our everyday life. Thus every legitimate purpose and every constructive act is God working through us.

13. *God Immanent* means God within us and within all creation. *God Transcendent* means God above, around, and greater than creation.

14. Man's mind is the place where he uses the Mind of God

15. The Mind of God was the power that Jesus used.

16. We do use the power that Jesus used because every time we think, we use the Mind of God.

17. Because the Law is a doer and not a knower, and because It is subject to our thought, It must always say "I will."

18. God in the Infinite World means Spirit or Intelligence as the Cause of all there is. Man in the finite world means this same Spirit individualized in man.

19. It is impossible to get away from the creative power of our thought since every time we think, we use the Creative Principle of Mind.

20. *The Father who seeth in secret* means that the Spirit is at the center of our own being and that the invisible Law responds to our thought.

The Wisdom of Jesus

Because the Life-Principle is not something separate from ourselves, but is the Supporter of our individuality, therefore, the more we understand and obey its great generic Law, the more fully shall we be able to make any specific applications of it that we like. This quotation from Troward's Chapter X, *The Teaching of Jesus*, reminds us that in dealing with the laws of our own mind we are dealing with a Universal Principle.

When Troward refers to the necessity of obeying the generic Law he means that we must come to understand what the Law is and how It operates through us. The Law of Mind is omnipresent; therefore It is at the center of our own being. Because of this each one individualizes It.

We are using this Law at all times and under all circumstances but mostly in ignorance of Its true nature. If we would bring the Law under conscious control and use It in such a way as to be certain that good alone can result, we must understand both the mechanics of the Law and the Spirit back of It. This means that we must bring our mechanical use of the Law under the control of Spiritual wisdom, for knowledge without wisdom might be dangerous.

Troward says, *We cannot impress upon ourselves too strongly the impossibility of living by two contradictory principles at the same time.* He continues, *But for the very same reason we cannot trifle with the Great Mind by trying to impress one character upon It by our thought, while we are impressing another upon ourselves by our actions.* This is equal to saying that we cannot walk two ways at once. We cannot make a red house green by painting it yellow. Lip service alone does not suffice. Inwardly we must become one with the words which we speak if these words are to have power. Only when wisdom speaks through knowledge can knowledge produce permanent freedom.

The true Law of our being is one of liberty but not one of license. Troward tells us that Jesus washed his disciples' feet to illustrate that we must first obey the laws of nature if we expect them to obey us. Obedience is a positive word in the Scriptures, signifying that the Law of Life becomes our servant when we unify with Divine Love and Wisdom. The Law of Itself is merely a blind force. It is a law of cause and effect which should always be used from the highest motivation. In *Fragments of a Faith Forgotten* we find this remarkable paragraph: *Grieve not the Holy Spirit which is in you, and put not out the Light which hath shone forth in you. As ye see yourselves in water or mirror, so see ye Me in yourselves.* In Romans we find this corresponding paragraph: *Love worketh no ill to his neighbor: therefore love is the fulfilling of the law.* And in I Corinthians this most famous passage: *Though I speak with the tongues of men and of angels, and have not charity, I am become as sounding brass, or a tinkling cymbal.*

Obedience to the Divine Nature is an essential part of the teachings of scriptures of all ages. Again and again we are admonished to remain true to this Nature, and repeatedly we are told what the effect of going contrary to this Nature must be. We are told to repent of our mistakes and enter into the salvation and joy of right action. *Repent ye therefore, and be converted, that your sins (mistakes) may be blotted out, when the times of refreshing shall come from the presence of the Lord* (Acts 3:19). Repenting from our sins means no longer continuing in our mistakes.

Since the mind cannot accept that which it rejects, nor believe that in which it has no faith, it follows that regardless of outward protestations, if our inward feelings contradict what we say, we are a house divided against itself. Jesus made it plain that there is no virtue in laying our gift upon the altar if we still have hatred in our hearts. Lowell said, *The gift without the giver is bare.* But obedience to the Divine Will is, as Troward suggests, not so much a submission to a greater power as it is the acknowledgment of and submission to a higher intelligence.

Troward points out that in the symbolic washing of his disciples' feet, Jesus was seeking, as was his custom, to personify the laws of nature before his followers. He placed himself in the position of a servant rather than a Lord and Master. Lord and Master is symbolic of the higher mind, the developed individuality. From a universal sense it symbolizes the All-Creative Wisdom and the Perfect Law or the Holy Spirit. Servant suggests that which obeys.

When the disciples remonstrated because they thought it sacrilegious to permit Jesus to wash their feet, he compelled them to submit, thus showing that nature's laws obey us when we first obey them. Swedenborg said, *To wash the feet is to purify the natural man.* Hence this becomes a symbol of the inner cleansing, since feet stand for the activity of will exercised on the lower plane. In Psalms we find this passage: *I thought on my ways, and turned my feet unto thy testimonies.* And in John*: Jesus saith to him, He that is washed needeth not save to wash his feet, but is clean every whit.* Here we may assume that feet correspond to the fundamental principles of our being, the foundation upon which our understanding is reared, the foundation of our mental habitation. Therefore the purification of this foundation makes the washing complete. Perhaps there was no more meaningful symbol used by Jesus than that of washing his disciples' feet, since it explains our whole relationship not only to the Infinite Mind but also to the immutable Law of Cause and Effect.

Troward makes it plain that Jesus was teaching a system of thought, a way of life, rather than a theological code or a code of speculative ethics. He states that the basis of the whole philosophy of Jesus was an understanding of the unity of God with man, and the absolute freedom of the individual life. Jesus testified that he came to bear witness to the Truth and that the knowledge of this Truth which he taught would make man free from sin and death; that is, would free him from the error of his ways and finally deliver him to endless bliss.

Troward points out that . . . *the perfect liberty of the individual must be in accordance with the will of God.* Let us not misunderstand his conception of the Will of God. When he uses this expression he means the Nature of the Divine Being. For example, if the Nature of God is happiness, how could Spirit decree or have any will toward anything other than happiness? Since the Nature of God is one of unity, we could not expect to use this Nature as a power to make us happy while we seek to make others unhappy.

The wisdom of Jesus clearly perceived this great principle. Therefore in his parable of the man who asked his Lord to forgive him while at the same time exacting a debt from someone else, Jesus asked in substance: "Does such a procedure make sense, or is it not a contradiction of Reality Itself?" This shows us that if we would be forgiven we must first forgive.

Troward points out that the wisdom of Jesus could not lead his followers into a rebellion against the Divine Authority. Rather it leads into the freedom of this authority through a knowledge of the Truth which is Love, Union, Cooperation, and Kindness, all of which signify spiritual wholeness. In speaking of the unity of God and man Troward says, *If we hold fast to the initial teaching of Genesis, that the Divine Principle makes things by itself becoming them, then it follows that when it becomes the individual man, it cannot have any other than its own natural movement in him. . .* The marvelous conception contained in this thought is the progressive and eternal expansion which it implies.

The wisdom of Jesus teaches that we are made out of God. Our being arises out of the necessity of the Spirit becoming expressed through us. There is no limit to the possibility of our expansion. But before the Divine Giving can be complete, there must be a receptivity in some degree equal to the giving. This closely follows another thought of Troward, running through all of his writings, to the effect that the Spirit can give us only what we take. Since our taking is a mental and spiritual act, the Divine becomes manifest in and through us in mathematical degree as we first embody Its nature. This is the very essence of spiritual wisdom, the essence of Reality Itself, and holds forth a promise so bright with hope that even our greatest flight of imagination can but dimly perceive its meaning. This is why the Apostle wrote, *For now we see through a glass, darkly. . .*

The significance of the wisdom of Jesus lies, as Troward suggests, in its utmost simplicity and in its implication that there is a Truth, which known and complied with, can provide us with the freedom we so earnestly desire. If we view the teaching of Jesus, together with his acts, as being representative of the true relationship between our innermost nature and the Divine, we shall see that his whole life was designed to reveal God to man; and in so doing to reveal man to himself.

It is interesting that at the very climax of his life, when he was about to withdraw from this plane, Jesus told his followers that the Spirit of Truth would make plain to them the meaning of everything he had said and done. Jesus taught a wisdom and a principle for practice which, before it can be understood and utilized, must become embodied. He plainly told his followers that if they would know of his teaching, they must do it.

There is an inner meaning to everything, as Troward suggests, and the inner meaning of the teaching of Jesus is the revelation of the Self to the Self. In the story of the prodigal Son we are taught the complete freedom of man, the Divine Individuality forever incarnated within us. This freedom is so great that it may even cause a temporary bondage. In spite of this experience, *our souls*, to quote Wordsworth, *have sight of that immortal sea which brought us hither*. Hence the Prodigal Son comes to himself, a spiritual intuition awakens him, and he returns to his Father's house. The Father represents the All-Creative Wisdom which turns to the son as the son turns to It. This, Troward has called the reciprocal action between the Universal and the individual; the laws of nature obey us when we understand them and live in compliance with them.

If sin (mistake) and punishment (consequence) are representative of an experience built upon a concept of disunion with good, then salvation, knowing the Truth and complying with It, must automatically produce the reward (the fruit of right action). Since man is an individual he is permitted to pluck the fruit of experience from the Tree of Life, but he must suffer the consequences (the fruits of his action), the Karmic Law, or the Law of Cause and Effect.

Troward suggests that the Prodigal's younger brother equally erred in not realizing that he was living in the Father's house; that he was one with the All-Creative Wisdom. The story of the prodigal Son, perhaps more than any other spiritual symbolism, has made a strong appeal to the imagination because it so perfectly describes what each man feels that he has been, is, or might become. Troward tells us that the only restriction imposed upon us is that of using our powers in a destructive manner. This is automatically stopped because it is a denial of the unity of Spirit. When we take the Law of Love as a foundation for our actions we shall always be safe. . . .*the Law of Power is one with the Law of Love*. Robert Browning arrives at the same conclusion when he says, . . .*all's love, yet all's law*. These are the two laws which must become synchronized if we are to arrive at a true conception of the wisdom of Jesus. There is no possible constriction or bondage in this conception, for it leaves ample room for the only freedom which is worth having: freedom under law, sustained by reason and guided by love.

Troward tells us *The Spirit of Truth will guide us into all Truth, and the possession of all Truth must carry the possession of all Power along with it*. It would be absurd to suppose that the Creative Spirit would or could desire anything for us other than the utmost self-expression, since our self-expression is the Spirit-Itself expressing through us. Therefore it is written that *God increases with the increase of man*.

The idea that we *cannot bear fruit except we abide in the vine* is one of conscious unity even while we are living in this world. Therefore not only is the Kingdom of God within us, but the day of salvation is at hand. If, as Troward suggests, we realize that our Liberty resides in the creative power of our thought, then by accepting the Divine Ideal as our own we provide the conditions under which the Undifferentiated Universal Subconscious Mind becomes able to differentiate Itself.

Perhaps the most meaningful paragraph in his entire chapter devoted to the teaching of Jesus, is the one where Troward suggests that in each one of us the Universal Mind attains an individualization capable of consciously recognizing itself, and to attain this is the aim of evolution. Perhaps this is what Jesus meant when he said, *The Father worketh hitherto, and I work*.

Just what do these two ideas really mean? Surely not some mystery which it would be impossible to understand, but rather the very essence of simplicity itself, so obvious that we have overlooked it. The life of man is the Being of God expressing Itself in, as, and through man. The Truth is One, and the essence of Power is One, and the two are One. Because we are ignorant of this fact, and because we believe that we are separated from good, the very Creative Power, which rightly understood would produce good, creates confusion.

Where, then, is the answer to our problem? And what would be the greatest lesson we could learn from the wisdom of Jesus, other than a true understanding of his saying, *I and my Father are one*? One in essence, One in spirit, One in law and order, One in power and manifestation. The distinction between the New Thought and the New Order which it must finally bring into the world, and the old order of thought, lies in our simple acceptance of the teaching of Jesus, not as something that was, but as something that is.

The so-called miracles of Jesus were logical outcomes of his spiritual wisdom. They were not miracles but mathematical manifestations of the creative power of a man's thought. He had penetrated the confusion and obscurity of disunion and discovered the *adequate cause* to which Emerson referred.

He never could have made this discovery unless he had first conceived of the Self of Jesus as One with the Self of God. It was from this Divine Center, this exalted realization that he spoke as never man spake before. His life, teachings, and acts remain clouded in mystery until they find a corresponding echo in our own consciousness—*This is my beloved son in whom I am well pleased.*

Substance and Supply or the Law of Opulence

Naturally we all want what we want when we want it. One of the many criticisms made of the New Thought has been that it is materialistic, since those interested are striving to better themselves materially. This criticism is based on a most materialistic foundation, since it divides Substance from supply, God from man, and Life from living. It makes the Kingdom of Heaven a far-off Divine event, and separates earth from the Eternal Glory. It is just the opposite of the simple but direct statement of Jesus when he said, *What things soever ye desire*, and, *The kingdom of heaven is at hand*.

The idea that it is wrong for man to pray for or treat to get what we call material good is based on the belief that reality and actuality are separated by a gulf which can be bridged only through individual suffering, impoverishment, and misery; that man may be redeemed from all this misery in some uncertain future, but not here and now. Yet Jesus stood in the midst of the *here and now* and proclaimed that the Kingdom of Heaven is within and at hand.

We find, then, that the teaching of Jesus is quite at variance with the idea that it is wrong to ask for what we desire, for did he not say, *What things soever ye desire when ye pray, believe that ye receive them, and ye shall have them* (Mark 11:24). He was announcing a principle, and all principles are universal, changeless, and ever present. All universal principles are available to those who understand them, and they immediately respond to anyone who subjects himself to the way in which they work. For instance, water will reach its own level by its own weight—water will flow down hill. We obey this principle. We use it. We apply it, but we cannot go contrary to that principle and compel water to flow up hill.

It is the same with electricity. The electrician can do anything he wishes to with his principle, provided he realizes that it flows from a higher to a lower potential, but he cannot make it act contrary to its own nature. So Jesus was proclaiming the nature of a certain principle, and teaching how to use it.

Jesus announced the principle of Substance and Supply or the Law of Opulence. He clearly taught that it is right for us to have what we want, provided we subject our desires to the Divine Will and the Divine Necessity. Just what do we mean by Divine Will and Divine Necessity? Divine Will means the nature of God or Spirit, and Divine Necessity means the Law of Cause and Effect.

Jesus announced that when our will complies with the Infinite Harmony, the Law of Cause and Effect has no choice other than to obey our will. We have elsewhere discussed the idea that the Divine Will is toward Life, since being the very Principle of Life It cannot contradict Itself; It must be toward Life. It is toward givingness, since in giving It expresses Itself. Therefore we know that as far as the Divine is concerned, it is always Its Will that we be self-expressed. For God is expressed through the expression of man.

There cannot be the slightest question but that the Divine Will is toward giving us what we want in the way in which we want it, provided we first have complied with the Divine Will which is harmony, peace, love, goodness, truth, and beauty. If we have complied with the Divine Will, the Law of Cause and Effect, which has no purpose of Its own to execute but is a blind but intelligent force, must bring the pattern of our desire to us.

Jesus stated this proposition in its most simple terms when he said, *Seek ye first the kingdom of God, and his righteousness and all these things shall be added unto you*. He was describing the necessity of our union with the Divine Will, to which all else is added, and the *all else* he included in *what things soever ye desire*. Whether these things be automobiles, undershirts, or sacks of beans makes no difference. Included within the *what things soever* must be all things, past, present, and future. Thus Jesus tells us to comply with the Divine Will.

Next he lays down the way in which the Law will answer us. This is the Divine Necessity, the Law of Cause and Effect. He said, . . . *believe that ye receive them, and ye shall have them*, and again, *For whosoever hath, to him shall be given*. Here he is stating the Law of Cause and Effect as It operates through human consciousness. In no place did this august teacher, this remarkable genius, deny man the right to possess and use the entire gift of God, wholeness of life and its manifestation.

When anyone tells us that it is wrong to use spiritual methods for promoting material well-being, we need not be misled. Such a philosophy contradicts the entire evolution of science, the inspiration of revelation, of Divine insight, and the unfoldment of human personality. It is a philosophy of materialism based upon the superstition that there is God and something else. We do not have to enter into theoretical discussions with anyone, but if we are wise we will remove all barriers from our imagination and come to the Spirit of Truth with a childlike mind, expecting to receive good.

Let us approach this idea of substance and supply and the Law of Opulence with a firm conviction that the Eternal is forever saying to the temporal, that the Father is forever proclaiming to the son: *All that I have is thine.*

Even though manna falls from heaven, we must accept it. The manna is substance, and our receptivity to it is our supply. The Law of Opulence is in us—an ever increasing mental equivalent of the good which we desire. The Law of Mental Equivalents is discussed in the main body of these lessons. It is that Law which says that we can possess any objective thing, provided we first have a subjective mental image of it, and provided that this subjective mental image is a real embodiment within our thought.

From what we know about any law in nature, it is safe to say that the more broadly we generalize a principle, the more completely shall we be able to specialize such a principle. This means that the more we know about the nature of the principle and the way it works, the more widely shall we be able to use it.

Jesus proclaimed that within the Kingdom of God is contained all gifts. In other words, he generalized the principle which is to be specialized. He announced that the right idea of substance may be applied to everyday needs. So he found money in the fish's mouth, fed the five thousand, brought the boat immediately to the shore, and did many other things which people looked upon as miracles, or Divine interference with universal law, but which Jesus understood to be natural and normal.

It was just as natural for Jesus to turn water into wine as it would be for us to draw a glass of water from the tap. He did not feel that he was concentrating any power or coercing any Divine favors. He did not even petition God; he understood the Law of Cause and Effect. He knew that substance takes form through faith, is shaped by conviction, and projected upon the screen of human experience through the mold of mental equivalents.

We should throw away all doubt, fear, and despair, and enter joyously into our inheritance. But the very Law which we are using should teach us that we shall arrive at the consummation of our desire only by starting from where we are. We are told to despise not the day of small beginnings. Each one must start with the mental equivalent he has today, and by enlarging upon it increase his capacity to receive.

In this connection we must remember that the Law of Cause and Effect, the Universal Subjectivity, has no intention or purpose of Its own relative to any individual. We make up Its mind for It. As far as we are concerned It has no thought for us other than the thought we ourselves entertain about life. It does not know that a million dollars is more money than ten dollars. It does not know that an ocean is larger than a fish pond; that a mountain is more than three feet high. And yet It creates form through idea, for as we have elsewhere stated, there is no big or little in the Law.

This is the crux of the whole matter—not two powers, but ONE. What we need to change is not the Law, but our use of It. We have no power of limitation to contend against, no evil to fight, no hell to cool off. How wonderful! How fortunate! And what a happy outlook! If we can become more in our inner consciousness we shall have more in our external environment.

The Law having no mind of Its own relative to us, and being compelled by Its very nature to follow the patterns of our thought, is and must remain our obedient servant. But we have affirmed a negation; have declared that there is not good enough to go around. Hence we lack the experience of that good which we fail to perceive.

We must not only know that there is good enough to go around but we must specifically announce this good. It stands to reason that if the Law knows about us only what we know about ourselves, and that if what we hold to be true about Life Itself furnishes us with our mental patterns, then the Law knows about us only what we believe about Life. Therefore the very belief in the reality of evil creates the evil believed in. Or as Jesus said, *All they that take the sword shall perish with the sword.* The belief that there is not enough good to go around makes it difficult, if not impossible, for good to be experienced by the one who entertains such a belief.

We must reverse all these beliefs and accept the simple proposition that God is Good, for this is fundamental to a correct idea of substance and supply and the operation of the Law of Opulence. God is

Good. This Good is ours now. This should be our permanent and increasing expectancy. We should expect so much Good that we should conceive of it as being more than we even have time to enjoy. We should feel the presence of this Good and appreciate its meaning and give thanks for its manifestation. There should be the combination of gratitude, expectancy, and joy. There should be an enthusiastic recognition that we are in partnership with the Divine and that God and Company cannot fail.

When it comes to actual and specific practice we should definitely know that the particular thing we desire, we already have. In this way we form a mold in our thought and a definite one around which the Creative Energy of Mind may play. This is our bowl of acceptance, catching, as it were, from the horn of plenty that which we are able to receive.

This Law of Mental Equivalents should never be overlooked, for It is the Law which decides how much of this infinite thing we are to experience. We cannot experience more than we can accept, but we can expect more than we have been experiencing. If we are willing to start from where we are today, creating a little bigger, broader, and better mental equivalent than we had yesterday, we shall progressively advance.

Since we are dealing with an Infinite Principle, no possible limitation can be placed upon our use of It, just as there is no number we can conceive of which cannot have a like amount added to it, or which cannot be multiplied by itself. And just as there is no place where this sequence of numbers can stop, there is no place where infinite possibilities can cease to unfold. The only place where they appear to cease unfolding is where our expectancy and understanding inhibit their action through us, for the operation of the Law is always mathematically correct. The Law of Cause and Effect having no mind of Its own as far as we are concerned, must follow the patterns of our individual thought.

In actual practice we make definite statements, as we have illustrated in the main body of these lessons. If you want a home, treat for a home. If you want an automobile, treat definitely for an automobile, and if you want a certain sum of money treat definitely for that sum of money. There is nothing materialistic about this since all things emanate from pure Spirit and return again to It.

In actual practice, having first complied with the Law and with the Spirit, do not hesitate to work definitely for what you want. Not to do so would be to deny the very Principle which you have affirmed, to inhibit the operation of the very Law which you have come to understand.

Any intelligent perspective of the operation of this Law should cause us to know that when we work, we should work definitely for what we want. There is no other way. The Spirit can give us only what we take, and our taking is mental. How can the mind accept what it rejects, entertain what it refuses to listen to, possess what it casts out, or have what it will not take? This is not only unthinkable; it is impossible.

Bibles of the World
Fragments from the spiritual history of the race revealing fundamental UNITY of religious thought and experience

JUDAISM and CHRISTIANITY—The Lord is my helper, and I will not fear what man shall do unto me.

Be strong, all ye people of the land, saith the Lord, and work; for I am with you . . . My spirit remaineth among you: fear ye not.

HINDUISM -

> Yea, God, Thou art our Father,
> Thou art a Brother and a Friend.
> So give us strength, that we may live.
> Be with us when we stray afar!
> Be with us when our home is nigh!
> Protect us with Thy help both near and far away!
> Protect us ever with Thy help!

BUDDHISM—So long as the brethren shall be full of faith, modest in heart, afraid of wrong doing, full of learning, strong in energy, active in mind, and full of wisdom—so long may the brethren be expected not to decline, but to prosper.

CONFUCIANISM—If a scholar have not faith how shall he take a firm hold of things?

Heaven makes hard demands on faith.

Hold faithfulness and sincerity as first principles, and be moving continually to what is right. This is the way to exalt one's virtue.

ISLAM—Put thou thy trust in God; for God loveth those who put their trust in Him.

If God help you, none shall overcome you.

In God then let the faithful trust.

Spirit, Soul and Body
Office of the Dean

My Dear Friend,

Our life is God and God is our life. We must build our faith on the supposition that there is no difference between the faith that we have and the Original Word that speaks everything into existence. This means that we must not only have faith in a power greater than we are, but a faith that passes into a simple acceptance that our word is the Presence, the Power, and the Reality of the Living Spirit.

In the life and teaching of Jesus we do not find him depending on a power separate from himself or apart from his own being. Everything he said and did was based on the supposition that the Spirit speaks through man. "I and my Father are one." There is no division, no separation. He carefully led his followers from a position of hope to a place of acceptance. We might say that this passes from faith *in* God to the faith *of* God, a faith in which there are no doubts.

This is the position we are all seeking to arrive at. Our endeavor is to pass from idle wishing and negatively stated affirmations to a place where we stand side by side with the Power greater than we are, as though we were in It and of It. This kind of affirmation admits of no denial.

In doing this you will soon discover that there is a Center in you that already knows. Try to develop the consciousness that flows from this Center, for it is the Secret Place of the Most High within you. You may be sure that all the power there is, is for you. Nothing is against you.

Sincerely,
Ernest Holmes

Lesson 11
pp.113 to 117

One Spirit, One Body, One Mind
The spirit of man is a microcosm within a Macrocosm. If we were to draw a large circle to represent the Life Principle, and within this large circle draw a small one to represent the individual, we should see that the center of the small circle is merely a point in the large one. Put a cross within the small circle and then erase the line around it. The cross is at the center of the large circle. This is what a microcosm within a Macrocosm means.

Man is an individualization of the God-Principle, a center of God-Consciousness in a Unitary Wholeness. Our definition on page 645 says, *When we speak of "the Whole," we are speaking of God*, or the Universal Creative Principle. It is because this Universal Creative Principle is always around us as well as within us that our thought is creative.

Thought is defined on page 638 as *the movement of consciousness*, and on page 641 the word *Universe* is defined as *the entire universe, the Cosmic World*. When we think within our own minds, we think upon or within this entire universe in which One Power alone acts, the Word of God. Our endeavor is not to find access to the Creative Power, but to use the Creative Power in such a way that our thought in It will be one of harmony instead of discord.

If you will turn to page 615 under the heading, *Obstruction to Thought*, and carefully consider the meaning of this explanation, you will see that because Mind is one complete unit, when you think into It in that particular place which you call your mind, you are thinking within the only Mind there is.

As we think into or upon what we call our own mind, we are thinking into and upon the One Mind. The avenue of our own thought is the only approach we have to this Universal Power.

Each one of us is individual and unique, separated at the stem but united at the root. We are all bound together in this common Mind. If you will read the definition at the top of page 599 you will see that we teach that each individual forever maintains his identity in the Perfect Whole.

Turning to page 603 under the definition of *Judgment*, you will note that while the Universe holds nothing against us, we are judged by our own acts and since we cannot act without first thinking, we are really judged by our own thoughts. Punishment and reward are automatic.

Follow this thought by reading the explanation of *Karma*. Note that Karma does not mean fate. It means the Law of Cause and Effect, that Law which judges us with the identical judgment by which we judge ourselves and others; by the thought we entertain about the universe and our relationship to it. Notice particularly the statement that Karma is both individual and collective. We shall discover later in our lessons that world thought or race thought does have a certain influence on each one of us, and will continue to have this influence until we free ourselves from it.

The Kingdom of Heaven, defined on page 604, is the consciousness of God, of harmony within us. This consciousness of God transcends the Karmic Law of previous experiences, and without neutralizing or destroying the Law of Cause and Effect places us in a different relationship to it. We might add that there is no sin but a mistake, and no punishment but an inevitable consequence.

Turn to page 500, *The Law Is No Respecter of Persons*. While God is natural goodness and pure loving kindness, the Law is a cold, hard fact. It is a doer and not a knower. When we are wrong, the Law punishes. This is the Law of Cause and Effect. This is the Karmic Law.

When our thought is contrary to the nature of harmony it hurts us. When it is in accord with harmony it heals us. From this Creative Power of thought we cannot escape, and since we cannot change the nature of the Universal Law we must learn to live in such harmonious accord with It that we shall be happy. Freedom always awaits our recognition of it, and the law which now binds us is the only law which can free us.

Turn to page 494, *Be Strong in the Lord*, and you will note that *if a man can change his inner concept his whole life will be changed*, for *all cause is from within*. Man's mind is the Mind of God working through him.

On page 113, the second paragraph, we learn that man may judge by appearances or his judgment may be based on spiritual intuition. We find that judging from appearances only, inevitably limits our use of the Law to those things which we have previously experienced. It is certain that we must reverse the order of our thought if we expect to reverse some particular effect of its creativeness, for as you will find in the lower paragraph on page 394, *the Law . . . has no intention for us other than the intention that we give It*. This is deeply significant since it means that there is nothing in the Universe against us but ourselves, or as the Scripture says, . . . *they could not enter in because of unbelief* (Hebrews 3:19). *They . . . limited the Holy One of Israel* (Psalm 78:41).

We must learn to rise above appearances if we expect to be successful practitioners, and by successful practitioners in this field we mean those who are proving the supremacy of spiritual thought force over all apparent material resistance.

When the disciples of Jesus failed to heal a certain person they asked him to explain the reason for their failure. He told them that they must have more faith. *Faith* is defined on page 591 as a mental attitude of affirmation which is so complete that it recognizes no opposite suggestion whatsoever.

To have faith in God is a good thing, but to have the faith *of* God would be absolute, and *The Absolute* is defined on page 575 as *that which nothing can limit; that which forever transcends any conceivable limitation*. To have the faith of God is to think God-thoughts, to judge not according to appearances but to judge righteously; therefore when Jesus said that we should have complete faith in God, he meant that our thought is to be so completely affirmative that we never doubt for one moment.

We do not instantly rise full-orbed into this complete faith, but through a study of the Science of Mind, through a correct understanding of its principles, and through a definite knowledge of its technique, we can gradually acquire this desired faith. This is what constitutes a science, and our text says that *science is Spirit inducing Its own laws. Intuition is Spirit knowing Itself* (page 113).

Now by Spirit inducing Its own laws we mean that what the Spirit knows, must be. When the Spirit knows, the very act of Its Self-knowing creates the Law which projects that Self-knowing into actual experience, which is but another way of saying that God makes things out of Himself through the act of Himself becoming the thing which He makes.

Intuition, as explained on page 603, means God in man revealing Reality to him. It is a marvelous thing to realize that when we conceive of a right idea, the Law which is destined to project that idea into manifestation is instantly created or set in motion. It is written that the Law of the Lord is perfect, and this perfect Law reacts to us as a law of reflection, casting back the images of our thoughts molded into form.

At the top of page 416 is the statement that into this world, that is into this Law, we project an idea of ourselves. We may or may not be reflecting freedom and happiness, but whatever we are projecting into this Law must be reflected back to us. Our spirit, then, is some part of the Divine (foot of page 113), and we must never try to separate Life from living for *we enter into the Spirit of Life only as we enter into the spirit of living* (top of page 114).

Next we have the idea that *the Essence of Reality is invisible, but the substance of the invisible is seen and heard* as part of our everyday experience. Faith, belief, and the affirmation of definite, accepted mental statements tend to project this invisible substance into visible supply, activity, objective forms, or personal experiences. We must believe in this invisible world if we wish to demonstrate its dynamic power. We must look into it and perceive, by some mystical interior awareness, that which the physical eye does not see.

Now turn to the Meditation on page 512, *O Soul of Mine, Look Out and See*. Repeat this over and over, permitting the words to sink deep into consciousness. In the last analysis the universe cannot be explained; it must be accepted. We do not see Causation but we do experience its effects. We have every justification for our belief.

Again we find the idea that subconscious does not mean unconscious but merely subjective to the conscious thought. The soul is that part of our being which is subjective. The Creative Medium is a thing we use; it is also subjective to the will that uses it, but the Subjective Mind being the seat of memory must create from the patterns which it has already received, and the new patterns which we give to it. If this were not true we should have no principle to demonstrate. The thing we must understand is that the Principle of Life appears to each one of us in the form of a savior or of a serpent, or in other words, good or evil.

If you will read carefully the section, *The Son of Man*, starting at the bottom of page 472 and continuing through to the top of page 475, you will find an excellent explanation of this principle of dual unity which is within all of us. This is written to explain that the Law is to us what we are to It.

There is a Law which obeys our will even when that will is vicious, but of course the wrong use of this Law punishes us until our very need for salvation wells up within our consciousness by Divine Intuition (the Savior, which is Emmanuel or God within us), and looking on the new image, that is, looking at perfection, we are saved. What are we saved from? Ignorance. Ignorance excuses no one from the Law of Cause and Effect. Only intelligence and enlightenment can free us, and there are no prophets other than the wise.

The Universe of Itself holds nothing against us (page 470), and no matter how many or how serious our mistakes may have been, we are still perfect within. The Universe cannot wish evil to anyone. As the prodigal returned to his Father's house, so must we return to conscious perfection. This return journey should not be morbid. It should be free of all sense of fear; it should be a joyous homecoming.

Read page 405 where it says that *the Spirit has not withheld good from us;* that *the gift of Heaven is forever made*. Certainly we must learn to receive this gift.

Since the soul or the Subjective Mind is the seat of memory, it contains the memory or images of everything that has ever transpired through us or has been handed down to us from the race consciousness. (Read definition of *Race Suggestion* on page 624). It follows, as our text says on page 115, that the sum total of human belief binds us until we lift ourselves above the law of averages. By the law of averages we mean above the race belief in any particular form of limitation. It is another way of judging not according to appearances or according to race belief.

There is at the center of your own soul a place which knows. This has been called the Secret Place of the Most High, the Shadow of the Almighty, the Secret Chamber, the Mystical Man of the Heart, the Christ Consciousness. It matters not what we call this place; it matters only that we enter into it, and having entered in, that we close the door and here make known our request with thanksgiving, knowing that when the door is again opened and we look out upon our objective world we shall see the manifestation of our inner thought and acceptance.

All objective forms are effects created by subjective images. All subjective images are then created by the spiritual Mind, the Mind which is consciously conscious. The second paragraph on page 117 says that *nothing could give form to a formless stuff, which has no mind of its own, but some Intelligence operating* upon this formless stuff, working through the medium of the Word. The Word is the starting point of any and every creation; God's Word in the Cosmic World, our word in our individual world. There is one Law, one Substance, but many words.

Jesus tells us that we are held accountable for every word which we speak (second paragraph on page 449). Of all the deep thinkers he most completely taught the power of the individual word. He placed implicit confidence and trust in the power of his word . There was no doubt in his mind about the Law reacting to it. We must ponder deeply on the meaning of life until we too arrive at such faith. We must know that our word is complete, that it shall not return to us void.

Turn to page 545 and meditate upon *The Word of Power*. Also the following Meditation, *The Unassailable Truth and the Irresistible Word*. Surely there will come to you a deep realization of the power of the Word. You must immediately put this principle into practice. To do is to know. Speak your word with calm faith, with implicit confidence, and believe with enthusiasm. You will find that practice is convincing yourself, for there is nothing else to convince if your mind is in, and one with, the only Mind.

On page 401 it says that the Law of Cause and Effect is not an entity, but is merely the way we use the Law of Life. It is because of this that we are able to change any effect through substituting one thought for another. A treatment is always definite, concise, and conscious. Mental treatment is not daydreaming; it is a series of spiritual statements declaring the presence of the All-Good, the presence of those experiences which are desirable and in harmony with the nature of All-Good. Whether the declaration is made for yourself or for someone else, it is always the Law which executes the will.

It seems strange that the freedom for which we have been searching we already have, but this is the great discovery that each must make for himself—that the very bondage which he suffers is merely the way in which he has been using the law of freedom. No greater unity than this can be conceived, and yet the liberty of this unity has produced all the discord we have ever experienced.

Just what do we mean by the liberty of this unity? We mean the inevitability of the Law of Cause and Effect remaining true to Itself. *Whatsoever a man soweth, that shall he also reap*. Heaven and hell are but two ends of one idea, just as are any other apparent opposites such as bondage and freedom, abundance and poverty. The Kingdom of Heaven is harmony, and if we would make the ascent from hell into heaven we must begin to think harmony, for that upon which we continuously meditate must some day come into our experience.

Summary

Man is a microcosm within a Macrocosm, a small circle within a great circle, or a center in the activity and consciousness of God.

All the Power and all the Presence there is in the Universe is theoretically at the point of the individual circle. Jesus said, *He that hath seen me hath seen the Father*.

Karma is not Kismet; it is not fate, but the Law of Cause and Effect in action.

Since any new action in thought can transcend all old ones, we should never consider past experiences, acts, or thoughts as anything other than effects which can be changed.

We must rise above appearances to the contemplation of complete freedom in God. Time, experience, and self-discipline alone can deliver this greater consciousness to us.

Through intuition we know that there is such an elevation of thought, and through experience we climb the ladder of Life to that place where intuition beckons us.

Strange as it may seem, the freedom we have been looking for, we already possess.

Big and little are one and the same thing.

Spiritual mind treatment is not daydreaming but a series of spiritual statements spoken and believed in.

Questions

Brief answers to these questions should be written out by the student after studying the lesson, and the answers compared with those which will be included in next week's lesson.

1. What is meant by the Macrocosm and the microcosm?
2. What is the practical lesson to be deduced from the theory of the Macrocosm and the microcosm?
3. How do we find access to the Creative Power of Mind?
4. (a) What is our approach to the Universal Power? (b) Is there more than one way of making this approach to the Universal Power?
5. Do we believe that man is an immortal entity?
6. Can we change the Karmic Law or the Law of Cause and Effect?
7. Why does freedom await our recognition?
8. Why must a practitioner rise above appearances?
9. What is the difference in having faith *in* God and having the faith *of* God?
10. What projects the invisible into definite form in our lives?
11. Can the Universe, in the last analysis, be explained?

12. Do the subconscious and the unconscious have the same meaning?

13. From what thought patterns does the subjective mind create?

14. Why does the Law of Life give back to each of us, as experience, what each believes about It?

15. What is the Gift of Heaven?

16. What and where is the Secret Chamber?

17. When will our word be as powerful as was the word of Jesus?

18. How can spiritual liberty and freedom produce personal discord and limitation?

Answers to Questions on Lesson 10

1. The Science of Mind explains the problem of evil by recognizing one Law and one Power to which there is no limitation. Our ignorant use of this Life Principle produces the bondage which we call evil.

2. The salvation and freedom from sin and mistake—which is ignorance producing bondage—is an intelligent and constructive use of the Life Principle.

3. Bondage and evil are not things of themselves; they are different ways of using the One Life Principle.

4. The reason we never say to those who are poor, sick, and unhappy, "Nothing ails you," is that we do not deny human experiences, but we do affirm that they can be changed.

5. By a Spiritual Universe governed by mental Law we mean that Spiritual Consciousness dictates, while mental Law obeys.

6. The reason good destroys evil is that good, being the nature of God or Reality, is permanent, while evil is but a suppositional opposite to good, having only the vitality we give to it.

7. By the phrase, *Being passing into becoming*, in our experience, we mean the Divine Creative Spirit passing through our imagination into creative action.

8. Steps essential in mental and spiritual treatment are to recognize the Christ of Perfection; that right thought neutralizes discord; that love overcomes fear; that a realization of the Divine Presence of Perfection within gives power to your word.

9. We should have an attitude of knowing in mental treatment because knowing implies no doubt.

10. To abide in the Truth means to have complete faith in the One Presence, Law, and Life, which is the Cause of and Power in and through everything.

11. We cancel doubt by denying its existence and affirming its opposite.

12. The law of averages means that we are subject to the race belief until we consciously realize our own freedom.

13. Divine forgivingness is a principle because while we are punished by wrong action, we are automatically released through right action

14. A law of bondage is but our use of the Law of Liberty.

15. We do not deny that man sins and is punished; what we do say is, "There is no sin but a mistake, and no punishment but a consequence."

16. We are forgiven only as we forgive, because the Law must give back to us that which we have set in motion.

17. In summing up the problem of evil and limitation of any nature, one might state that evil is a mistaken use of the Law of Good, and limitation is a mistaken use of the Law of Freedom.

The Great Surrender

Troward tells us that the doctrine of the forgivingness of sins is the mainspring of the Bible. He also reminds us that on several occasions Jesus accompanied his miracles of healing with the words: *Thy sins are forgiven thee*. It is evident that there is some connection between forgiving and healing.

An insight into the Laws of Mind, as understood both in psychology and metaphysics, will be of great service in helping us to understand what the Principle of Forgiveness really is. It is a wiping out of those psychic congestions which fester in the soul, inhibiting the free flow of the Universal Spirit through man's consciousness.

It makes no difference whether we take the position of psychology that conscience is the result of a conflict between desire and forces that inhibit it, or the viewpoint most commonly accepted that there is something within us that instinctively knows right from wrong, since both positions finally arrive at the same conclusion.

In all probability what we call conscience is a combination of these two. It is born both from human experience and from the fundamental nature of the Universe Itself. Psychology has proved that many sincere persons are smitten with a conscience which, when analyzed, has no vitality whatsoever. In such instances this conscience reaction arises from a conflict between the desire to express the self and an opinion that inhibits this desire, which opinion is based upon a false assumption. Consider the position of two men going fishing on Sunday. One has been brought up to believe that Sunday is no different from Monday; the other believes that Sunday is especially set apart as a day for prayer, worship, and meditation. The man who believes that Sunday is no different from Monday would have no conscientious pangs about fishing on Sunday, while the other man probably would.

One could repeat the possible illustrations of this principle in innumerable ways. The point is made when we arrive at the conclusion that everything which operates under the guise of conscience does not necessarily make sense. At the same time if a person has certain fundamental convictions which he violates through his actions, he will become inwardly disturbed. This is why the Apostle said that a man who does not condemn what he permits himself to do is happy. In other words he has a clear conscience.

Certainly if we consider the fundamental nature of the universe to be goodness, truth, unity, and harmony, it would follow that the whole foundation of our mental and spiritual life is rooted in this nature. We can agree with the psychologists that much in the field of conscience is born out of human frustration, without denying that there is a true cosmic basis in the conflict between right and wrong. But in reconciling these apparent opposites we should be careful not to confuse the issue with the belief in any ultimate duality in the universe.

Our conflict between right and wrong is not a conflict between two fundamental principles in the universe, but between two uses of one unified Principle. And what is right and wrong, in so far as we humans can understand it, other than conflict between that which works out constructively and that which is destructive?

Since we are dealing with the Law of Cause and Effect, the mistake punishes itself while the correction of the mistake automatically heals. In no way does this alter the nature of Reality; it merely becomes the play of our own act upon the Law of Cause and Effect. The Universe automatically protects Itself against false aggression.

Most people have a deep, unconscious sense of guilt, even though it seldom rises into conscious perception. It was this sense of guilt which Jesus removed in order to permit a fresh, spontaneous flow of life through the consciousness of those whom he healed. This was both metaphysically true and psychologically sound. For anything that congests the spontaneous flow of life is bound to find a corresponding reaction in our physical bodies and in the body of our affairs.

On some occasions when Jesus forgave people he told them to go and sin no more for fear that a worse condition might come upon them. We cannot assume that one with the wisdom of Jesus would threaten anyone; he was merely stating a law of cause and effect. He tells us that not everyone who says "Lord, Lord," enters into a state of harmony, but only those who truly interpret the Divine Nature.

In Chapters XI and XII, Troward deals exhaustively with the idea of forgivingness as being a necessary part of the Divine Nature. Being a man capable of tremendous abstract conclusions relative to spiritual things, he was too clear a thinker to believe that the act of sin or mistake is a violation against anything other than our own nature. If the violation of that nature produces suffering, the correction of such violation automatically restores harmony, provided we do not continue in the mistake.

By way of illustration we might say that writing out the proposition that two times two equals five is a sin or a mistake; in no way does this violate the principle of mathematics or confuse anything in nature other than those who believe in the mistake. By the same token, changing the proposition to make it consistent with reality and saying that two times two equals four, automatically corrects the mistake. As Isaiah infers, it blots it out so that it is no longer remembered against us; that is, it no longer operates. But just to affirm that two and two equals four while making them appear to equal five would never solve a mathematical problem. The mistake must be understood, corrected, and no longer indulged in. The problem is then healed by no longer remaining a problem. It is solved by knowing the truth.

Since we believe that Jesus healed through the right interpretations of the laws of nature and the relationship between God and man, we may be sure that he never did anything without adequate reason. When he told a certain man that his sins were forgiven him, he backed up this statement which the priests thought blasphemous by commanding the man to get up and walk. Consciously and scientifically he removed the obstruction which impaired the man's progress. In doing this he was consistent with a true understanding not only of the Law of Cause and Effect, but of the nature of the Divine Being.

Troward points out that the life and substance of all things must subsist as images in Divine Mind before they can come into manifestation; that true Man subsists eternally in the Divine Imagination. Like Plato he conceives of archetypal ideas; that is, Universal Natures as preexisting our experience. Hence he tells us that the real nature of sin is turning our mental mirror the wrong way, and so reflecting the limited and negative. Sin means going contrary to the Divine Nature of our own being, temporarily violating its nature. Since we cannot conceive of the Eternal violating Itself, it follows that our own false experiences must finally prove to us, and generally through suffering, that there is something wrong somewhere. This wrong does not exist in the inspirational power but in the misuse of our forces. The correction which comes through the experience of suffering becomes a taskmaster leading us back to Christ, or the Truth.

If we have a deep sense of Divine Forgiveness, that there is nothing in the Divine Nature which holds anything against us, we shall carry at the very center of our being a healing power. It was this healing power which Jesus exercised when he forgave people their sins. Troward tells us that the logical root of healing must be in the removal of the sense of separation, and the assurance that all the transgressions and shortcomings of the past have been blotted out forever.

It is interesting to note that in psychology as well as in theology there is a concept of conversion known as *the transformation of a repressed mental state, or effect, into a physical manifestation* . . . This means that the repressed emotional energy finds a new and better outlet for self-expression. It is also interesting to note that in analytical psychology a person would not be considered a good analyst should he hold the slightest sense of condemnation about his patient. The analyst must have enough human understanding (which in religion we might call compassion) to realize that he is trying to heal a mistake rather than attempting to change the nature of Reality. It would be impossible for a spiritual mind healer to do his best work it he held his patient in condemnation. All arbitrary opinions and judgments must not only be laid to one side; they must not be there at all.

Both the psychologist and the metaphysician can agree on this; each is trying to correct something which is wrong rather than create something which is right. He does not condemn; he reveals. This means that love and human understanding should always be considered the chief characteristics in these two fields if one is to do effective work. Perhaps this is why Jesus said to judge not lest we be judged by the very judgment we have used against another.

To speak of the wrath of God is to imply the illogical proposition that the Originating Power could operate against Itself. We are Itself, individualized, and It could no more condemn us than It could condemn Itself.

In making the forgiveness of sins one of its main teachings, the Bible is correct, for everyone labors more or less under the burden of condemnation. The child who is always told "Don't do this" and "Don't do that," becomes either repressed or, if he is a self-assertive child, arrogant. Unconsciously he sets up a protection against the aggressiveness of his parents. Of course neither of these psychological conditions is desirable. The child should be taught that destructive methods will make him unhappy and will also make everyone else around him unhappy. He should be taught that he is part of the community life.

This is not as difficult as it seems to be. Creating what Kunkle calls a *We* psychology is teaching the child to cooperate. This is done by taking him into full partnership with the parents and others around him.

For instance, if the child breaks a dish, instead of the mother rushing up and saying, "You naughty child! You have broken my precious dish!" she would say, and with deep understanding arising out of her love for the child, "Isn't it too bad we have broken this pretty plate—now we shall not be able to use it again. We are going to be very careful and not break another, aren't we?"

It is easy enough to see that if this *We* psychology were carried throughout life it would be effective of much good, for all society is made up of different combinations of *We.* Suppose as the child grows up he is taught that we are all One and that we never wish to harm each other because it would make us very unhappy and we would always feel bad; that we really wish to help each other. With such an attitude from infancy, the child would not grow up with any inward sense of condemnation. This does not mean that he would lack a true conscience; it merely means that there would be neither self-condemnation nor condemnation for others. Enlightenment and understanding would have established a unity.

When we consider how important the reactions of infancy are to adult life, and what a dominant role they play in the drama of future experience, we shall see how far-reaching this *We* attitude really is. It is based upon something fundamental in the universe, the unity of good; for it is only when we have arrived at the conclusions which make it impossible for us to harm others that we ourselves shall be free from being harmed by others. If the parent on earth symbolizes the Parent Mind in Heaven (in the within of Reality), it follows that we should have a *We* attitude toward the Supreme Being Itself. There should be a sense of the Divine partnership, free from condemnation and its blight.

From this viewpoint alone we can see the necessity of understanding that givingness and forgivingness are two ends of one Principle. If the actions in our lives follow the dominant suggestions or realizations of the mind, then a person who has lived from a sense of guilt must not only have a different outlook on life but his entire actions and reactions must be modified by such a belief. This is why a sense of forgiveness has played such an important role in both psychological and spiritual confession.

If a person has the intellectual capacity to think abstractly he will arrive at these conclusions through logic and reasoning. If he lacks such capacity his understanding will come by intuition and if even this capacity is lacking he can learn by example. This, Troward tells us, was the purpose of Jesus; to provide an example of the Divine Forgivingness and to do so in a manner that would satisfy every man's need. His philosophy was never one of illusion or delusion; it was one of self-revelation.

We are all children, not so much of a larger growth as of a greater experience. Instinctively we sense the necessity of some relationship to the universe which makes the pattern of human parenthood symbolic of the Divine Pattern inherent in the nature of Reality Itself. It was this Divine Pattern which Jesus felt and upon which his entire teaching was based. The Father turns to us as we turn to the Father; the Law obeys us as we obey It; always there is a Divine partnership and companionship. To know that our sins (mistakes) are blotted out and remembered no more against us forever, will do more for us than any other single attitude of mind.

There was nothing harsh in the philosophy of Jesus, and yet he never departed from the necessity of eternal justice. The Universe is always for us unless we are against It; even then It is for us. That which makes it appear as though we were being punished is a working out of the Law of Cause and Effect.

One of the fundamental propositions in spiritual mind healing is the necessity of removing the guilt complex; of clearing the avenues of psychic energy to find constructive release rather than destructive repression. There is nothing chaotic about this release; it is merely sublimating one form of psychic energy by transmuting it into an expression of constructive and happy action. The practitioner removes the sense of guilt, first by explaining the nature of Reality and next by silently working to remove all sense of guilt and condemnation, while at the same time pointing out in no uncertain way but in a kindly manner what the inevitable fruits of action (the Karmic Law of Cause and Effect) must be.

Having penetrated more deeply into the nature of existence than most others, Jesus sought to make his life an example of the true relationship between man and the Divine Being, which is one of kindness and compassion always balanced by law and order. It might truly be said that the idea of constructive forgivingness, which turns one from destructive action into the channels of happy and constructive self-expression, should be the chief characteristic of all spiritual instruction.

We are indeed children on the pathway of life. We cry out over its hurts and are bewildered by its apparent contradictions. Happy is the individual, who with Jesus, sees that Divine Forgivingness, like Divine Givingness, is at the root of all being. What untold misery and misunderstanding would be eliminated by this simple recognition! The Universe is both just and compassionate. It is always giving, but our receiving must be consistent with Its nature. We cannot expect a complete psychic clearance in our individual experience until we have granted the same clearance to others. Therefore we are told that the law of justice sees to it that we are condemned by and through the same condemnation which we have toward others.

The Universe is just. Harboring nothing against us, having no condemnation at Its center, It remains true to Itself. If we would come to the altar of our faith for true cleansing (whether we consider such a confession from a psychological or metaphysical viewpoint makes no difference) we must first be sure that outside the temple gates of our own consciousness we have left everything that hurts.

The Holy of Holies is entered through the archway of love. Somewhere along the line of experience, humanity must learn this great lesson—who would find his life must lose it. This is the great surrender; the giving up through renunciation of the "thee and thine," the "me and mine," and the taking hold and grasping the full meaning of the "We." Humanity will struggle on through tears and suffering, both individually and collectively, until this lesson is learned.

Why Talk So Much About God?

You may ask why we else the words *God* and *Spirit* so frequently in these lessons, and why it is when we explain the Science of Mind that we so often speak about the nature of God or Spirit.

When we use the word God or Spirit we mean the Intelligent Life Principle which the philosopher calls Reality, and what all religions mean when they refer to that something in the universe which responds to our consciousness. It is self-evident that such a First Cause and such an Intelligent Cause exists.

Haldane says, *Materialism, once a scientific theory, is now the fatalistic creed of thousands. But materialism is nothing better than a superstition on the same level as a belief in witches and devils. This* eminent scientist is telling us that it stretches our imagination more to disbelieve in God, or a Universal Consciousness, than it does to believe that there is such a Universal Consciousness. Or as the sage of antiquity said, *He that planted the ear, shall he not hear? He that formed the eye, shall he not see? He that teaches man knowledge, shall he not know?*

People are more interested in God than they are in religion, because religion has been more or less mixed up with superstition, theology, and ecclesiasticism. But people never have ceased being interested in the nature of God, and there is nothing that gives greater satisfaction than to believe in a Supreme Intelligence with which we may commune, and an Infinite Power with which we may consciously deal.

When we use the word God or Spirit we do not mean a tribal God, but the Supreme Mind and Power back of all created form, the Intelligence which responds to us, the Intelligence which rises through the mineral, vegetable, and animal kingdoms, and blossoms in the human mind as it approaches the conscious recognition that it is one with this Oversoul. It would be impossible to discuss philosophy, science, or religion without continually referring to the nature of man's being, and the nature of man's being is God.

We wish more than a blind acceptance of God. We need to know with scientific certainty that there is a Consciousness and a Power in the universe that responds to us definitely, directly, and dynamically. Each individual must arrive at a place in his own consciousness where this contact is so immediate and so dynamic that if every other living soul denied it, he would still know. Without this inner conviction neither faith nor understanding are possible. We would be depending on a forlorn hope which might vanish in the hour of need.

It is enough for the intelligent person to know that the entire planetary system manifests intelligence and organization; that is, it manifests intelligence plus direction, and intelligence plus direction means consciousness. It implies both will and representation; both an Infinite Will and an Infinite Manifestation.

There is within each of us a deep awareness, a subjective and a spiritual consciousness which by pure intuition knows that the Universal Intelligence which we call God exists. We do not need to turn to the Bible for such declarations, for the real Bible is inscribed on the walls of our own consciousness and is *the true light which lighteth every man that cometh into the world.* The inner consciousness of our union with Good is Supreme. Not only is it the highest hope and inspiration of the human mind, but it has ever been its greatest realization.

It is self-evident that we exist because we experience existence. It is self-evident that an Infinite Mind exists, since we can think. It is self-evident that this Mind is a Unity, since as individuals we recognize each other. It is self-evident that we can commune with this Infinite Mind, since we can commune with each other. We cannot disbelieve these self-evident propositions, for we must accept that which it is impossible to deny.

Now everything starts from this certainty of our own being. It is the only fact in the entire universe of which we are absolutely certain. Man's whole being consists in thinking, and if his thinking is based on knowing, this knowing must be built upon a consciousness of his own existence and of his relationship to the Infinite. It is this spiritual discernment of which Jesus spoke when he said, *Ye must be born again.* With scientific certainty the intellect is being led back to the necessity for a new birth.

We must believe in Spirit if we are to use spiritual power effectively. The consciousness of Spirit, the inner realization of the presence of Perfection, the willingness to meditate upon this Perfection, to understand Its operation and to sense Its presence, is the power back of all effective mental treatment.

Whether it be the healing of physical disease or the control of conditions, consciousness must be back of the Word. This consciousness does not contradict common sense or the best use of the intellect. It is never necessary to contradict common sense in arriving at the Truth, for fact and faith need never conflict.

We talk about God throughout these lessons because everyone instinctively feels that God is, and because human experience proves the necessity of such a supposition in order to explain the facts we do know. We start with the simple induction that since man is and has consciousness, he must live in consciousness. Consciousness or pure Spirit must be the cause of everything that is, including the physical universe.

Since the Universe exists as a harmonious whole, the consciousness back of it must be a perfect, indivisible Unit.

After having established these two simple premises we go on to the conclusion that since man is, and since there is an Infinite Consciousness, this Infinite Consciousness in man is man. Man's thought becomes creative not by well-wishing, prayer, supplication, or desire, but through necessity.

Consciousness in Its Infinite sense is what we mean when we use the word God. Consciousness in the individual sense is what we mean when we use the word man. This in no way shuts out any department of knowledge, but includes them all within the realm of consciousness since knowledge could not exist unless someone were conscious of it. Our entire inquiry, then, is an inquiry into the relationship between God and man, and so far as we establish a right relationship we shall have a corresponding power.

When people ask, "Why do you talk so much about God?" or when they say something to the effect that they are not interested in religion, be sure to explain to them that you are not offering them a new religion; you are merely seeking to give them an interpretation of life. You are not even trying to convince them that your philosophy is correct; you are trying to give them a reasonable basis for what they already believe.

Always be careful to explain that what you are giving them is just as much theirs as yours; it does not belong to any person, but like the principle of mathematics this knowledge of God can be used by all.

Every normal person wishes to believe in God, and you are giving the student a reasonable explanation for that which he already believes, and trying to help him understand what he already feels must be so.

You may be certain that if you approach your teaching from this viewpoint everyone will agree with you. Always make people feel that you are adding to that which they already have, never taking anything away. The very fact that God is already in them as the Principle of their own life needs to be explained.

When you explain to them that the God Power within them is independent of another person's consciousness, that they stand alone in the Divine Reality with the power to demonstrate as much of It as they can conceive at any moment, you will have established them in their relationship to the Universe. Reality Itself must always exceed any individual's understanding, because with an expanded consciousness a larger Good is understood.

Do not be afraid to use the word God or the word Spirit. All we need to avoid is any superstitious use of the term, and we most certainly should avoid all dogmatic uses of it. In this work we are making the greatest experiment which the human mind can undertake. We are determining whether or not there is a Universal Intelligence which responds to us in a creative manner. We are engaged in an endeavor to see how much joy we can take out of this Oversoul for ourselves and for others.

Bibles of the World

Fragments from the spiritual history of the race revealing fundamental UNITY of religious thought and experience

JUDAISM and CHRISTIANITY—

> Bless the Lord, O my soul!
> And all that is within me, bless his holy name!
> Bless the Lord, O my soul!
> And forget not all his benefits!
> Who forgiveth all thine iniquities,
> Who healeth all thy diseases,
> Who redeemeth thy life from destruction,
> Who crowneth thee with loving kindness and tender mercies.

For if ye forgive men their trespasses, your heavenly Father will also forgive you. But if ye forgive not men their trespasses, neither will your Father forgive your trespasses.

And be ye kind one to another, tenderhearted, forgiving one another, even as God for Christ's sake hath forgiven you.

For he shall have judgment without mercy, that hath showed no mercy; and mercy rejoiceth against judgment.

HINDUISM –   Strength might be vanquished by forgiveness.
                Weakness might be vanquished by forgiveness.

There is nothing which forgiveness cannot accomplish.

ISLAM—He who forgiveth and is reconciled shall be rewarded by God himself.

BUDDHISM—The whole length and breadth of the wide world is pervaded by the radiant thoughts of a mind all embracing, vast and boundless, in which dwells no hate nor ill-will.

CONFUCIANISM—If a ruler be not able to love men, he cannot possess his own person.

If a man love others, and no responsive attachment is shown to him, let him turn inwards, and examine his own benevolence.

Meditation

As I center my consciousness in Infinite Being, I realize that Its Essence is LOVE, and that this Love is in and through everything and everyone.

I know that this Love Essence, the very Substance of Life, the Creative Principle back of everything, flows through my whole being—spiritual, emotional, mental, and physical. It flows in transcendent loveliness into my world of thought and form.

I am conscious of this Divine Circuit which Love is. I feel It as a golden stream of force flowing from God through me and out to all that my thought rests upon, and returning to God. I know that this force is ever flowing, ever renewing, vitalizing, bringing joy and harmony and blessing to everything and everyone it touches.

Consciously I attune myself to this stream of Perfect Love. In Its flow I see It as an ever-widening spiral of continuous right action, bringing me into ever-widening fields of expression.

I, who am Love, share myself, my Love, with all humanity. I know that in Love there can be no separation, for Love unites. Love sustains and protects Its own.

I know that the Love I express, blesses all who are in any way touched by it. It heals every condition and brings my own to me.

I am immersed in Love.

Principle and Law Are Unlimited
Office of the Dean

My Dear Friend,
Always remember that this teaching is for the purpose of practice. We are not introducing a new religion or a new philosophy into the world. These lessons should make religion and spiritual consciousness practical in everyday life, something you can take hold of and use, something you can put your teeth into.

While these truths have been believed in throughout the ages, the conscious use of this Principle is something new in the world. You have embarked on the experiment of proving that there is a Power greater than you are that you can use.

All sense of strain or stress must be carefully avoided. All forces of nature flow spontaneously. You identify your treatment with the person or the place or the condition you are working for, and then seek to arrive at a definite realization about this person, place, or condition. Your thought never leaves your own mind because you are using the only Mind there is, which Mind is everywhere present.

As you watch your thinking take definite form, you will come to realize that you are using the most dynamic and the most creative power ever discovered, and you will also understand the complete simplicity of the way it works. It works in you, through you, as you. This could not be true unless you were One with the Principle, the Presence, and the Power.

I know that you will be successful in your use of this Power.

Sincerely,
Ernest Holmes

Lesson 12
Limitless Medium, p.118 through p.122

In the first paragraph of this lesson we find these words: *The Universal Subjective Mind, being entirely receptive to our thought, is compelled by Its very nature, to accept that thought and act upon it no matter what the thought may be.* This is perhaps one of the most significant truths of our science; the availability of Law plus the realization that Its reaction to us is entirely mechanical even though intelligent.

We can never ponder too deeply the meaning of such an impersonal law in the mental world. Our text reveals that since this Law is infinite, we are dealing with an Infinite Creative Power which is limited in Its reaction to us only by our reaction to It.

We must have a mental equivalent of our desire. The Glossary defines *Mental Equivalent* (page 610) as the *subjective idea of the desired experience.* This mental equivalent is a subjective embodiment of our desires. So what we have to change is the subjective reaction to our thought, for as stated in our last lesson the subjective state of our thought is the medium between the Absolute and the relative. By *Absolute* we mean that which is undivided and by *relative* that which depends not upon itself but upon the Absolute.

On page 627 *Relativity* and *Absoluteness* are defined. The Absolute is the cause, while the relative is an effect. That which is relative means related to something else. When we hold an image in front of a mirror the reflection in the mirror is relative to the image, for without the image there would be no reflection. Remove the image and the reflection vanishes with it. The image cannot be rubbed out of the mirror; it must be removed from in front of the mirror. Yet the object which we place in front of the mirror is also relative to our choice. We are absolute first cause; we place the image there and we can remove it. The reflection in the mirror has nothing to say one way or the other; it merely reflects the image held before it.

If the subjective state of our thought is like the image held before the mirror, and if our objective conditions are like the reflection in the mirror, then the subjective state of our thought is the cause of our conditions. Now the subjective state of our thought, like the image in front of the mirror, is itself in relationship to that which projects it, which is our conscious mind. That is the reason why the conscious mind, by changing the subjective state of thought, can change the reflection in the mirror.

It follows that our use of the Absolute may be consciously determined; if this were not true we should not be free. This is also why a person who thinks poverty year after year will attract it to himself. His subjective image held before the mirror of Creative Law is one of impoverishment, and the Law being no respecter of persons returns to the thinker only what he thinks into It.

That we are surrounded by such a Law there is no doubt, and that we can consciously use It for definite purposes, thousands upon thousands have proved. That you are able to demonstrate this is certain, but the extent to which you will demonstrate it depends upon your use of it, and your use of it depends upon your understanding. Our lesson states that the laws of attraction and repulsion are entirely subjective.

We all come into the world with a certain mental background, a subjective inheritance so to speak, and if this subjective inheritance is one of impoverishment we must be certain so to enrich our consciousness that lack and limitation will be converted into abundance. This is done not by fighting the limitation but by conceiving that which is less limited. This is the meaning of the saying taken from the Bible: *Pray without ceasing*, which you will find discussed at the top of page 497.

To recognize the good and affirm its presence, to claim that you are surrounded by love and friendship, by right action and happiness, is scientific, and the statements which you make will be true in reality; in actual experience—they will be as true as is your conviction. Read the Meditation on page 527, *The Things I Need Come to Me*. This should help you to achieve a sense of certainty, a feeling that the Power with which you deal is immutable, and that you cannot fail to demonstrate your good.

Read on page 502 the paragraph, *Now Are We the Sons of God.* You will discover that we are sons of freedom and not of bondage. Not tomorrow, but today the Kingdom of Heaven is at hand. This Kingdom which already is, appears to us as our vision becomes clarified. But how can our vision become clarified while we doubt? We must heal ourselves of doubt. And how are we going to heal ourselves of doubt? By repeatedly affirming that *now* are we the Sons of God, not by and by.

On page 544 read the statement, *My Word shall bear fruit. My Word is Law. My Word is complete and perfect.* Try to sense that because you now are the Son of God, your word has Divine Power. The Kingdom is not far off, but at hand. *The word is very nigh unto thee, in thy mouth . . . that thou mayest do it.* Man must be and is some part of the universe, a fragment of God with the same essence as the Divine. His word is creative because his word is the Word of God individualized through man. The same power which Jesus used is in each one of us. Emerson speaks of it as the power to stand and to walk. It is the power to execute the Divine Will and Purpose in human experience.

You will find on page 350 the statement that each person is surrounded by a mental atmosphere. This mental atmosphere is the result of the subjective state of his thought. It is continually repelling or attracting conditions. This silent process of attraction or repulsion goes on at all times, and no matter what we may say objectively, unless the subjective state of our thought is changed, we shall still attract negation. Fortunately we do have the ability to change the subjective state of our thought, and in this way bring new conditions into our lives.

This changing of conditions is the purpose of mental treatment, and as stated on page 119 in our text, the method is direct. Whatever we think about long enough will become a part of our subjective mental state. Thus it will become automatic, and it is this automatic thought process or mental atmosphere within us that is silently attracting or repelling. We must learn to realize more if we wish to experience more.

On page 120 there is a discussion of *Christ and Antichrist.* Let us first turn to the definition of *The Christ* on page 578—*The Word of God manifest in and through man.* The Christ means the idea of sonship. It means our conscious unity with the Perfect Whole. The man Jesus understood the Christ Principle, and because of this he was able to perform the so-called miracles which were in reality Divinely natural.

As stated on page 485, the Inner Spirit bears witness to this Divine fact, so that by pure intuition we recognize that the Christ dwells within us. This is the Spirit bearing witness with our spirits that we are heirs of the Kingdom of Heaven, of Reality, and joint heirs with Christ.

On page 422, the last paragraph, you will find an interpretation of the mystical conception of Christ, in which it says that we comprehend the Infinite only to the degree that It expresses Itself through us. We know God in such degree as we consciously permit the Divine to be incarnated in us, and in such degree we become the Christ. A complete change of thought must take place before we can become such an embodiment of the Christ Principle; we must first have harmonized with truth and beauty.

Emerson tells us that God will not make Himself manifest to cowards. We must overcome fear. Nothing can overcome fear but faith and perfect love, for faith and perfect love cast out all fear. To fear a thing is to bring upon one that thing which one fears. To remove the fear is to dissolve the thing. Here is the image and the mirror, the reflector and the reflection.

The power of thought is creative. We can never alter this fact, we can only use it. The spirit of Christ and Antichrist, referred to on page 120, refers to two uses of the one Law. The Bible is full of warnings against the wrong use of this Law. It tells us that our thought is creative, and then goes on to explain what happens when we use this creative power constructively and what happens when we use it destructively. It is careful, however, to explain to us that any destructive use of this Law is but temporary. The dire results which it brings upon us produce so much pain and suffering that we instinctively turn again toward the light. Just as light overcomes darkness by its presence, good overcomes evil by remaining true to its own nature.

Wherever good is recognized, evil disappears. To know the truth about evil is to realize the presence of good where evil appears to be. We should never fear the negative use of this Law, for no form of mental suggestion can affect us unless we permit it to. We do not teach a system of mental influence, for if we admit that we can influence others, we are admitting that others can influence us. This would become a question of willpower, and we are not practicing willpower.

We are practicing the Presence of Good, and the knowledge of the Presence of Good automatically dissolves evil. Right where evil appears to be, keep on declaring that Good is the only presence there is. Persist in this declaration, compel yourself to believe it by any and every argument or realization that you can conceive. Do not take *No* for an answer. Good is the only presence there is. If you know this you will see evil vanish into its native nothingness. We never try to influence people; there is no hypnotism, mesmerism, or mental suggestion in our practice; it is entirely an explanation and re-education.

Turn to page 368, the last two paragraphs, for a definition of the Christ Principle, and as you use the Meditation following these two paragraphs, try to sense the Divine Presence as being the reality of your own life.

Returning to our lesson section at the top of page 121, we note that subconscious mind is the servant, since it is Universal Law and available at the center of our own thought. The practitioner never goes outside himself to give a treatment. We recognize that man in his physical body is in complete unity with the entire physical universe, and his mind is in complete unity with the Universal Mind. We recognize that the self-knowing or conscious mind of man, whether it is acting on the plane of intellect or the plane of intuition, is the avenue through which Divine Wisdom flows. Therefore the self-knowing or conscious mind has absolute precedence over every previous experience. It creates a new present as it dissolves the past. It creates the present and projects the future.

If the power which you seek to use were something separated from your consciousness, your objective discerning faculties; if the Christ Consciousness or Subliminal Mind were separated from your self-knowing mind, it would be impossible for you to attain this Christ Consciousness. Our self-knowing mind is the place where we recognize God, while our subconscious is our use of the Universal Law of Cause and Effect.

What a marvelous truth to contemplate! This is what Jesus meant when he said, *All power is given unto me in heaven and in earth*. This same power which Jesus exercised is our power now. We must never lose sight of the fact that, as Emerson said, *God is, not was; speaks, not spake*. We must learn to speak the Divine Presence into objective form. This is the purpose of spiritual treatment: to demonstrate that we have control over all negative situations, to prove that there is such a thing as Spiritual Power and that we do have access to It, and that we can use this Spiritual Power for definite purposes.

Summary

The Universal Subjective Mind cannot refuse to accept your thoughts, because It is entirely impersonal. But because It acts creatively on all thoughts, we need a mental equivalent of our desires, a conscious and subconscious mental picture or embodiment of our desires.

The Law of Mind is a mirror reflecting only the images in front of It. If this were not so, the conscious mind could not change these reflections and their attendant conditions.

We all have inherited subjective tendencies of the race. Whether we call this the carnal mind, the mortal mind, or race suggestion makes no difference. Realizing that the Kingdom of God is at hand today, we seek to rise above all negative suggestions, whether they come from our own thoughts or those of the entire human race, to a new place in consciousness where limitation has no acceptance. We do this by knowing that evil disappears when we replace it with the contemplation of good.

We do not use mental influence; we use the Law of Mind when we practice the Presence of Good. This is called the Christ Consciousness or the Subliminal Mind. This consciousness is always at hand within the upper atmosphere of our own thinking. It has been called *Christ in you, the hope of glory*.

Questions

Brief answers to these questions should be written out by the student after studying the lesson, and the answers compared with those which will be included in next week's lesson.

1. Why is subjective mind compelled to act creatively on our thought?
2. What do we mean by the mechanical reaction of mental law?
3. What is meant by the terms *The Absolute* and *the relative*?
4. Why is the subjective state of our thought the cause of our conditions?
5. What can change the subjective state of thought?
6. Do we control the Absolute?
7. What conditions our use of the Law?
8. When will the Kingdom of God be revealed to us?
9. When will the good we desire automatically and continuously become a part of our experience?
10. What is the meaning of the Spirit of Christ and Antichrist?
11. Does the Spirit of Christ and Antichrist imply two powers?
12. How do we treat to dissipate evil or negation from our lives?
13. Does hypnotism, mesmerism, or mental suggestion enter into our practice?

14. What is the difference between the self-knowing mind and the subconscious mind?

Answers to Questions on Lesson 11

1. The *Macrocosm* means the big world, the Universe, the Absolute Spirit, God, the Universal Mind. The *microcosm* means the entire nature of God which is individualized in man, as man.

2. The practical lesson to be deduced from the theory of the Macrocosm and the microcosm is wholeness and unity. Hence when man thinks within himself he is automatically thinking within the Creative Mind of God.

3. Since the Universal Creative Mind is always at the center of our own being, we do not need to discover, uncover, or find access to Its Power; we already have It and need only to use It.

4. (a) Our approach to the Universal Power is through our own thought. (b) Yes, there are many ways, faiths, and methods through which one may realize the Divine Presence and Power. The most simple method, however, is to realize the Divine Power at the center of one's own thought.

5. We believe that man is an immortal individualized entity in Universal Spirit.

6. The Karmic Law or the Law of Cause and Effect of Itself is changeless. There is nothing fatalistic about this, since we can change Its effect in our lives by reversing our thought. Karma is the law which binds the ignorant and frees the wise.

7. Freedom awaits our recognition because the very idea of freedom implies choice. Without choice there could be no freedom.

8. A practitioner must rise above appearances because the objective world is in the realm of effects, while the practitioner's work is done in Mind, which is in the realm of causes.

9. To have faith in God means to have faith in a Power to which all things are possible. To have the faith of God means not only to believe in but to make use of this Power.

10. The invisible is projected into form through faith and belief in its reality and its responsiveness to us, followed by definite statements and affirmations.

11. In the last analysis the Universe cannot be explained; It must be accepted. What we explain is the way laws work, not the reason for their being.

12. The subconscious and unconscious do not mean the same thing. The unconscious is a psychological term designating that aspect of the subconscious life which is so deeply buried that neither the will nor the act of memory can bring it back to conscious experience. In the Science of Mind the unconscious means the deeper aspect of the subconscious memory.

13. The subjective law of mind creates from the thought patterns held in memory and from the thoughts which we consciously give it. Conscious thoughts can change subconscious patterns.

14. The Law of Life gives back to man as experience what he believes about It because, being an individual, man must experience the result of a sum total of his belief. This belief is largely unconscious, arising from the collective experience and belief of the race.

15. The Gift of Heaven is the conscious intuition or inner sense of Reality which we all have.

16. The Secret Chamber means the Christ Consciousness or Spiritual Awareness wherein there is neither doubt, fear, nor uncertainty. It is located in man's own consciousness.

17. Our word will be as powerful as was the word of Jesus when we live in as complete harmony with life and have as complete faith in the Law as did he.

18. Spiritual freedom of itself is perfect, harmonious, and limitless. It is the Law of Liberty. But this Law must be to each as each is to It.

The Outpouring of Spirit

Let him take hold of my strength that he may be at peace with me, and he shall make peace with me. In this way Troward finishes his chapter, *The Divine Giving. All things are possible to him that believeth. If ye have faith . . . nothing shall be impossible unto you.*

Troward tells us . . . *Free Givingness is a necessity of the very being of the All-Originating Spirit.* Since we have nothing to give Life other than the living of It, it follows that we, as Emerson said, become beneficiaries of Its effulgent glory. Our business is to receive and to use. Why then Troward asks, should we not take up the position of grateful and expectant receivers? In the Apocrypha it says, *But to Him who is both life and deathless, endless light, and who pours forth upon men gladness sweeter than honey, to Him alone bend thy neck.*

Jesus, with the direct simplicity of one who held long communion with nature, said, *Consider the lilies of the field, how they grow; they toil not, neither do they spin.* All nature proclaims the silent outpouring or givingness of the creative genius of the universe. The Koran tells us, *Make the best of things; and enjoin what is just, and withdraw from the ignorant.*

To assume the attitude of an expectant and enthusiastic receiver of the Divine Gifts is to cooperate with the Divine Giver, for how can a gift be fully made until it has been received?

Jesus told his followers that it was impossible for him to instruct them unless they listened, or to convert them unless they believed. Throughout his whole teaching he emphasized the necessity of cooperation with the Supreme Spirit. The Mahabharata says, *There is nothing impossible of attainment by persons of virtuous behavior.* And in Proverbs: *Her (wisdom's) ways are ways of pleasantness, and all her paths are peace. She is a tree of life to them that lay hold upon her: and happy is everyone that retaineth her.*

We should, as Troward suggests, take up the position of grateful and expectant receivers. And he tells us the reason we have not done so is because we have not believed in the Divine Givingness. We have placed every sort of block in the pathway of our good. The chalice of our acceptance has not been held upward that the heavenly outpouring may fill it with the Divine Gifts. We do not expect manna from heaven. Our wilderness of despair is so dense that the heavenly light cannot penetrate its shadows. Troward remarks that this is because of our inability to see beyond secondary causes. We judge the possibilities of the future by viewing the experiences of the past. Our present is sandwiched between two impossible outlooks, one of introspective morbidity and the other of expectant calamity.

The negation looms large. By judging according to secondary causes Troward means that we are forming our thought patterns after the image of conditions rather than penetrating with a clear spiritual insight into the possibility of the Infinite which surrenders Its entire nature to our use. We do not think the thoughts of God after Him, and yet Proverbs tells us, *For as he thinketh in his heart so is he.* Hermes said, *Then, in this way know God: as having all things in Himself as thoughts, the whole cosmos Itself.* And from one of the ancient sayings we gather this remarkable metaphor: *Churning your milk assiduously with knowledge, so that what is hidden in it may be disclosed.*

Troward states that we do not perceive this invisible good, but judging from secondary causes alone we limit the flow of life to our thought patterns of negation; that we are slow to realize that . . . *just as the Spirit can create the thing we desire, so it can also create the way by which that thing shall come to us . . . .* Effect is hidden in cause as the butter is hidden in the cream. If our philosophy of life were based upon the proposition that, that which we see comes out of that which we do not see, and that *the invisible things of God* are projected in our experience through faith, we should give heed to the Divine Promises.

The question might arise at this point—How do we know what the Divine Promises are? Has God made any promises? The answer to this interrogation is self-evident—the Divine Promises are inherent in the nature of the Divine Being Itself. All Reality is delivered to our use, of a necessity; nothing can be withheld. Jesus proclaimed this through the admonition given by the prodigal's father to his elder son who remained at home: *Son, thou art ever with me, and all that I have is thine.* And Life is forever proclaiming this truth to each of Its sons.

The Bible speaks of *the lamb slain from the foundation of the world. Lamb* symbolizes the Divine Sacrifice or Givingness. It refers to the gift of Life. This is but another way of saying that the entire nature of the Divine is delivered to our use. The Divine Promises, then, constitute a Divine Givingness which is a necessary complement of the Infinite Being Itself. Browning said, *It is Thou God who give, it is I who receive.*

To this givingness Troward tells us we should fix no limits. He insists that we should have faith in the universe and that this faith should be founded on the unquestionable fact that the universe exists. He explains that the logic of this proposition lies in the fact that since the universe exists and is projected out of nothing (that is, nothing physical or material) it must be a thing of thought. Since we also are some part of this projection, fundamentally we are beings existing in, by, and through consciousness alone. This in no way contradicts or denies the objective universe which becomes thought clothed in form. This is the way the Spirit works.

Troward tells us, *In the beginning there were no antecedent conditions, and the whole creation came out of the desire of the Spirit for self-expression.* We also have the desire for self-expression. It is, as psychology points out, the mainspring of all our action. Indeed *libido* is defined as *an emotional craving toward self-expression.*

In one of his marvelous spiritual abstractions at which Troward was so adept, he points out that since the universe is a thing of thought, and since we are centers of consciousness in it, *then our thought inspired by the promise, is, so to say, reflected back into the mind of the Universal Spirit in direct relation to ourselves . . .* This must be what Jesus meant when he said, *The Son can do nothing of himself but what he seeth the Father do: for what things soever he doeth, these also doeth the Son likewise.* Man reproduces the Creative Spirit, re-enacts the Creative Cause, and in countless individual ways proclaims that he is not (if by man we mean something separated from Spirit), but is Spirit Itself as man. He is not an attribute but the essence.

If we accept Troward's idea that God makes things out of thought and that man reproduces the Original Creative Energy, it follows that our thought, as he suggests, *. . . is as unhampered by antecedent conditions as was the original cosmic creation itself.* In *Fragments of a Faith Forgotten* we find this paragraph: *Seek for the great and the little shall be added unto you; seek for the heavenly and the earthly shall be added unto you.* And from the Text of Taoism: *Take the days away and there will be no year; without what is internal there will be nothing external.* From Tin Fu King: *If one observes the Way of Heaven, and maintains Its doings (as his own), all that he has to do is accomplished.* In the Upanishads we find this saying: *Where is the locality of truth? In the heart, for by the heart man knows truth; the heart therefore is the locality of truth.* From the *Book of the Dead*: *My soul hath built for me a habitation.*

Jesus said that the Kingdom of Heaven is within; that we must be converted and become as little children if we are to enter into this heavenly paradise; that the one who shall humble himself as a child shall exercise the greatest power in this kingdom. Lao Tze asks this question: *Can you maintain an entire simplicity? Can you become a little child?*

Troward said that it is this childlike faith in the Invisible which makes the Divine Promises come true in our lives, because our thought reflected in It becomes Its thought reflected back to us. And he goes on to say that the Bible promises are nothing else than the statement of the essential creativeness of the All-Originating Spirit when operating in reciprocity with the individual mind. This is an abstract way of saying that the Law of Mind responds to us by corresponding with our mental attitudes.

Troward continues, *It is for this reason that the Bible lays such stress on belief in the Divine promises as the way to receive the blessing.* In other words, we must all believe to receive, and he points out that this is all in accord with the Law of Cause and Effect. When we come to understand any law of science we need not go into the laboratory analysis of it when we use it. So he suggests we should accept the Divine promises or the Law of Reciprocal Action between the Universal and the individual as a fact, and have as much faith in It as we would in the law of electricity or any other law of nature.

We all alike have to come back to the standpoint of a simple faith in the vitalizing working of the energizing power, whether God or electricity. . . Even the one who does not technically understand electricity but who has faith in it may use it. It is not so much a technical knowledge of the Law as it is a childlike and implicit faith in It which produces the desired result. Our confidence is built not only upon an intellectual understanding, but also upon an unwavering faith.

The Bible both analyzes the Law and assumes a childlike attitude toward It. This is consistent with all scientific methods. Naturally, the one who knows the most about any law can the most effectively use it. For faith and fact need never collide. We should come either by simple faith, through intuition, by logic, or by Divine revelation into the knowledge of the spiritual laws of cause and effect. We must gain a mental equivalent of these spiritual laws in order to use them. Our individual faith is this mental equivalent, and since we are dealing with a Law infinite in Its potential possibility we can set no limit to Its capacity—It is able, ready, and willing to give us all or more than we can take.

Troward makes it plain that we are not under bondage to the Law; It is our servant. Therefore we should have a restful enthusiasm in using It but at the same time there should be a persistent and insistent determination to think straight. As an ancient scripture says, *Success forsaketh the person whose heart is unsteady, or who hath no control over his mind, or who is a slave of his senses.*

Coupling this determination with joy and enthusiasm, one becomes a Divine artist, picturing life not as some forlorn hope destitute of good, but as a glorious proclamation of Spirit. It was from this state of exaltation that Jesus proclaimed, *For my yoke is easy, and my burden is light.* And from *Fragments of a Faith Forgotten*: *So he gave them Glory, Joy, Jubilation, Gladness, Peace, Hope, Faith, Love, and Truth, imperishable. This is the nine-fold which is given unto them who have fled from matter. And they have become blessed and perfect, and have recognized the True God, and known the mystery which is given to the man.*

Jesus said that everything is included in the Kingdom of God. *All these signs shall follow them that believe; In my name shall they cast out devils . . . they shall lay hands on the sick, and they shall recover. In my name* means in the nature of Reality, following the example of Jesus, in conscious union with good. Speaking in the name of Truth means to speak from a consciousness of the union of all life; from a realization that the reality of earthly things has a pattern in Heaven. From *Fragments of a Faith Forgotten* we inherit this statement: *If ye make not the below into the above and the above into the below, the right into the left and the left into the right, the before into the behind (and the behind into the before), ye shall not enter into the kingdom of God.*

Troward tells us that we must exchange . . . *the burden of Law for the peaceful liberty of Faith in the Divine Goodness, the All-givingness of the Heavenly Father.* In this way the burden of life is laid aside and the yoke becomes easy.

When we consider that the Divine Promises must always be consistent with the eternal nature of Reality, we shall see that they include everything worthwhile; not only Joy, Peace, Meekness, Love, Long-suffering and Compassion, but also Beauty, Harmony, and Accomplishment. We should always realize with Hermes that *with Him, therefore, is there no difference with one another; there is no partiality with Him. But they are one in Thought . . . They have one mind—their Father,—'Tis Love Himself who worketh the one harmony of all.*

The Divine Promises should teach us to overcome fear—*The Lord is my light and my salvation; whom shall I fear? The Lord is the strength of my life; of whom shall I be afraid?*

We should expect nothing less than wholeness to proceed from the perfect Law—*Be ye therefore perfect, even as your Father which is in heaven is perfect.*

We should expect absolute unity—*One God and Father of all, who is above all, and through all, and in you all.*

We should expect permanence—*I know that whatsoever God doeth it shall be forever: nothing can be put to it, nor anything taken from it.*

We should expect such a complete unity that there is neither separation from it nor enmity toward it— *The Lord God omnipotent reigneth . . . Whither shall I go from thy Spirit? or whither shall I flee from thy presence? . . . I will contend with him that contendeth with thee.*

We should expect all problems to be solved through our knowledge of the Law—*Fear them not therefore; for there is nothing covered, that shall not be revealed; and hid, that shall not be known . . . I wisdom dwell with prudence, and find out knowledge of witty inventions.*

We should expect substance from the Law—*That I may cause those that love me to inherit substance; and I will fill their treasures.* Also from *Echoes from the Gnosis*: *O, primal Origin of my origination; Thou Primal Substance of my substance; First Breath of breath, the breath that is in me.*

We should expect healing—*For I will restore health unto thee, and I will heal thee of thy wounds, saith the Lord.*

We should expect guidance—*To give light to them that sit in darkness and in the shadow of death, to guide our feet into the way of peace . . . And I will bring the blind by a way that they know not; I will lead them in paths that they have not known.*

We should expect security—*For he shall give his angels charge over thee, to keep thee in all thy ways . . . He that dwelleth in the secret place of the most High shall abide under the shadow of the Almighty . . . Who redeemeth thy life from destruction; who crowneth thee with loving kindness and tender mercies . . . The eternal God is thy refuge; and underneath are the everlasting arms.*

Above all, we should expect peace and love. *And we have known and believed the love that God hath to us. God is love; and he that dwelleth in love dwelleth in God and God in him . . . For God hath not given us the spirit of fear; but of power, and of love, and of a sound mind . . . Because he hath set his love upon me, therefore will I deliver him: I will set him on high, because he hath known my name.*

The Bible also affirms, *If ye know these things, happy are ye if ye do them.* Since the statement of one's conviction in a principle is different from the use of such principle, it becomes necessary not only to understand the Law and accept the promises; we must live as though they were true while making definite use of the Law of Cause and Effect. Realizing that our thought patterns are reflected into the Mind Principle to be reflected back to us as conditions, we must guard these thought patterns as we would the very treasures of heaven itself.

Having assumed that Spirit is the only Presence and Power in the universe and that this Presence is forever guiding us into the fullness of joy, we should anticipate fruitful action and accomplishment.

Consciously and joyfully we should approach the Temple and enter into the Secret Place of the Most High without fear, for there alone is the bond of absolute union.

What is the meaning of life? What is the pathway of human experience? What is the goal of existence? What but a realization that the Divine Partnership is forever formed; that the eternal Spirit Itself goes forth joyfully through us into self-expression. Life should become, as Emerson suggests, the triumphant march of a jubilant and a beholding soul.

Troward begins his *Bible Mystery and Bible Meaning* with the statement: *The Bible is the Book of the Emancipation of Man. The emancipation of man means his deliverance from sorrow and sickness, from poverty, struggle, and uncertainty, from ignorance and limitation, and finally from death itself.* In many ways he explains to us that the very nature of Reality presupposes the necessity of such an emancipation. He points out that there is a Universal Creative Spirit of warmth, color, and light personal to each one of us because It is personified at the center of every man's being. This is God, the Living Spirit Almighty, the Presence with which we commune. From this indwelling and overshadowing Presence we are to receive inspiration and guidance.

Troward also makes clear that we are immersed in a universal Law of Cause and Effect, an intelligent creative Force having no volition of Its own but being compelled by Its very nature to receive the impress of our thought and act upon it. This he calls the Universal Subjective Mind. It is law and not person. It is a mathematical Principle, intelligent but un-choosing. It is the supreme Law in nature. Since this Law reacts automatically but creatively to our thought, having no choice of Its own, It will bring upon us freedom or bondage according to the use we make of It. Therefore we should seek the inspiration of spiritual realization that we may impress the Law with those images of thought which will produce goodness, truth, and beauty.

Having laid before us his profound system of thought, Troward tells us to accept and stop arguing about it. He says, *Try it!*

Affirmations and Denials in Treatment

There are two methods of giving a mental treatment, two ways in which one may approach spiritual mind healing in its practical application. These two methods are called *argumentative* and *realization*.

The argumentative method is one wherein a series of mental arguments is used to erase a negative mental conviction. In the method of realization no argument is used, but a state of consciousness is induced, the result of which is such a harmonious reaction that the physical discord disappears. Let us consider, then, the use of affirmations and denials in spiritual mind healing.

As we have frequently stated, Science of Mind practice is built on the supposition that Spiritual Man is perfect, Nature is perfect, God is perfect, Being is perfect. Spiritual Man is a part of Spiritual Being. Spiritual Man is the manifestation of Spiritual Being. Spiritual Man is the Consciousness of God as man.

In spiritual mind healing it is necessary to establish a consciousness of this foundation of Truth. The treatment seeks to bring man back to the Principle of his being; to the Perfection of his being. In doing this the practitioner meets what we call the argument of negation.

It may seem strange to speak about the argument of negation, but this idea is rapidly being accepted by many psychologists. Out of years of practical experience they have learned that the inertia of thought patterns is so great and so difficult to remove from the consciousness of the patient that they sometimes speak of these thought patterns as actually arguing back, refusing to be dislodged.

When we speak of the argument of negation we are speaking of a very real mental activity, and the practitioner must meet this argument of negation by an opposite argument. If a child says two times two equals six the teacher explains to him that two times two equals four, never more and never less. There is no emotional strain in delivering this message to the child, but there is the necessity of convincing the child's mind that two times two really does equal four, always and under every circumstance.

So the practitioner starting with this Principle of Perfection argues that disease is neither person, place, nor thing. It has no law to support it. The condition from which his patient suffers has no location; it has no duration; it has no beginning and no development and no end. His argument is as definite in his own thought as though he were explaining that two and two always make four. There never began to be a time when two and two made five. Two and two put together never evolved to a place where they made six, and no matter how many people believe to the contrary or experience the negative result of such a belief, two and two never made seven.

In the wrong working out of an example it is the teacher's duty to point out where the mistake arose. This is what the argumentative treatment is. It is the activity of thought establishing not only a correct premise, but an equally correct conclusion.

Diagnosis in mental treatment is for the purpose of discovering why the person thinks as he does, upon what false premise his thought is based, what belief in the opposite of good he is entertaining. Of course the negative beliefs which he entertains are mostly subjective. As they are subjective he is not conscious of them; they are operating through him. To the all embracing Intelligence, the Infinite Mind, man is held as being perfect and complete, and two and two never equals anything but four in this Intelligence. There is no negation of mind in this Intelligence, and as the practitioner reverses the negation the wrong argument disappears from the patient's thought.

By the wrong argument we mean that which attends the wrong argument, which is the negative condition. The practitioner does not feel that he is fighting an adversary or contending with a real opponent. He rearranges the facts which his patient has misarranged. He reverses the mental process by knowing that two and two make four; he knows the truth about them.

Each individual who presents himself to a practitioner represents an individual problem to be solved, or an individual opportunity to be met. The practitioner denies that perfection can produce imperfection. He declares that his patient is a spiritual idea forever perfect. He knows that health is indestructible, while disease is a negation. He knows the belief that two and two equals five never was the truth; therefore it does not have to disappear nor can it reappear—it has no appearance. He knows that from the standpoint of the spiritual man, disease never started; lack, want, and limitation never had any beginning, operation, or ending in the Spirit of Truth.

The practitioner handles the experience of negation as though it were only a belief in negation. And this is an important point in mental healing, for unless the practitioner of this science could resolve things into thoughts he would have no mental method of procedure which would sound reasonable, sane, or scientific. Unless disease originates in consciousness, consciousness cannot change it. Whether we are aware of the fact or not makes no difference—it has nothing to do with the truth of the matter.

In dealing with negation the practitioner does not feel that he is separating the negative from the real as though they were two different things, for that would be to fall under the hypnotic suggestion that No is equal to Yes, that evil is lord over the kingdom of good, and that the Infinite has a rival equal in power to Itself.

The practitioner deals with That Which Is, and not with that which is not. Therefore when That Which Is appears in the form of negation, even this negation is part of the activity of That Which Is, but is a wrong use of It. This wrong use of That Which Is implies no negation of That Which Is, no separation from That Which Is, and no disunity with That Which Is. It implies merely a negative use of It. Hence the practitioner never deals with the negative as though it were a thing of itself—it is but a state of consciousness.

In analyzing a case for argument (that is, for the affirmation and denial method of procedure in spiritual mind healing), the practitioner starts with this premise: A patient has presented himself for help. It follows that something is wrong. The argument is that there is a place where this negation is experienced. There was a time when he began to experience this negation. There is a real substance which takes the form of this negation. This substance is separate from Mind, Spirit, or Perfection. Consequently he is actually experiencing a negation, and the negation which he experiences has a form. This form is seen by others. It is a fact even though it is not a truth or an eternal verity. This negation may have taken the form of disease, unhappiness, poverty, domestic infelicity, loneliness, fear, or any other of the myriad forms which deny good. This is what the patient presents to the practitioner.

Having accepted the premise, how does the practitioner proceed? He begins to deny that anything is wrong. He knows that negation is neither person, place, nor thing. He knows that negation never began, just as two and two never began to be five. He knows it in the same way, dispassionately but with absolute certainty. He knows that there is no place where negation can be true, nor is there any place where it can be thought to be true. It has no one to support it, no one to believe in it, and no one through whom it can operate. It is exactly nothing and is cancelled by knowing that it is nothing.

There is no time but the present and the present is perfect. The practitioner knows that the Allness of Truth precludes the possibility of any opposite. Then he pays particular attention, in his thought, to affirming the presence of the desired good. From this viewpoint the specific negation is met by the opposite and specific affirmation. The denial is used to clear the consciousness; to sweep it out, as it were, and to make room in thought for the opposite affirmation, which recognizes God as the Only Presence, Power, and Person.

The practitioner deals with the argument of negation which appears as wrong things, or wrong conditions, by using the opposite argument of Truth based upon the reality that God is all there is. The mental argument continues until the mind of the practitioner is satisfied with the evidence he has produced. In this practice it is evident that the practitioner deals with the negation more as though it were a hypnotic suggestion than as though it were a reality. He is conscious that his patient is suffering from this condition, but he is equally conscious that he need not suffer from it.

Suppose a patient came to a practitioner and said, "I am an elephant." The practitioner would not believe that he was an elephant; he would not believe that he ever began to be an elephant or ever developed into an elephant. He would not believe that there was any law compelling him to be an elephant.

But suppose the patient should tell the practitioner that there was such a law and that that law was inherited; that he had inherited a tendency toward becoming an elephant. What would the practitioner handle; the elephant or the wrong belief in the patient's mind? It is obvious that he would handle the wrong concept. The practitioner knows that his patient is not an elephant. He knows that he does not inherit any tendency toward being an elephant, but he does know that he suffers from his wrong conception. He heals him, not from being an elephant but from the illusion that he is an elephant.

Now suppose the patient were to tell the practitioner that he is an elephant because he was born on the second day of July and that the stars control the whole thing—it is a matter of fate. Would the practitioner treat fate or the belief in fate? The answer is self-evident. He would deny that the stars had anything to do with this man's being an elephant or not being an elephant. He would know that the only sign is the sign of God or the sign of Perfection. He would deliberately remove the hallucination; he would not try to remove the influence of the planets because they have no influence.

But suppose on reading the history of humanity he should have discovered that many millions of people had believed that at certain times in their lives they must become elephants because of the time of year that they were born into this world. Would the practitioner agree to this hypnotic suggestion? Not at all. He would say to himself, "It does not matter how many people believe that this man is an elephant, or that because he was born under a certain sign he must become an elephant; I know that this is a lie. He is not an elephant, never was, and never will be."

Let us carry the proposition into a more subtle field of argument and suppose that millions of people were to say, "We can prove to you that this thing works mathematically; all people born under certain signs have the inclination to become elephants." What would our practitioner do in a case like this? How would he detect this subtle argument of negation? By following this line of argument: *I realize that whatever the whole race holds to be true about itself appears to be true, because thought works with creative power and with mathematical precision. But even so, I know that the whole thing is an illusion; that even though thought does work with mathematical precision and with creative power, and even though countless millions of people have acted as though they were elephants and believed that they were, they never have been elephants at any time.* This line of argument may be used to heal any belief in horoscopes, inherited tendency, prenatal influence, or race suggestion.

The practitioner must never be tempted to believe that the negative condition is a thing of itself or that it ever had a cause. He denies every aspect of belief about it. In the argumentative method he affirms that man, being perfect, is not born under race belief and does not suffer from signs in the heavens. Two and two are always four no matter what anyone believes. His entire argument is affirmation and denial swinging around the central theme of spiritual being and perfection, and that God is all there is, ever was, or ever will be.

The practitioner recognizes that we all suffer from race consciousness and that what millions of people have believed in operates to some extent through all of us. But this does not make it so. He must learn that much which appears to be true in experience is not true in Principle, and he must reverse the use of thought until the experience is transcended. In doing this he resolves everything into mind—planets, people, peanuts, kings, and cabbages. The entire human experience and the latest event in the experience of his patient are theoretically resolved into mind and into thought.

Next he knows that the only activity of mind is thought. He knows that the activity of his thought destroys the activity of the negative thought, and that what is left is perfect. Hence the sooner he recognizes that what is left is perfect, the sooner his denial becomes an affirmation. Affirmation always follows denial in order that realization may be built up. This realization is a realization of the Presence and the Perfection of God.

The practitioner deals with the mentality alone. Having theoretically resolved the physical universe into a thing of thought, he handles thought. Negative thought is not evil of itself and is not a law unto itself. It is merely a mistreatment of Principle and belongs to no one. Therefore it must be dealt with as though it were an impersonal thought force operating through someone's belief. Correct mental practice means dealing with this negative thought force as though it were a belief, and removing it as though it were merely a mistaken conclusion.

The practitioner, then, deals with the negative condition, whether it is impoverishment or physical illness, as though it were an objective argument or combination of wrong thoughts. Seeing it in this light he untangles the wrong thought, leaving the field to that nature which is perfect. He seeks to arrive at a realization and recognition of the Allness of God, the Omnipresence of Good.

In this entire process the practitioner deals with nothing but his own thought. His affirmations, denials, and realizations take place at the center of his own consciousness, and he never attempts to project nor suggest. He makes no attempt whatsoever to concentrate. His treatment is a moving, conscious, animated thing.

This practice would be impossible unless the practitioner could sincerely and truthfully resolve things into thoughts in his own imagination and proceed upon the basis that all manifest life is a thing of thought in form. He must be thoroughly and sincerely convinced that there is a spiritual man and that this spiritual man is perfect; that the Kingdom of Heaven is now and that a statement of Truth has actual power.

Moreover he must be certain that as far as he is concerned the answer is taken out of it, not put into it. Otherwise he will be trying every form of mental coercion, will power, suggestion, and concentration.

Bibles of the World

Fragments from the spiritual history of the race revealing fundamental UNITY of religious thought and experience

ISLAM—What ever good betideth thee is from God, and whatever betideth thee of evil is from thyself.

From your thoughts proceeds destruction, when from time to time evil thoughts occur to you. Ah! cast out of your head these vain imaginations. Ah! sweep out of your heart these evil suggestions. Cry, "There is no power nor strength but in God!"—to evert the Evil One from the world and from your own soul.

BUDDHISM—When a mirror is covered with dust, it cannot reflect images. It can do so only when it is free from stain. It is even the same with all beings. If their minds are not clear of stain, the Absolute cannot reveal itself to them.

HINDUISM—Even here on earth everything is overcome by those whose mind remains balanced, therefore they are established in the Eternal.

TAOISM—Who uses well his light, reverting to its source so bright, will from his body ward all blight.

CONFUCIANISM—The superior man acts before he speaks, and afterwards speaks according to his actions.

Is there any one word which could be adopted as a life-long rule of conduct? Is not sympathy the word? Do not do to others what you would not like yourself.

SIKHISM—Where there is forgiveness, there is God himself.

The true teacher, having taught me love, hath caused me to meet God. Without love for God there is no emancipation. Grasp the love of God; dismiss doubts.

Made in the USA
San Bernardino, CA
27 December 2013